RAILWAY
DISASTERS
OF THE WORLD

Patrick Stephens Limited, an imprint of Haynes Publishing, has published authoritative, quality books for enthusiasts for more than a quarter of a century. During that time the company has established a reputation as one of the world's leading publishers of books on aviation, maritime, military, model-making, motor cycling, motoring, motor racing, railway and railway modelling subjects. Readers or authors with suggestions for books they would like to see published are invited to write to: The Editorial Director, Patrick Stephens Limited, Sparkford, Nr. Yeovil, Somerset, BA22 7JJ.

RAILWAY DISASTERS
OF THE WORLD

Principal passenger train accidents of the 20th century

PETER SEMMENS
MA, CChem, FRSC, MBCS, MCIT

Patrick Stephens Limited

First published 1994

British Library Cataloguing-in-Publication Data;
A catalogue record for this book
is available from the British Library.

ISBN 1 85260 323 2

Library of Congress catalog no. 94–77766

Patrick Stephens Limited is an imprint of
Haynes Publishing, Sparkford,
Nr. Yeovil, Somerset, BA22 7JJ

Typeset by MS Filmsetting Limited, Frome, Somerset

Printed in Great Britain by Butler & Tanner Ltd of
Frome and London

Contents

Safety and the Railways

Safety is an emotive matter. It is, furthermore, one about which most of us have ambivalent attitudes, consciously or otherwise. If our persons or property are damaged by others, we expect someone to be held responsible for the inadequate safety. On the other hand, how often can we not be bothered to follow the well-known safety procedures for everyday activities, like using safety glasses or fastening our seat-belts, quite apart from not obeying speed limits when we are driving our cars? These may seem trivial precautions with which to conform, but the same attitude often applies in the work-place, where danger can be real, invisible and very close. In 1815 George Stephenson and Humphrey Davy both invented safety lamps which were universally welcomed because they provided illumination in coal mines without the danger of naked flames causing explosions. However, it later became necessary for these lamps to be designed so they could not be opened underground, for any reason, such as to light a pipe. Miners began to be searched regularly before they went down the shaft to ensure they were not carrying smoking materials. On the railways too, boilers of the early steam locomotives frequently blew up because the safety-valves were tampered with, *Locomotion* killing its fireman in that way less than three years after the opening of the Stockton & Darlington Railway.

It is also all too easy for us to overlook the fact that throughout life we are at risk from something or other. The likelihood of death by accident in the home is only marginally less than that of dying in a road accident (86 per million compared with 98.)[1] Our deliberate or subconscious failure to appreciate this may well stem from the fact that the only 100 per cent certainty all of us face is death, and the ability of the media, politicians and activists to arouse concern about potential or actual disasters has the same origin. It is all too easy therefore for the vast improvements in transport safety which have taken place this century to be overlooked. A study of the world railway scene over this period can thus help readers to appreciate the way in which science and technology have improved this aspect of the quality of life we enjoy in the developed world.

When looking at accidents or disasters, even over the last 90 years, it is important to consider each of them in the light of the contemporary technology, as well as the public expectations and attitudes of the time. From the 1820s onwards, the British inventions of the railway and the steam locomotive had given a major impetus to the industrial revolution. It is at times fashionable only to equate the coming of Blake's 'dark satanic mills' with these momentous changes, but it must not be overlooked that most of the subsequent rise in population came from a lowered death-rate, rather than more births. Although railways were at their most prosperous and influential during the first decades of the twentieth century[2], railway technology in the 1900s, as well as the contemporary standard of living, differed vastly from today's.

In the first few years of the twentieth century, a few experimental trains reached speeds of 100mph[3], and in 1904 a steam train could reasonably be said to have attained such a velocity[4]. The coaching-stock then provided for passengers was broadly the same as that available 50 years later, at least in this country, although a smaller proportion was provided with through corridor connections. The inventions of telephone and radio were yet to come, but, thanks to the electric telegraph, it had been possible for many years to send messages giving the whereabouts of trains in advance of their arrival. This had made perhaps the biggest single contribution to railway safety, particularly on single-track routes, which are still today the majority of those in the world. The introduction of the block signalling system also relied on the use of telegraphic equipment, but such arrangements were not, by any means, universal in 1900.

Most of the potential dangers associated with the steam locomotive were understood by 1900, and systems had been worked out to make their widespread use acceptable, although the twentieth century was still to see the occasional boiler explosion, one of which even reached disaster proportions[5]. New problems were, however, to arise as size increased, the introduction of Pacifics in France causing a number of bad accidents because of signal-sighting difficulties in 1910[6]. There were also a few problems with some designs of bogie which had a tendency to leave the track, but these never attained epidemic proportions.

Electric traction had already been introduced in places, and this innovation was, by and large, not to cause any specific changes in the level of railway safety. Electric tramways had also appeared in many cities, and, heralding the rise of motor traffic, were the cause of many accidents. In the year ending on 30 April 1908, 105 people were killed and 1,003 injured by them in Britain[7]. The replacement of oil and gas lighting in trains by electricity was, however, a big step forward from the safety point of view, as the older systems often caused the wreckage to catch fire after an accident, significantly adding to the number of fatalities. At the turn of the century, wood was still the main material of construction for passenger coaches, but this too was to change fairly quickly. Although some countries switched to all-steel construction, wooden bodies on steel underframes were still used elsewhere for many years. In Britain the railways did not completely give up the use of wooden bodywork for new construction until the 1950s.

Petrol-engined railcars began to appear early in the twentieth century, but the use of such an inflammable fuel presented an added danger in any accident[8]. The widespread adoption of the internal-combustion engine for railway traction was to await the development of the diesel motor. After a comparatively slow start, this form of motive-power was to combine with electrification to sweep steam off the railways of the world from the 1950s onwards.

It was the combination of these two forms of motive power which was to revolutionise railway speeds in the second half of this century. Led by the Japanese Shinkansen from 1965, speeds of 125mph or faster became commonplace, with the French TGVs now running in regular service at 186mph. Fast though that may seem, our neighbours across the Channel reached no less than 320mph on a trial run in 1990. Nor were these 100 + mph service speeds confined to new lines, and, a few years ago, British Rail was operating more trains at speeds of over 100mph than any other country, the majority of these being diesel-powered, running on routes that were up to 150 years old. Safety standards with these new railways have been extremely high, the most outstanding example being the Japanese 'Bullet Trains', which have never caused a single passenger fatality in nearly 30 years of operation.

The weather still lies outside our power to control, but technology has enabled some of its dangers to be tamed, particularly as more reliable methods of forecasting were developed. The introduction of track-circuits, colour-lights and cab-signalling have done a lot to overcome the clammy and often deadly grip of fog, replacing the fog-man with his detonators and brazier on the lineside. Prior to the days of clean-air legislation, the 'London peculiars' or 'pea-soupers' used to be worse than they are today, but it is now the road user who gets involved in massive pile-ups in fog on motorways. Trains have occasionally been blown off the line by high winds, but the worst dangers result from heavy rain, which can cause landslides and flooding. The frequency with which trains have been pitched into swollen rivers after a bridge or embankment has been weakened by floods is amazing. Such disasters have occurred throughout this century, right up to the late 1980s[9]. Even in Wales three died in October 1987 when the bridge across the River Towy at Glanrhyd collapsed, precipitating a diesel railcar into the floods. The 'wrong sort of snow' continues to disrupt railway operations in many countries — not just Britain — but disasters due to this type of precipitation have been rare this century.

As early as 1913, the annual total of road fatalities in this country had risen to 2,099, with more than 43,000 being injured[10]. By the mid-1930s the numbers killed in road accidents had increased to more than 7,000 annually, and such totals continued into the 1970s. In 1990, however, in spite of all the additional traffic, the figure was down to 5,217, with 341,141 people being injured.[11] Most of these occur in ones or twos, and this, plus their frequency, means that most of them do not make the headlines in the national media. On the other hand, the very rarity of railway accidents causes them to be splashed across the front pages of newspapers and on our television screens. There were only two fatalities in the buffer-stop collision at Cannon Street, although a large number of passengers were injured, but the media, presented with this story on their doorstep when other news was in short supply, had a field-day. It is this newsworthiness of railway accidents which has meant that the local press agency or 'stringer' has sent the stories from around the world to the press in this country, and this has provided much of the information in the Chronology that follows.

Alongside the advances made in transport hardware in the last few decades, engineers and others have developed a far greater understanding of the risks connected with repetitive operations, ranging from the frequency with which a skilled typist hits the wrong key to the expected failure of some vital component in an airliner. Several years ago, Professor Trevor Kletz, one of my colleagues in the chemical industry, worked out with me the statistical chance of a train driver passing a signal at danger, and it was roughly a tenth of what one would expect from a comparable non-railway activity. On the other hand, if traffic builds up, as it did on Network SouthEast in the late 1980s, drivers encounter far more signals at caution or danger, particularly in the rush-hour. This increases the overall risk of a Signal Passed at Danger (SPAD), and one can see how the need to cancel the Automatic Warning System each time might subconsciously become an automatic reaction to the hooter, rather than a trigger to check the aspect of the signal ahead. In a way one can understand the attitude of Sir Richard Moon, one-time chairman of the London & North Western Railway, that 'These mechanical appliances were all inducements to inattention on the part of signalmen and drivers'. However, following that line of argument ignores the other side of the risk factor, and it is balancing them which is very difficult.

More than ten years ago the Royal Society set up a study group on risk, and later widened its membership to include social scientists as well as engineers and authorities in the field of the natural sciences. A second report has now been published, looking at the different perceptions people have of it.[12] There is a useful summary by Sir Frederick Warner in the Winter 1992 issue of *Science & Public Affairs*, published by the Royal Society and the British Association for the Advancement of Science. A lot of the problems with the public attitude to accidents lies in the way we subconsciously set different standards for involuntary risk (travelling by public transport) and voluntary risk (our own skill in not getting involved in road accidents.) It is all too easy for politicians and their advisors to demand the expenditure of large sums on safety measures to avoid the former, which puts up fares and so pushes more people into the higher-risk voluntary mode.

There is another aspect which one has to consider with disasters, and this is the way in which they can form 'clusters', purely as the result of random chance. At any given time the incidence of a major public-transport accident probably depends on this factor to a large extent. Under the criteria I have had to adopt in the Chronology, that element must have been reinforced by the fact that inclusion of a particular accident is primarily based on there having been 20 or more fatalities. When a particular crash occurred, it was only chance that determined whether the number killed was 19 or 20.

On the other hand, there were undoubtedly longish-term trends in the severity and frequency of railway accidents. As an example one can quote the statistics for the United States of America. In the 1920s the incidence of disasters was quite high, but in the mid-1930s there was a period of 15 months when not even a single passenger was killed on that country's railways. Unfortunately the situation changed for the worse after the United States had entered World War II, as will be seen in the Chronology. One can ascribe the earlier improvement to the major 'Safety First' campaigns, and the subsequent decline to wartime conditions. It would be very difficult, if not impossible, to produce any world-wide correlations of this sort that were statistically valid, and I have not attempted to do so. Overall there must nevertheless be some correlation between the safety record for a particular form of transport and the investment put into it. To take two railway extremes, one can compare what was happening in France in 1911 with the exemplary record they have achieved with the introduction of their world-beating TGVs during the last 15 years. However, a lot of carefully-managed development work has gone on with these new high-technology railways. Simply throwing money at every safety problem perceived by the public or politicians is not the way to optimise the cost:benefit equation, let alone bring about the maximum reduction in risk.

In writing up the various accidents, I have had to interpret the reports in the light of other specific or general railway knowledge. Back in 1961 I wrote a tongue-in-cheek article, 'A cub reporter's guide to British Railways'[13], in which I poked fun at some of the

stock phrases that were trotted out on many occasions. The classic
one was to stress the fact that every train hit from behind by
another was running late, a throw-back to the days of time-interval
operations, long-since replaced by the block system imposed by
our Railway Regulation Acts. During the work on this book I have
come across some other similar stock reasons which do not ring
true, and have commented on them in the appropriate place. The
most widespread has been the suggestion that, if part of a train
becomes uncoupled, this is enough to cause the rear section to be
derailed. In most cases the sequence of happenings must have been
the exact reverse.

Any study of railway disasters also has to look at the lessons
learnt from them, and this is again an aspect on which I have
commented as appropriate. My ability to do this depends on the
attitude of the country or railway authority concerned to carry out
an 'open' investigation and publish the results. When Russia
started imposing summary sentences of up to ten years' imprisonment for breaches of discipline in 1931, this, of itself, hardly
encouraged an open investigation of any accident. This was especially true if there was any suggestion that the actions were
deliberate, as this could invoke the death penalty[14]. After more
than 35 years of such a regime, it was interesting to see how the
reports of an accident at Kamensk-Shakhtinsky in August 1987
changed as *Glasnost* progressed in the USSR[15]. Other countries can
also be secretive. When I was working on the early stages of this
book, Maurice Holmes, BR's then Director of Safety, told me that,
in his previous role of Director of Operations, he had been
interested in certain accidents that had taken place on the mainland
of Europe. In spite of his membership of the Movement Committee of the *Union Internationale des Chemins de Fer* (UIC), he
found it very difficult to obtain the correct detail and information.
(It is worth remarking that the USSR was not a member of the
UIC, nor are its successor republics.)

The United States of America currently prides itself in having a
liberal policy of access to official information. In that country the
Interstate Commerce Commission (ICC) carried out much of the
federal investigation work into railway accidents this century, but
their reports are not widely available, even in that country,
although that seems to be due more to library-purchasing policies.
At one time, however, their periodic summaries, comparable to our
own Railway Safety Annual Reports, did not disclose the location
of particular accidents, nor the name of the railway concerned.

In Britain, for over 150 years the Railway Inspectorate has
carried out an inquiry into any accident which involved the death
of a passenger, as well as many others. The results of these have
all been the subject of an official report, available for anyone to
buy. In the Library at the National Railway Museum, the bound
copies occupy some 15 feet of shelf space, and form a valuable

archive for anyone wanting to study the subject. Back in 1946 the author happened to be in Hatfield on the evening of 15 July when the down 'Aberdonian' was derailed, and was able to help passengers recover their luggage from the wrecked coaches. I later ordered a copy of Lt Col. G. R. S. Wilson's report on the accident, and was fascinated to read how the cause had been pinpointed to a shortcoming in the side-control of the V2's leading pony-truck, which was actually the only wheel-set of the locomotive still on the rails. Over the years that followed I regularly purchased these reports, and learnt a lot about railway rules and regulations from them, as well as gaining an insight into the way in which accidents can occur, which was of value in my industrial career. The layout and clarity of these reports also set an example to be followed when I had to write technical reports in later years.

Until recently the Railway Inspectorate consisted of former senior officers from the Royal Engineers, who had man-management experience, and had supervised activities in the field, even if these may not always have been under wartime conditions. Although their formal approval for new railways and works was mandatory, the recommendations from their investigations into the cause of accidents were only advisory. Originally they were part of the Board of Trade, but later migrated to the Ministry of Transport, and, and after a spell with the Department of the Environment, returned to the *Department* of Transport. Now formally entitled Her Majesty's Railway Inspectorate, they are part of the Health & Safety Executive, which comes under the Department of Employment, but the military connection has lapsed.

The style of some of the accident reports has changed too. In the old format, the details of the accident and where it occurred were set out clearly, and these were followed by a summary of the evidence, after which came the conclusions, remarks and recommendations. By contrast, in the *third paragraph* of a recent report there is a list of twelve questions '. . . which required to be examined and answered (if possible) . . .' Anyone logically reading the report from the beginning has at that stage no information on the significance of these, or even their meaning. One of the questions is incorrectly phrased too, as it asks whether the driver was misled by a route being set and then cancelled, implying that it had happened. The actual question being posed was 'did the signalman set one route and then cancel it, thereby misleading the driver?', which is significantly different. The crisp military phraseology has also been lost in some cases, long sentences of more than 70 words appearing in one recent report. In successive paragraphs one finds the phrases 'quite pessimistic assumptions' and 'extremely pessimistic assumptions', but there is no way in which one can quantify what the author of them is trying to imply.

After the Cannon Street accident there was a lot of media discussion about the effects of a buffer-stop collision on standing passengers. The general inference was that Network SouthEast was making travel unnecessarily dangerous by failing to provide sufficient seating accommodation on rush-hour trains. There were suggestions being bandied about that no standing passengers should be allowed, and the wearing of seat belts made compulsory. The Health & Safety Executive therefore decided to commission some studies using dynamic modelling techniques. Seven months after the accident, the press were invited to view two 'unique computer simulations which help to show why and how so many people were injured in the Cannon Street accident'. While watching it, Richard Hope of *Railway Gazette International* spotted that the representations of human figures on the video screens lost all control of their muscles the moment the shock occurred[16]. He asked for the simulation to be rerun with a zero impact-speed, and the 'passengers' collapsed in heaps on the floor! When the final report appeared in March 1992, it referred to the modelling work being undertaken in two stages, and the second of these did make allowance for the mathematical dummies bracing themselves.

Since 1871 there has been provision for the public inquiry system to be used to investigate the causes of a railway accident, rather than for it to be carried out by the railway inspectorate. This has been invoked very much more often in recent years. The Hixon level-crossing accident in January 1968[17] prompted only the second such inquiry, but both the King's Cross Underground fire[18] and the Clapham Junction collision[19] were given this treatment within 13 months of each other in 1987/88. Such inquiries are inevitably more wide-ranging, as are their recommendations, which totalled 157 and 93 respectively in these instances. The former rated them into five different categories of importance, but, although there had been a dialogue on this subject with London Underground, it is not clear whether the classification was based on any sort of cost:effectiveness analysis, or an assessment of the speed at which they could be introduced.

In the wake of these two accidents, a widespread, 'over-the-top' attitude developed on safety matters. Various involved parties commented on different aspects of railway operations, making recommendations which should be carried out regardless of cost. The concern about fire on the London Underground almost reached the point at which every item of machinery was expected to operate without lubrication, as any oil or grease was inflammable and so could start a fire. On hundreds of subsequent occasions the slightest smell of smoke caused the station concerned to be closed until the fire services had checked that everything was all right. This was tackling a single risk in isolation, and overlooked the fact that frustrated passengers, or would-be ones, suddenly diverted into the street, were subject to significantly higher risks from other causes than they would experience travelling on the Underground. As Sir Frederick Warner pointed out in *The Times*, the annual risk of death in a road accident is more than 30 times greater than on the railways.[20] The situation was made worse by the fact that as many as three out of every four such incidents resulted from false alarms, albeit well-intentioned.

This policy culminated in an incident on the Central Line at Bethnal Green in February 1991. This '. . . could have ended in an unparalleled disaster and it well illustrates the way that different kinds of risk can interact, the difficulties of operational control and the importance of balancing risks', to quote Brian Appleton's subsequent report.[21] A bomb alert had occurred when an unattended briefcase was left on Bond Street station. Trains were stopped and another similar case was then left on an Underground train at Liverpool Street station by someone getting out of it. As a result seven trains were trapped in the tunnels, and there were thus more trains to evacuate than stations at which to carry out the operation.

The drill is then for trapped trains to be moved up to each other, so passengers can walk through the one ahead to the next station. As Mr Appleton said, 'That is a tricky process, itself not without risk.' In this instance two trains touched, and there was a short-circuit. The electrical resistors in the rear train began to smoke, and that started to drift down the tunnel. Power was then cut off, and the fire brigade called as the instructions required. However, their arrival upset the evacuation arrangements which were in the hands of the police and the railway staff, and 'Inevitably there was confusion as to who was in control'. It took several hours to evacuate all the 6,000 passengers involved, but, although about 70 people had to be taken to hospital with heat exhaustion, no one was seriously hurt. Brian Appleton, who had been the chairman of one of the old divisions of ICI, and an assessor on the Piper Alpha disaster inquiry, was able to bring the experience of the chemical industry in dealing with potentially dangerous situations. His main conclusions and recommendations are too detailed to quote here, but it is perhaps significant that the evacuation of three times as many passengers from Central Line trains after the power-failure on 24 November 1993 was carried out without a hitch.

Before leaving these overall aspects of safety on the railways, there is one other matter worth mentioning. In the reports of the accidents in the USSR at Porbelo in January 1935[22], and the one in June 1936 at Karymskaya[23], I have referred to the extreme measures taken by the Soviet authorities against any railway staff they considered had caused an accident. One of the things that comes through the study of the Railway Inspectorate's accident reports has been the openness of those involved. The difference was most marked with a passing involvement the author had with a mining mishap where the evidence had subsequently been deliberately 'muddied.' My colleagues had been surprised at this, but the comment by the mining inspectors was that such happenings were commonplace in their experience. It would be very unfortunate if we were to lose our open attitude to railway enquiries, and the danger of this happening is one reason why I have included a report of the Purley accident in March 1989 in the Chronology, even though there were only five fatalities[24].

A few years ago two InterCity 125s were involved in a minor collision on the King Edward Bridge outside Newcastle station, after one of the drivers had passed a signal at danger. He was subsequently taken to court and fined £30. This was in spite of the well-established body of evidence, referred to above, that even the most conscientious persons carrying out repetitive jobs will make mistakes from time to time, whether they are 'driving' a type-writer, a train, or even a police car. In this connection I cannot do better than conclude this essay on Safety & the Railways by quoting a letter connected with the Purley collision from Stanley Hall, a former British Rail signalling and safety officer, whose own books on railway accidents are listed in the bibliography.

> It seems to me that the present trend of seeking a scapegoat and revenge for serious transport accidents is unwholesome. Rather than cause any improvement in real safety standards, it is likely to result only in people and institutions seeking to cover their tracks. What purpose, other than revenge, is served by sending to prison a train driver who inadvertently failed to stop at a red signal? Does it make the railway any safer? The prime objective in accident investigation must be to discover in what way the system was flawed, so that it can be put right. Systems must provide for the possibility of human error because people make mistakes, however unwittingly. You will not change that by sending them to prison[25].

[1] Health & Safety Executive & Consumer Safety Unit figures for 1989.
[2] Professor Harold Perkin, *The Age of the Railway*, Routledge & Kegan Paul (1970.)
[3] Murray Hughes, *Rail 300*, Appendix: David & Charles (1988.)
[4] P. W. B. Semmens, *City of Truro - A Locomotive Legend*, pages 10–19: Silver Link Publishing (1985.)
[5] San Antonio, Texas, USA: 12 March 1912. (See page 40.)
[6] See page 39.
[7] *Railway Gazette* **9** 85 (1908.)
[8] Collision at Tipton Ford, USA on 5 August 1914. (Page 49.)
[9] See pages 170, 173.
[10] *Railway Gazette* **20** 405 (1914.)
[11] *Great Britain Transport Statistics*, HMSO.
[12] *Risk: Analysis, Perception and Management*, The Royal Society, ISBN 0 85403 467 0 (1993.)
[13] *Trains Illustrated Annual 1961*, pages 48–49: Ian Allan.
[14] *Railway Gazette* **54** 170 (1931.)
[15] Page 170.
[16] *Railway Gazette International* **147** 573 (1991.)

[17] A report of this is not included in the Chronology as it involved a level-crossing accident. It was published by HMSO in July 1968. (Cmnd. 3706.)

[18] This was not a train accident, and is not therefore included in the Chronology. The title of Desmond Fennell's report is *Investigation into the King's Cross Underground Fire*, HMSO (ISBN 0 10 104992 7.)

[19] See page 174.

[20] Sir Frederick Warner, Letter to *The Times* (17 January 1991.)

[21] *Appleton Inquiry Report*, HMSO (1992.)

[22] See page 80.

[23] See page 81.

[24] See page 176.

[25] Letter to *The Times* (21 September 1990.)

Chronology

Abbreviations of Railway Companies' Titles

BRB   Bangladesh Railway.

BRC   Burma Railways Corporation.

CBTU   Brazilian Urban Train Company   *Companhia Brasileira de Trens Urbanons.*

CDE   Ethiopian Railways   *Chemin de Fer Djibouti-Ethiopien.*

CFM   Mozambique Ports & Railways.

CP   Portuguese Railways   *Caminhos de Ferro Portugueses.*

CPPR   Chinese People's Republic Railways.

DB   German Federal Railways   *Deutsche Bundesbahn.* From the beginning of 1994 the railways of the former East and West Germanies combined under the initials DB, which is now short for *Deutsche Bahn.*

DR   German State Railways   *Deutsche Reichsbahn.* This title was adopted by the German Railways from April 1920, and continued in use in East Germany (the Democratic Republic) until the end of 1993. On 13 December 1951, the state railways in the Federal Republic (West Germany) took the title *Deutsche Bundesbahn* (DB.)

EFE   Chilian State Railways   *Empresa de los Ferrocarriles del Estado de Chile.*

ER   Egyptian Railways.

FNdeM   Mexican National Railways   *Ferrocarriles Nacionales de Mexico.*

FS   Italian Railways   *Ente Ferrovie dello Stato.*

GRC	Ghana Railway Corporation.	
JNR	Japan National Railways, now split into six regional passenger railways and a national freight company.	
JŽ	Yugoslav Railways	*Zajednica Jugoslovenskih Zeleznica.*
KNR	(South) Korean National Railways.	
NMBS	Belgian National Railways (see also SNCB)	*Nationale Maatschappij der Belgische Spoorwegen*
NS	Netherlands Railways	*Nederlandse Spoorwegen.*
NSB	Norwegian State Railways	*Norges Statsbaner.*
ONCFM	Moroccan Railways	*Office National des Chemins de Fer du Maroc.*
PJKA	Indonesian State Railways	*Perusahaan Jawatan Kerata Api.*
PKP	Polish State Railways	*Polskie Kokeje Państwowe.*
PR	Pakistan Railway.	
SAR	South African Railways, later part of South African Transport Services (SATS), and now known as Transnet.	
SLR	Sri Lanka Government Railway.	
SNCB	Belgian National Railways (see also NMBS)	*Société Nationale des Chemins de Fer Belges.*
SNCF	French National Railways	*Société Nationale des Chemins de Fer Français.*
SNCZ	Zaïre National Railways	*Société Nationale des Chemins de Fer Zairois.*
SNTF	Algerian National Railways	*Société Nationale des Transports Ferroviaires.*
SRC	Sudan Railways.	
SRT	State Railway of Thailand.	
SZhD	Soviet Union Railways.	
TCDD	Turkish State Railways	*Türkiye Cumhuriyeti Deviet Demiryollari.*

Introduction

The following chronology provides as comprehensive a list as possible of all the railway disasters involving more than 20 fatalities which occurred anywhere in the world between 1900 and 1990. Collecting the information has not been easy, and the figure of 20 was chosen because it was likely to be large enough to prompt mention of the event in the British press. My task was made a lot easier by Francis Voisey's willingness to place at my disposal his notes on the subject, compiled from studying *The Times* for this period, together with some of the other quality papers in later years. In addition, I have searched through the weekly issues of *The Railway Gazette* up to the mid-1960s, when it ceased to report most major railway accidents when they occurred. For accidents in the United Kingdom there are, of course, the reports of the Railway Inspecting Officers available, made to whichever ministry was responsible for their activities. As described in Safety and the Railways these are an invaluable source of factual information, as well as pinpointing the cause of the disaster. The availability of the complete series since 1843 in the National Railway Museum Library has complemented my own extensive collection. Unfortunately the even more numerous corresponding reports from the Interstate Commerce Commission in the United States are not available in Britain, nor widely kept in libraries in their country of origin. However, Professor Robert Shaw's masterly 1978 analysis *A History of Railroad Accidents, Safety Precautions and Operating Practices*, provides an invaluable summary. It is the extended, second edition of his *Down Brakes*, produced in 1961, which suffered from the English publisher going bankrupt. The distribution of the enlarged version also left a lot to be desired, and I was fortunate to be presented with a copy by the Transport Museum Association at St Louis, and have drawn on it extensively in the sections that follow.

Each entry for an accident has a number of headings, the first being the date. On the few occasions where it is given in brackets there is some doubt about the exact day on which it occurred. Reports from the other side of the world are not always precise with this information. In addition, some totalitarian states, communist ones in particular, frequently did not admit publicly that such disasters could occur in their 'excellently-run' economies, and any information that ultimately became available only did so long after the event.

The next heading gives the location of the disaster. In many cases, especially with head-on collisions on single-track sections, the accident is said to have occurred between two points, or 'near' somewhere. In the heading or the text I have given either all the information that is available, or provided sufficient to identify the location to a station or town. Over the period covered by this Chronology many place names have changed, but I have used whatever was current at the time. In some cases, involving large cities such as St Petersburg, I have made mention of the changes that have occurred during this century, but there is no way in which this could be done for every entry. Similarly the name of the country used is that current at the time of the disaster.

Wherever possible I have then given the name of the railway company or organisation on whose tracks the accident occurred. This was not always clear, and, where there is any doubt, I have omitted the entry, rather than confuse the issue by assuming an ownership which could be incorrect.

The final heading entry gives the number of casualties. Again the information available is not consistent, and the only press reports in this country were often only preliminary ones. Many figures for the numbers killed and injured are thus approximate, being quoted as such, or given in round figures which makes one suspect their accuracy. In these cases I have put the figures in brackets to indicate this. In some other cases the report from the scene may refer to 'More than x killed', and in these cases I have entered the figure with a plus sign (+) after it. Sometimes different figures for the casualties appear in separate reports, both apparently equal in reliability, and in these cases I have quoted both of them. The numbers of people killed include any who have been reported as dying subsequently from their injuries. There are undoubtedly cases where such deaths pushed the total killed in a particular disaster over the 20 limit, although the initial figure in the press report was not high enough to meet the general criterion for inclusion. On the other hand, the totals can, at times, go the other way. On 1 July 1917 a car on the Niagra Gorge Railway — a Canadian interurban along the river below the Falls — fell into the river after an embankment 'washout'. The initial reports indicated that 27 were killed. In this particular instance I was able to get Dr R. V. V. Nicholls, the President of the Canadian Railroad Historical Society to check the details for me, and it turned out that there had been confusion about the number of people on the car. Although not all the bodies had been recovered, the accepted total of fatalities was only ten, so the disaster has not been included in the Chronology.

The entries differ in length considerably. Clearly those accidents of more than usual significance need longer descriptions, if information is available. 'Significance' is not confined to the size of the casualty list, but includes many of those accidents which were responsible for important changes in the railway's subsequent operating practices. Particularly unusual sets of circumstances which caused the accident are also given where appropriate. I have also included a few accidents in which there were less than 20 fatalities. The reasons for selection vary, but in most cases it was to record some interesting facet of operation, to remind readers of the diversity of different railway systems throughout the world, many of which had their own particular hazards and systems to cope with them.

As a deliberate policy I have not quoted the names of any individuals involved in the disasters, except when I have referred to the inspecting officer making the report. While it would be difficult to provide a more detailed description of an accident without doing this, the purpose of this book is to highlight the accident itself and any lessons which resulted from it. It thus did not seem necessary once again to parade the names of any responsible individuals before the reader.

There have been numerous instances when trains have been maliciously wrecked, rather than involuntarily involved in an accident. Such deliberate acts fall into two broad classes, depending on whether the action was that of disgruntled individuals, on one hand, or the organised forces of rebellion or an enemy, on the other. Some of the more notable railway disasters which have happened, or have been claimed to have happened, during wars and rebellions are described in a separate chapter. If the victims of the disaster have predominantly been innocent civilians, an entry is included in this Chronology, but the dividing line is, at times, a fine one.

All the disasters listed in the Chronology involve train accidents. There have, however, been many others on railway property, some with very high death rolls. Thirty-nine workmen were killed, for instance, when a trench collapsed at Alexandra Dock, Newport in 1909. Considerable numbers of workmen have also lost their lives in single incidents while tunnels were being constructed. The Lötschburg in Switzerland was particularly unfortunate. Twelve were killed by an avalanche which buried the construction camp at Goppenstein in February 1908, but five months later disaster struck in the bore itself. A blasting charge holed-through into a buried valley, and the rush of glacial debris into the northern end of the tunnel killed all except one of the 26 Italian workers present. During World War I another 25 workmen were killed in a tunnel collapse, between Visé in Belgium and Aix-la-Chapelle (Aachen) in Germany, on a new line being built to provide better transport to support the German front line in Flanders. Railways in the past were noted for their 'vertical' business interests, which have, in places, even included coal mines. In one of these, 53 fatalities were caused by an explosion which occurred in the East India Railway's Joktiabad Colliery at Giridih in July 1935.

Railway shipping is better known, and there have been several marine disasters involving these, in war as well as in peace. The Great Western Railway's *St Patrick* was bombed and sunk in June 1941 during one of its commercial services between Fishguard and Rosslare. Thirty lives were lost, but one of the stewardesses, Miss Mary Owen, was awarded the George Medal for her efforts in saving some of the passengers. Two examples of railway ships that have sunk since World War II are the *Princess Victoria*, which went down in the Irish Sea on 31 January 1953, and Japan National Railway's train-ferry *Toya Maru*, which capsized in a typhoon in September 1954 with the loss of over 1,000 lives.

Accidents to railway staff working on the line are also not included. Many have been killed by passing trains while working on the track, although the numbers in an individual incident are now usually small. The worst such incident the author has come across took place in World War I, when the German railways employed considerable numbers of young women on track work. (They also had women locomotive drivers at that time.) In late 1916 there was an incident which assumed disaster proportions when no less than 19 were killed, and three more badly injured. They had stepped off the up line while a military train passed on its way to Berlin. While waving and shouting to the troops aboard who were returning home from the Eastern Front, the 'girls' failed to get clear of the down track, and were hit by the Balkan Express travelling at speed in the opposite direction[1]. It was a classic case of people who work in dangerous situations allowing their attention to wander, and failing to concentrate on the laid-down safety procedures. Before the war there had also been an incident on the Berlin line, when six trackmen were killed by a train making a trial trip. Familiarity, as the proverb says, breeds contempt, and an *unexpected* happening has often been the cause of an accident[2]. Another similar case occurred when a party of men was caught out by an unusual working on the Forth Bridge in 1915. A 'company of artillery' marching across it — no doubt to one of the forts on Inchgarvie — was surprised by a train running 'wrong line.' Two gunners were killed and six injured[3]. Fifty years on, ten members of a track gang were killed in 1963, including an assistant inspector, and 13 injured, when their trolley, laden with 38 lengths of rail, fouled the wall of a tunnel on the Western Railway in India[4].

In Britain there were many fatalities amongst railwaymen generally at the end of the last century. In 1874, for instance, 788 were killed, but contemporary deaths were probably also high in mills and mines. There have also been some multiple fatalities on our railways this century, four platelayers being killed at Old Oak Common in May 1910, for example[5]. In that particular year one in every 737 permanent-way men was killed on the railways of Britain, but the mortality amongst shunters was higher, one in every 428 of them dying on the track that year[6]. It must be remembered that lineside lighting was virtually non-existent at that time. Some railways managed better than others, the City & South London Railway, for example, not recording a fatal accident to any of its employees for the 21 years between opening and 1911[7]. By 1974, however, the number of staff deaths on our railways had been markedly reduced, reaching a total of 39. Even this now seems high, as the highest number killed on the line by being struck by trains in the years 1987 to 1991/92 was eleven[8]. By mid-1994, well over a year had elapsed without any such fatality.

In addition there have been disasters on railway property affecting passengers, like the fire at King's Cross Underground station on 18 November 1987, in which 31 people died. Space does not permit any more detailed listing of such accidents, and their causes are, in any case, not unique to railway operations, like those involving trains. Most level-crossing accidents have also been omitted. This is a huge subject in its own right, and, as it involves the undisciplined road user, as well as the railway, a whole section would be required to explain the ways in which the safety of such crossings is controlled. The only such accidents included in the text are those in which there were more than 20 fatalities among people aboard the train involved in the collision.

To enable readers to obtain more information where it is available, I have included references to some of the more readily available books on the subject which give specific descriptions of the accident. Also included are references to The Railway Gazette and other periodicals. I have not included references to Stanley Hall's two excellent recent books, which are well worth reading on their own account, as their strength is that they follow particular causes or themes through a number of similar incidents. Full references to all the known books on accidents are included in the separate Bibliography.

References in Chronology
When a reference is given to a weekly or monthly periodical, the volume appears first in bold type, followed by the page number(s), and then by the year of publication in brackets. In the case of a newspaper, the date only is quoted (day, month and year) in brackets.

Where a page number is in italics, it refers to an illustration, usually accompanied by some text. In several books all the illustrations are in sections between two numbered pages of text. In these cases the page number is given in the form 66/67.

Hamilton	Hamilton J. A. B.: *Disaster Down the Line!*
Holloway	Holloway S.: *Moorgate — Anatomy of a Railway Disaster*.
MR	*Modern Railways*, Ian Allan, Weybridge.
Nock	Nock O. S.: *Historic Railway Disasters* (paperback edition.)
Pearce	Pearce, K.: *Broken Journeys*.
Rolt	Rolt, L. T. C.: *Red for Danger*.

Ritzau	Ritzau, H. J. and Hörstel, J.: *Die Katastrophenszene der Gegenwart — Eisenbahnunfälle in Deutschland Band 2.*
Reed	Reed, Robert C.: *Train Wrecks — A Pictorial History of Accidents on The Main Line.*
RG	*The Railway Gazette*, London. From 1971 the publication's name was changed to *Railway Gazette International*, currently part of the Reed Business Publishing Group, Sutton.
RM	*The Railway Magazine*, IPC Magazines, London.
Schneider	Schneider, A. and Mase, A.: *Railway Accidents of Great Britain and Europe.*
Shaw	Shaw, Professor Robert R.: *A History of Railroad Accidents, Safety Precautions and Operating Practices.*
T	*The Times*, London.
Vaughan	Vaughan, A.: *Obstruction Danger.*

Further details of these books are given in the Bibliography.

It should not be overlooked that there is an official report on virtually every accident in the British Isles which involved a passenger fatality. Because these exist for every UK disaster quoted in the Chronology, no specific reference to them is given.

[1] RG **25** 699 (1916.)
[2] RG **19** 656 (1913.)
[3] RG **23** 366 (1915.)
[4] RG **118** 183 (1963.)
[5] RG **12** 568 (1910.)
[6] RG **16** 373 (1912.)
[7] RG **14** 427 (1911.)
[8] *Railway Safety — Report on the safety record of the railways in Great Britain during 1991/92,* (HMSO p58.)

1900–1904

23 June 1900

McDonald, Georgia, United States of America
(Southern)

35 killed

A stone arch bridge over a stream was washed away in front of a train taking a work crew to repair another washout. The train plunged into the gap, and the wreckage which remained above water caught fire. Only the occupants of the sleeping car at the rear of the train escaped.

Shaw, p305.

30 August 1900

Nyack, Montana, United States of America
(Great Northern)

36 killed

In the foothills of the Rockies, 18 wagons loaded with shingle broke free from the rear of an eastbound train and ran backwards 16 miles to Nyack station. Here they overtook and collided with the rear of a passenger train which was just leaving. The last vehicle was the private business car of Mr Davis, the railway's Assistant General Superintendent, and he, his son, and cook were all killed. The next coach contained 46 of the company's Scandinavian workers from Duluth, and 33 of these were also killed. The wreckage caught fire, but three coach-loads of passengers escaped injury, although the vehicles in which they were travelling were destroyed.

8 September 1900

Bolivar, Texas, United States of America
(Gulf & Inter State)

85 killed

In the teeth of a developing hurricane, unsuccessful attempts were made to load the train from Beaumont on the ferry to continue its journey. These had to be abandoned, and the train set back towards Beaumont, but was destroyed by the force of the hurricane. All those who remained aboard it were killed, although those who had earlier taken refuge in a nearby lighthouse were saved.

27 November 1901

Seneca, Michigan, United States of America
(Wabash)

20 killed

The driver of eastbound train No. 4 misinterpreted his train order altering the normal crossing point with westbound No. 13. This had been changed from Sand Creek to Seneca, four miles further west, because both trains were running late. They met in the dark on the single line just outside the latter station. Most of those killed were immigrants.

Shaw, p123.

the central pier of a bridge had been washed away by floods. All the first-class passengers survived, including several Roman Catholic prelates. In addition to the bodies, some of the mail bags were subsequently recovered down-river, and their contents sent on.

30 March 1902

Between Barberton and Kaapmuiden, South Africa

44+ killed

On a falling gradient, the driver lost control of an early-morning passenger train, which was derailed on a sharp curve approaching a bridge over a gully or *donga*. The locomotive and the first three vehicles piled up on the side of the line, while the fourth fell into the *donga*, causing 22 of the fatalities. Most of those killed were soldiers travelling in the wagons immediately behind the locomotive, although two civilians were killed jumping from one of the coaches which, although derailed, safely negotiated the bridge.

1 September 1902

Berry, Alabama, United States of America (Southern)

21 killed

A passenger train was derailed for reasons unreported.

11 September 1902

Mangapatnan, India

62 killed

The locomotive and seven of the eight vehicles forming the Madras–Bombay mail train fell into the river at night after

27 September 1902

Arleux, near Douai, France (Nord)

20 killed, 41 injured

An express for Cambrai was diverted into a siding at full speed, the locomotive and six of its seven coaches being derailed. The signalman was thought to have operated the points irregularly.

20 December 1902

Byron, California, United States of America (Southern Pacific)

27 killed

A rear-end collision occurred between two trains after the first had come to stand because of an overheated axle-box.

26 December 1902

Wanstead, Ontario, Canada (Grand Trunk)

28 killed

A head-on collision occurred between westbound passenger train No. 5 and a freight, which it was due to cross at Wanstead. Because of a misunderstanding over the telephone between the dispatcher and the operator at Watford, the latter failed to give the passenger driver the train order changing the meeting point to Watford. The two trains collided on the single line near Wanstead

Shaw, p145.

27 January 1903

Graceland, New Jersey, United States of America (Central of New Jersey)

23 killed

A local train was switched on to the fast line to pass a freight train ahead, but was then forced to slow down because of a hot-box. Meanwhile the 'Reading Express' was following on the fast line, and the driver was distracted by a broken injector. As a result he missed the signals and collided with the rear of the local train. All the casualties, many of them from the dormitory town of Plainfield, were in the latter, three coaches of which were telescoped in the collision, and subsequently caught fire.

Shaw, p239.

27 June 1903

San Asensio, Spain

90–100 killed, 69 injured

A train fell into the Najerilla River at San Asensio, on the line between Bilbao and Zaragoza. Reports about the accident were vague and conflicting, while the work of clearing the debris was delayed by arguments between the civil and military authorities.

7 July 1903

Rockfish, Virginia, United States of America (Southern)

23 killed

A head-on collision occurred between a passenger and a freight train, because the conductor of the latter misread a train order, and the driver did not read it himself. The fatalities included four members of the train crews.

Shaw, p125.

7 August 1903

Durand, Michigan, United States of America (Grand Trunk)

22 killed

The Benjamin Wallace Circus was moving its location by rail after its show at Charlotte. In the early hours of the morning the first section of their special train came to a stand with its caboose foul of the main line. While awaiting clearance to enter the yard at Durand, its rear-end was protected by the brakesman. The driver of the second section was far from alert, failing to notice the warning fusee until roused by his fireman. The air-brake system had not been properly charged after the previous stop, and the train could not be halted clear of the one ahead. In addition to the human fatalities, two camels and an elephant were killed.

Shaw, p227.

10 August 1903

Paris, France (Compagnie de Chemin de Fer Métropolitan de Paris)

84 killed

This fire, which occurred on what is now Line 2 of the Paris Métro, was the worst railway disaster in France up to that time. Multiple-unit operation had not yet been developed, and the stock used by the Compagnie de Chemin de Fer Métropolitan de Paris (CMP) had a large controller in the leading cab. A power line connected the two motor cars at the ends of the train, and all this equipment was at full line voltage. It was possible for arcing to take place in the controller, and smoke started coming from the one on train No. 43 in the evening rush hour. The staff evacuated the passengers and arranged for the following train to propel it down the line, after its passengers had, in turn, alighted. Unfortunately the points were not set for the siding at Belleville as planned, so it was decided to propel it to the terminus of the line at Nation.

While this slow journey was taking place, the smouldering in the leading wooden vehicle of the cripple turned into flames at Ménilmontant station. This coincided with the arrival of the third train (No. 48) at Couronnes, the station behind it. Seeing the smoke coming out of the tunnel, the station master and the guard repeatedly tried to evacuate the passengers to safety. Having already had to leave at least one train, many were reluctant to do so again, a number of them being worried about losing their fares, while some even struck the staff. When the fire caused the lights to fail, a rush out of the station began, but the escaping passengers were impeded by others entering it. Many of those who escaped only did so by walking back through the tunnel to Belleville, the next station in the rear. Until more modern equipment could be introduced, the two motor cars in this type of train were coupled together at the front.

Hardy, B.: *Paris Metro Handbook*, p50, Capital Transport Publishing (1993).

14 November 1903

Kentwood, Louisiana, United States of America
(Illinois Central)

32 killed

A rear-end collision occurred as a result of the crew's failure to protect a stopped train. It was hit by the one behind it, which was effectively running on the time-interval system, as was standard on many of the country's railways at that time. Instructions for the places where trains travelling in opposite directions would cross on single lines were given by the train-order system, but trains following on the same line had to be stopped by the brakesman or conductor going back with detonators or fuses.

23 December 1903

Laurel Run, Pennsylvania, United States of America
(Baltimore & Ohio)

53 killed

Some heavy timbers, which had fallen from a wagon in a freight train, derailed the 'Duquesne Limited' express, which was travelling at high speed. Steam escaping from the sheared-off dome of the locomotive enveloped the smoking-car, killing all its passengers. Fire also broke out, although the two Pullman cars at the rear of the train escaped damage

Shaw, p211.

3 July 1904

Litchfield, Illinois, United States of America
(Wabash)

24 killed

A passenger train was derailed as a result of sabotage to a set of points.

7 August 1904

Eden, Colorado, United States of America
(Missouri Pacific train on Denver & Rio Grande tracks)

(88) killed

The Denver to St Louis express was wrecked at Steele's Hollow, when a wooden bridge over a minor stream was washed away after a cloudburst. Within an hour the water flowing down the stream increased a hundred-fold, and a weaker road bridge upstream of the railway line carried away. Its remains hit the train as it crossed the swollen stream at a very slow speed. Debris from the tender and front three vehicles was carried half a mile down stream. The exact number of fatalities was never established accurately, as some of the bodies were never recovered

Shaw, p303.

24 September 1904

Hodges, Tennessee, United States of America
(Southern)

63 killed

The dispatcher had issued instructions for eastbound train No. 12 from Chattanooga to Bristol to cross train No. 15 from Bristol to Knoxville at New Market. The crew of the latter ran through New Market without stopping. The reasons for this were never discovered, as the two men were killed in the resulting collision on the single line.

Many of the fatalities occurred in two lightly-built coaches in the eastbound train, which were crushed between the heavier vehicles either side of them

Shaw, p136.

10 October 1904

Warrensburg, Missouri, United States of America
(Missouri Pacific)

29 killed

An eastbound passenger train was running in two parts, the second carrying a special party to the World Fair at St Louis. The crew of a westbound freight train did not observe the indications on the first passenger locomotive showing that a second section was following, and pulled out of the siding into its path. The collision took place at a combined speed of about 30mph. Most of the casualties occurred in the first vehicle, which was not the customary baggage car. The crews of the two locomotives jumped clear beforehand and were not killed.

Shaw, p315.

1905–1909

11 May 1905

Harrisburg, Pennsylvania, United States of America
(Pennsylvania)

23 killed

In the early hours of the morning, a 68-wagon westbound freight train was flagged to a stop because of a shunting locomotive ahead. Although only travelling at a low speed, the driver stopped sharply, which caused the unbraked rear vehicles to force two of those ahead off the track into the path of the second section of the 'Cincinnati Express' on the adjacent fast line. The resulting collision was not sufficient to kill any of the crew or passengers, but one of the derailed vehicles contained 50,000 lb of dynamite, which was ignited by the fire from the express locomotive. In the resulting explosion three railwaymen and 20 passengers were killed.

Shaw, p213.

17 June 1905

Patapsco, Maryland, United States of America
(Western Maryland)

26 killed

A head-on collision on a stretch of single line was caused by the crew of one of the trains disregarding the instructions in their train orders.

27 July 1905

Hall Road, England
(Lancashire & Yorkshire)

21 killed

A terminating electric multiple-unit had been put into the central reversing siding, situated between the running lines beyond Hall Road station. The signalman found he was unable to reverse the points and clear the signal for the following electric train, which was not booked to stop there. After a second, unsuccessful, attempt to reset the points, they were left aligned for the siding. Failing to note this, and, with the protecting semaphore locked at danger, the signalman gave a green hand-signal to the motorman of the second train. The unit accelerated into the siding, where it collided at approximately 40mph with the standing train.

Hamilton, p15.

6 October 1905

Rostoff-on-Don, Russia

27 killed, 35 injured

The mail train for Vladikaukas was derailed.

31 December 1905

Lebedin, Russia

30 killed

A collision in the station caused the deaths of 30 recruits and 'railway delegates'.

31 December 1905

Between Znamenska and Trepovka, Russia

20 killed

Two military trains collided between stations, the fatalities all being soldiers.

16 March 1906

Florence, Colorado, United States of America
(Denver & Rio Grande)

34 killed

During a snowstorm in the early hours of the morning, the dispatcher was trying to decide where to cross an eastbound train with the westbound 'New Mexico, Utah & California Express'. He called the operator at the outlying station of Beaver to find out if the express had gone through, and was told it had not. However, the 25-year old at the remote location had been on duty for 19 hours, and had dozed off for a very brief period, during which the train had passed. In the light of this false information, the dispatcher decided to move the 'meet' to Adobe, further east than usual. He instructed the operator at Beaver to give the driver of the express the necessary train order, which was, by that time, impossible. The express continued non-stop through Adobe, and the two trains collided head-on between that station and Florence. The two front coaches were crushed, and fire broke out. Once again many of the casualties were immigrants on their way to the Northwest. (Even in England emigrants

to the New World were involved in railway accidents during this era, two being injured when a double-headed special was in collision with a coal train at Woodhouse in 1908.)

Shaw, p146. RG **8** 601 (1908).

1 July 1906

Salisbury, England
(London & South Western)

28 killed

Three minutes before 2am, the up boat train from Plymouth to Waterloo failed to slow for the sharp curves through Salisbury station. The locomotive and coaches left the track and struck a milk train travelling in the opposite direction. Only the last of the express's five vehicles was comparatively undamaged, and 24 of the train's total of 43 Trans-Atlantic passengers, all travelling in the three central vehicles, were killed.

These expresses had been introduced in 1904 in connection with the arrival of the America Line's ships at Plymouth, and were the only trains which did not stop at Salisbury. The locomotives were changed at Templecombe on these trains, which had a start-to-stop average of 57.9mph between there and Waterloo. In the light of the observations made by railway officials on the first of these workings, a speed-limit of 30mph was fixed for the passage through Salisbury station. The third Special Traffic Notice underlined this by giving passing times at the two signal boxes there, which corresponded to a speed of less than 26mph. On the night concerned, the boat train's speed though the curve was probably just over 60mph, and this was sufficient to cause the locomotive to overturn and come into contact with the milk train.

One of the interesting points in Major Pringle's report for the Board of Trade is the fact that, at that time, it was not customary to detail speed restrictions in British railway companies' Working Timetables. He recommended that this should be done, although the widespread provision of speedometers was not to be adopted for almost another half-century.

There is one significant point about this accident which, to the author's knowledge, has not previously been noted. On the following day, the GWR was to begin passenger services over its Castle Cary–Cogload 'cut-off', which meant that the LSWR would lose its distance advantage between London and Plymouth.

In early 1907 the *Railway Gazette* reported that the executors of five of those killed in the accident had settled for an average of £1,300 each, with twelve of the injured averaging £495. Two years later, however, one of the women passengers who had been in the accident was awarded £7,000 for her injuries. The total compensation paid to passengers came to £32,854, with a further £350 being paid to employees' dependants. Surprisingly the cost of the damage to the locomotives (£246) was less than that to the track and station (£608). Both were minor compared with that for the stock (£4,400), but several of the coaches had to be scrapped, while both locomotives were repaired and returned to service.

Hamilton, p19, *p92/93*. Nock, p81. Rolt, p166. RG **6** 146 (1907), **10** 159 (1909). RM **139** *v* (April 1993).

18 September 1906

Dover, Oklahoma, United States of America
(Chicago, Rock Island & Pacific)

20 killed

A northbound passenger train from Fort Worth to Chicago fell into the Cimarron River when a bridge collapsed, having been damaged by flood water from a severe storm on the previous day.

28 October 1906

Atlantic City, New Jersey, United States of America (Pennsylvania)

57 killed

An electric excursion train was derailed at 40mph approaching an open drawbridge across the tidal Elizabeth River. The driver had never worked over this line before, but, in spite of the fixed warning signals and the open span being clearly visible, he made no attempt to stop. Although the conductor's emergency brake valve was opened in a late attempt to save the train, the first two cars followed the locomotive off the bridge into deep water.

In the following year a report was published about railway 'drawbridges' in the New York State. There were no less than 41 of these, and the inspector considered that, although they were all protected by signals, a standard arrangement should be adopted. Not less than 500 feet from the 'draw' there should be derailers, with a home signal 50 feet before it. Advance warning should be given by a distant signal 1,500 feet away.

Similar installations still exist in many states, and in recent years a photographer actually got a series of pictures of runaway diesel locomotives, without a driver aboard, falling into the water.

Reed p90, 100. Shaw, p194. RG **6** 280 (1907).

12 November 1906

Woodville, Indiana, United States of America (Baltimore & Ohio)

43 killed

A collision occurred between an eastbound freight train and the second section of westbound passenger train No. 47. The freight was held in the loop at Babcock to cross the two sections, but, in the snowstorm, the crew failed to see the green marker flags on the locomotive of the first section, and the corresponding green lights had gone out. They nevertheless acknowledged the special whistle signal made by the crew of the first passenger train, but failed to realise its significance. The freight moved off which brought it into collision with the second section of train No. 47, and the wreckage caught fire. Many of the victims again were immigrants, this time from eastern Europe.

29 December 1906

Elliot Junction, Scotland (North British & Caledonian Joint)

22 killed

In the severe snow-storms affecting the east coast of Scotland, the 7.35am from Edinburgh reached Arbroath over an hour late. Meanwhile a southbound freight train had run into a snow-drift beyond Elliot Junction, south of Arbroath, and the train had split. The driver decided to take his locomotive forward, cross over to the other line and return to Elliot Junction to propel the separate portions of his train southwards. The operation took far longer than expected, and the wagons then became derailed. Single-line working had to be instituted, but the block system was put out of action by the snow on the telegraph wires.

By 3 o'clock in the afternoon the staff at Arbroath were anxious to send their snowbound trains back south. The first to be dispatched was a local, the passengers getting into the rear carriages because only this portion of the train could be put into the platform. Fifteen minutes later the express left with its locomotive running tender first through the blizzard. Before he departed, the driver was twice warned to travel cautiously under the time-interval system, and this was again repeated at Arbroath South box. He did not do so, and collided at an estimated speed of 30mph

with the local train, which was standing at Elliot Junction waiting for the pilot-man to conduct him over the wrong-line stretch to Easthaven.

The official report was critical of many aspects of the organisation of the joint line. Although the conditions were difficult, no news of the accident reached Easthaven, $2\frac{1}{2}$ miles away, for nearly four hours, and it was not until 11pm that the information was relayed to the North British headquarters in Edinburgh. There was no suitable rescue equipment available locally, not even heavy jacks, to deal with the wreckage, and the breakdown train did not arrive until the early hours of the following morning. The driver of the express, who had accepted a drink from passengers at Arbroath 'to keep the cold out', was convicted of culpable homicide, although his 5-month prison sentence was later reduced.

Hamilton, p30. Rolt, p121.

30 December 1906

Terra Cotta, Washington DC, United States of America (Baltimore & Ohio)

43 killed

In foggy conditions, an empty-stock train ran through signals at Tacoma and collided with the rear of a late-running excursion train from Frederick to Washington. The latter was standing in Terra Cotta station picking up passengers. Immediately after the accident most of the railway staff concerned were arrested, leading the Baltimore & Ohio to announce that it could not make its own investigation because all its vital witnesses were in prison.

Shaw, p168.

2 January 1907

Velland, Kansas, United States of America (Rock Island)

31 killed

At Velland the operator had only worked in that capacity for three days. In his application for employment, he had stated he was 23 years old instead of 18, and falsely claimed to have had six years' experience on other railways. The westbound 'California Fast Mail' had been held at Velland to cross a train in the other direction, and the dispatcher, after enquiring whether it was still there, issued orders for it to be held for a second eastbound train. While the operator was writing this out, the Mail started to reverse on to the main line. Instead of ensuring that it was stopped to receive the new orders, the operator merely reached out and moved the train-order board, but failed to put it into the 'stop' position. The train continued to reverse, but the operator still did nothing, thinking that the locomotive was going to the water column. Only belatedly did he rush out and unsuccessfully try to attract the crew's attention. Realising a collision would be inevitable, he then ran away. Although the eastbound train involved in the collision was only travelling at about 10mph up a bank, a tramp travelling on the roof of one of its cars was killed. In the other train, the baggage car of the westbound Mail telescoped into the smoker, which was filled with Mexican labourers, 30 of whom were killed.

Shaw, p148.

16 February 1907

The Bronx, New York City, United States of America (New York Central & Hudson River)

23 killed

Three days after the introduction of electric traction by the New York Central, an evening express for White Plains was derailed on a curve near 205th Street. The two locomotives and the leading coach remained on the track, continuing for a further 1600 feet, while the vehicles at the rear of the train fell on their sides and slid for some distance. At the time the motorman was thought to have underestimated his speed because of the much smoother riding of the electric locomotive. There was also some debate about the state of the track, but tests showed that the $4\frac{1}{2}$-inch super-elevation provided for the 60mph limit was safe at 75mph. The sleepers had, however, moved in the ballast during the faster run, which may have explained why some of the press representatives invited to take part had left the train after the first trip, carried out at 50mph. At that time the authorities in the United States were considering the need for more systematic investigations into railway accidents, 321 passengers having been killed in 1906. The investigation work in this case included detailed calculations of the track forces produced by electric and steam locomotives. The official conclusions were that more spikes were desirable on track where electric locomotives were operated in pairs, and that the responsibilities of the construction and operating departments should be kept 'clear and distinct.'

Shaw, p296. RG **326**, 525 (1907).

28 March 1907

Colton, California, United States of America
(Southern Pacific)

22 killed

A derailment was caused by a 'misplaced switch' (pair of points).

11 May 1907

Surf, California, United States of America
(Southern Pacific)

33 killed

The second section of a northbound train was derailed at a pair of points, two of the coaches finishing up on the beach. While the locomotive itself passed safely over the points, they opened under the tender, possibly due to some item of equipment being pulled along the track. The locomotive was dragged off the rails, and the first five coaches were also derailed, although the last two safely passed over the points, the position of which was 'detected' and interlocked with the automatic signalling. The cause of the accident was not positively determined.

Shaw, p319.

20 July 1907

Salem, Michigan, United States of America (Pere Marquette)

30 killed

The misreading of a badly-written train order caused a head-on collision between a freight train and an eleven-coach excursion carrying railway employees on their annual outing from Ionia to Detroit. The writing on the order slanted upwards, although the vital time was connected to the station concerned by a dotted line. However, the crew of the freight, who did not read the order over to each other as laid down, connected the time at Plymouth with Salem, and the collision occurred in a deep cutting between the two stations. The freight locomotive was turned end-for-end by the impact, and finished up side-by-side with the other, both facing east.

Shaw, p124.

4 August 1907

Pont-de-Cé, France (État)

27 killed, 15 injured

One of the arches of a bridge across the Loire collapsed under an Angers–Poitiers train, the locomotive, tender and two coaches falling into the river. Two companies of infantry from Angers helped local fishermen with the rescue work. The injured passengers were visited in hospital by the Minister of Public Works, who presented the local Prefect with FF3,000 for their immediate needs.

15 September 1907

Canaan, New Hampshire, United States of America
(Boston & Maine)

26 killed

In the early hours of the morning, an error in the number on a train order was responsible for a head-on collision between a freight and a passenger train. Although the numerals were always repeated in words, either the dispatcher or the operator put down 34 instead of 30. That night train No. 34 was running 20 minutes behind No. 30, but the information given to the freight crew made them believe that No. 30 was running half an hour later than it was. They therefore pressed on towards the siding at West Canaan, as allowed by the rules, only to collide with No. 30 before reaching it. The tender and the baggage car at the front of the passenger train telescoped into the smoker behind them, causing the fatalities.

Shaw, p157.

19 September 1907

Encarnaćion, Mexico

(63) killed, 43 injured

An El Paso express and a freight train came into head-on collision on an incline with such severity that both locomotives and several carriages of the express were destroyed. The crew of the freight had continued beyond the siding where they should have awaited the express, and disappeared afterwards. The driver was later arrested when he entered his native United States, and was reported to have admitted responsibility for the accident.

25 November 1907

Between Hospitalet and Cambrile, Spain

20+ killed

The Valencia express was completely derailed approaching a river bridge between the stations at Hospitalet and Cambrile, and, with the exception of the rear two vehicles, fell into the river. Of the estimated 70–90 people aboard, only two of the survivors were uninjured.

25 December 1907

India (North-Western State)

22 killed

Two passenger trains collided after an assistant stationmaster had given a 'Line Clear' for the down mail, after accepting one in the other direction.

In the following year it was announced that more public information would be provided about railway accidents in India,

RG **8** 632 (1908), **11** 5 (1909).

20 April 1908

Braybrook Junction, Victoria, Australia (Victoria State)

44 killed, 140 injured

Late at night two trains for Melbourne collided in the station at Braybrook Junction, which was also known as Sunshine. The first to enter the station was from Ballarat, and it was just pulling out when the one from Bendigo crashed into its rear, wrecking the last five coaches of the departing train. The drivers of the double-headed Bendigo train claimed that their brakes failed, but they had worked satisfactorily at the previous booked stop and when two passengers pulled the communication cord because they wished to alight at Macedon. At the very lengthy inquest into the deaths, a large number of signalling irregularities at Braybrook Junction came to light, and the stationmaster, as well as the two drivers of the Bendigo train, were committed for trial.

25 April 1908

Gargantua Siding, near Maltrata, Mexico

28 killed

The collision involved a train carrying pilgrims on their return from the shrine at Guadeloupe.

May 1908

Moradabad, India

(120) killed, 50+ injured

As a result of a failure in the tablet system, one was withdrawn at *both* ends of the single-line section between Ghaziabad and Dasna. The two passenger trains collided at 40mph on a curve, and the six coaches were wrecked. Gas from the lighting systems ignited, and the fire spread to the coal on the locomotives. As a result it was not possible to determine the exact number of dead.

RG **8** 574C (1908).

21 May 1908

Contich, Belgium (Belgian State)

40 killed, over 100 injured

A morning passenger train from Antwerp to Brussels was unexpectedly diverted into a loop outside Contich station, a few miles after starting. It managed to negotiate the points at 40mph, but then collided with a stationary train for Turnhout. The two old third-class carriages at the rear of this were badly damaged. Most of the casualties to the workmen, soldiers and pilgrims took place in these vehicles. Between 19 May and 14 June, 56 people had been killed, and over 300 injured in railway accidents in Belgium, so there was considerable public disquiet. A detailed inquiry was held into the Contich disaster, and the results were made public.

The locking in the signal box at Contich was being renewed, which involved the removal of the levers from the frame, one at a time for a period of 2–3 hours. The one for the signal protecting the points had been removed on the day in question, and a man placed by the line outside the box, who pulled the end of the disconnected signal-wire when instructed to by the signalman. After the arrival of the local train the points were not returned to normal. Even though the lever for them, and that for the facing-point lock, was clearly 'reversed' in the frame, the signalman told the man on the ground to clear the signal for the express.

RG **8** 545 (1908), **9** 361 (1908).

25 September 1908

Young's Point, Montana, United States of America (Northern Pacific)

23 killed

The collision occurred on a single-line stretch, the crew of one train having failed to observe the standard rules to give priority to a superior train running in the opposite direction.

26 September 1908

Berlin, Germany (Berlin Hoch-und-Untergrundbahn)

21 killed, 18 seriously injured

Two trains came into collision on the elevated triangular junction between Möchermstrasse, Leipziger Platz and Bülowstrasse. The one from Leipziger Platz ran past signals and collided with that from the Bülowstrasse direction, one car falling 30 feet to the ground. Both members of the crew of the former train were arrested, and the driver was given a prison sentence of 21 months.

RG **9** 401 (1908), **10** 230 (1909).

14 October 1908

Metz, Michigan, United States of America

35 killed

Severe forest fires in the states of Michigan and Wisconsin had surrounded the village of Metz, and a relief train was sent to evacuate the inhabitants. Laden with them and their goods, it tried to travel north, but could not get through the blaze. It was attempting to escape in the opposite direction when it came to a trestle across a culvert, which had been weakened by the flames. The train overturned into the ditch. Most of the fatalities were women and children.

1908

India

The Indian Railways report for 1908 referred to two other accidents not reported elsewhere. On the Oudh & Rohilkhand State Railway 79 were killed and 119 injured when two passenger trains were allowed into the same single-line section. The other, involving 26 fatalities, occurred when an express and a goods train collided on the Bombay, Baroda & Central India Railway. The former had run past signals at danger, but some of the rules had also been disregarded by the staff.

In the year 1908 there were 77 passenger train collisions in India, 46 of them serious ones, with fatalities totalling 131. There were also 73 serious derailments among the 204 recorded, but these only involved three deaths.

RG **11** 5 (1908).

15 January 1909

Dotsero, Colorado, United States of America (Denver & Rio Grande)

20 killed

A head-on collision occurred on the single line near the eastern end of Glenwood Canyon, due to the crew of one train failing to obey their train order.

24 February 1909

Riobamba, Ecuador

25 killed, 40 injured

A northbound main-line train left the track because of a displaced rail, and fell over a 100ft cliff.

1909 (first quarter)

United States of America

20 killed, 28 injured

Reference was made in the January–March report of the Interstate Commerce Commission to an accident where a westbound passenger train had ignored the order to stop at a particular loop. Instead it passed through ten minutes early and collided with an eastbound freight.

RG **11** 298 (1909).

21 April 1909

Cardiff, Wales (Rhymney)

3 killed

The boiler of 0-6-2ST No. 97 blew up in the company's sheds, after the driver had returned with it, saying he could not get the injectors to work. As a result of the explosion, which was heard over much of the city, the boiler and firebox were thrown 60 yards, and then bounced a further 30. This accident is discussed in more detail in the chapter on boiler explosions. The contemporary reports were confusing, an impossible explanation for the accident being given by the coroner's jury, although the Board of Trade's boiler inspector had very quickly discovered that the safety valves had been wrongly assembled, and were incapable of operating.

Hewison, p115. RG **10** 556 (1909).

28 November 1909

Sapperton, British Columbia, Canada (Great Northern)

22 killed

The accident occurred because of a washout.

13 December 1909

New York State (New York Central and Lake Shore)

Considerable number killed

The 'Twentieth Century Limited' sleeping car train from Chicago to New York collided at 60mph with a stationary Lake Shore passenger train because of a signalman's error.

RG **11** 820 (1909).

1910–1914

21 January 1910

48 miles west of Sudbury, Ontario, Canada (Minneapolis, St Paul & Sault Ste. Marie)

37 killed

The 'Soo Express' for Minneapolis, which had departed from Montreal the previous night, left the track just before a bridge across the Spanish River. A first-class carriage and the dining car plunged 30 feet through the bridge into the icy water, while a second-class coach hit the abutment of the bridge, killing 20 of its occupants.

The injured guard displayed great heroism, cutting a hole in the side of the dining car with an axe to release seven passengers, and was subsequently awarded the Albert Medal.

1 March 1910

Wellington, Washington, United States of America (Great Northern)

51 killed

In severe winter weather two electric trains had been held up by snow drifts at the west end of Cascade Tunnel since 25 February. They were being used as living quarters for their passengers until the line was cleared, but were overwhelmed by an avalanche just before dawn on 1 March. Two days previously some of the passengers, concerned about the possibility of such an accident, had asked for one of the trains to be moved into the tunnel, but the superintendent said they were in no danger.

21 March 1910

Green Mountain, Iowa, United States of America (Chicago Great Western)

55 killed

A main-line train was derailed on a stretch of track which was not in sufficiently good condition to cope with the unusual combination of weight and speed.

Shaw, p204.

30 March 1910

Mülheim (Ruhr), Germany

20 killed, 41 seriously injured

The 'Lloyd Express' from Hamburg to Genoa over-ran signals and collided with a troop train travelling to Metz, which had been part of Germany since the Franco-Prussian war. The 'Lloyd Express', one of the best-known *trains de luxe* in Germany, ran regularly in conjunction with the sailings of the Nord

Deutsche Lloyd's liners. The driver missed one of the signals.

RG **12** 436 (1910).

18 June 1910
Villepreux-les-Clayes, France (The former Ouest section of État)

18+ killed, 90 injured

Owing to a breakdown of the locomotive, a local train from Paris had been detained for about 45 minutes outside the station, when the express for Granville over-ran signals and hit it at a speed of approximately 60mph. The dining car and three carriages of the express were destroyed, as were the guard's van and three carriages of the local. Fire broke out, but when the fire brigade arrived they could not find a source of water. A photograph taken subsequently showed little more than piles of wheels and bogies. The driver of the express, who was unhurt, took to his heels with a group of peasants after him, and was subsequently arrested. The driver of the local train was said to have become 'temporarily insane', while, according to one account, the stationmaster, 'after an alternation of objurgations and appeals for mercy, had locked himself in his office, the terrible scene having momentarily deprived him of reason'. The casualty list was fortunately reduced because many of those travelling in the local train had alighted to while away the time.

The French Minister of Public Works said that the Ouest Railway, on whose tracks the accident occurred, had been handed over to the government in a very defective condition, but the *Railway Gazette* commented that the Ouest had been continually hampered by him when it tried to get sanction for renewals, etc.

RG **12** 704 (1910).

23 June 1910
Manzanillo Line, Mexico

37 killed, 50 injured

An accident occurred to a troop train, when four of its rear coaches broke loose and ran backwards down a steep incline.

4 July 1910
Middletown, Ohio, United States of America (New York Central train on Cincinnati, Hamilton & Dayton tracks)

20 killed

Just after lunch on Independence Day, a head-on collision took place 25 miles south of Dayton. The westbound 'Twentieth Century Limited' had been diverted on to the CH&D because of another accident at Sharon, Pennsylvania. It hit an eastbound freight, the crew of one of the trains not having been given the necessary train order.

14 August 1910
Saujon, France (Paris-Orléans)

43 killed, 50 injured

An excursion train from Bordeaux collided with a goods train about 25 miles from Saintes on the line from Paris to Royan. Most of the victims were young girls, and the Minister of Public Works cancelled his journey to Switzerland with the French President to go to the scene of the accident. The President also asked the Swiss authorities to curtail the festivities during his visit to their country as a mark of respect.

21 September 1910

Indiana, United States of America (Fort Wayne & Wabash Valley)

34 killed

At the time, this was the worst accident to happen on the electric interurban systems which operated extensively in North America. Clear of the built-up areas, these lines had their own segregated rights-of-way through the open countryside, and high speeds were reached. This accident occurred when a southbound extra working was driven past its assigned crossing loop, as well as the next, and collided with an empty-stock working in the opposite direction.

Shaw, p376.

4 October 1910

Staunton, Illinois, United States of America (Illinois Traction)

36 killed

Less than two weeks after the previous interurban disaster, a second occurred, with a larger number of fatalities, making it the worst such accident to be recorded in the United States. A southbound train was running in two sections, the second carrying an excursion party to the parade of the Veiled Prophets at St Louis. A local train in the opposite direction was booked to cross it at Staunton, and, in spite of its driver having been warned that the other one was running in two parts, set off as soon as the first had passed. The conductor unsuccessfully signalled him to stop and was making his way forward to the cab when the collision occurred.

Shaw, p376.

24 December 1910

Although the number of fatalities in none of them was as high as 20, on this particular Christmas Eve there were six railway accidents in England, the United States and France, and a seventh occurred in France on the following day. Such a spate of disasters is very unusual, and it could have been that peoples' thoughts were straying on to the coming festivities, rather than being concentrated on everyday safety.

Hawes Junction, England (Midland)

12 killed, 21 injured

The first of the two English accidents was at Hawes Junction (now Garsdale), when two light engines were incorrectly sent off by the signalman ahead of a down express. Fire followed the collision.

Bolsover, England

Three children were killed and another three injured when they were hit by a train on a level-crossing, after gaining access through an open wicket gate.

Upper Sandusky, Ohio, United States of America (Pennsylvania)

Eight people were killed in a collision.

Montereau, France (Paris, Lyon & Méditerranée)

1 killed, 7 injured

The sleeping-car attendant was killed and passengers injured when the Paris–Modane express collided with a goods train.

Marmande, France (Midi)

Twenty people were injured.

Arbanats, near Bordeaux, France (Midi)

A rear-end collision occurred between the Toulouse express and another passenger train after the first had been stopped in the station because of the accident at Marmande further along the line. The driver had missed the signals.

25 December 1910

Near Châteaudun, France (Paris–Orléans)

6 killed

An express hit a horse-drawn carriage on a level-crossing, and six occupants were killed.

The French accidents mentioned above only represented a small fraction of those that occurred at this time. In mid-February 1911 the *Railway Gazette* reported that there had been 30 during the previous two months and, on a number of occasions, had paragraph headings such as 'The Weekly Railway Accident in France'. The most serious (at Courville near Chartres) resulted in twelve fatalities, but major steps had to be taken to deal with the crisis. Many trains were taken off, and others slowed until the permanent way could be reconstructed. One of the problems turned out to be the sighting of signals from the new Pacific locomotives. An engineer investigated this for the Ministry of Public Works, and recommended changes in the height of signal posts, and the provision of automatic detonator-placers. The locomotives also suffered from smoke and steam obscuring the driver's view. There had been a strike of French railwaymen in the autumn of 1910, and many of them were not subsequently taken back, but it is not clear whether this had any bearing on the accident record.

RG **13** 542 (1910), **14** 47, 219 (1911).

22 April 1911

Blaauwkrantz Bridge, Cape Province, South Africa (Kowie)

30 killed

The passenger portion of the Port Alfred–Grahamstown train was derailed on the approach to the bridge, probably because of a sharp flange on one of the goods wagons. It ran across the structure, but on the other side a van and four carriages fell 250 feet into the ravine. The inquest determined that the poor condition of the track and rolling stock was responsible for the derailment, and recommended an immediate inspection of the railway, with annual ones thereafter. The line's manager was subsequently found guilty of culpable homicide.

25 August 1911

Manchester, New York State, United States of America (Lehigh Valley)

28 killed

A double-headed train of 14 wooden coaches was taking a party of Union veterans and their families home from a reunion at Rochester, when it was partially derailed by a faulty rail as it approached a bridge over the Canandaigua River. The locomotives and the first five coaches remained on the track, but one bogie of the sixth vehicle was derailed, followed by the rest of the train. Although the track across the bridge was protected by check-rails, the seventh coach fell 40 feet into the river, landing on its roof, and most of the fatalities occurred in it. The rail was found to have a manufacturing defect, which caused it to break into at least 17 pieces.

Reed, p97. Shaw, p202.

23 September 1911

Montreuil-Bellay, France (État)

22 killed, 27 injured

The accident was caused by flood damage to a bridge across the River Thouet, eight miles from Saumur. A single pier collapsed, precipitating the two locomotives and the first three coaches into the river. Some of the passengers who had climbed on to the roofs of the coaches were drowned before they could be rescued.

The accident record of État again became the subject for national concern, one Senator commenting that there had been 37 accidents in the previous six months causing death or injury. He added that the current journey times were longer than they had been in 1856. In his response, the Minister of Public Works said that the railway administration was being reorganised, and the permanent way would be improved to enable Pacifics to be used on all passenger trains from 1 July 1912.

18 March 1912

San Antonio, Texas, United States of America (Southern Pacific)

28 killed, 40 injured

During a test after a 2-6-0 locomotive had been overhauled in the railroad's workshops at San Antonio, it was destroyed by a boiler explosion, which also severely damaged the surrounding buildings. One 7-ton portion of the boiler was thrown 400 yards, while a smaller piece, weighing 8cwt, damaged

the side of a house nearly a mile away. The Inter-State Commerce Commission (ICC) inspector's comment was: 'I cannot recall an instance where the destruction was so complete, and in which the loss of life has been so appalling.'

Three different theories were put forward by the team carrying out the inquiry. There was some industrial trouble in the works at that time, and an army officer considered that the accident was caused by someone setting off a charge of high-explosive. The ICC inspector's view was that the cause was excessive pressure, although the boiler had been hydraulically tested two days before, and considered capable of withstanding a pressure of 956 psi(g). The manufacturers of the injectors said they would not work at pressures higher than 240 psi(g), and they were operating at the time of the explosion. Pictures of the incident show that the firebox was ripped into several pieces and badly distorted, which also strongly indicated that a low water level in the boiler was the most likely cause of the explosion. This accident is also referred to in the chapter on boiler explosions, as some of the statements referred to above do not stand up to a proper scientific/engineering analysis.

Reed also illustrates two other boiler explosions on the Southern Pacific that year, one in the roundhouse at Hondo, Texas, and the other out on the track, when the boiler was blown off the locomotive on to the side of the line. The latter incident occurred within a month of the San Antonio disaster.

Reed, pp163, 164, 166-8. RG **17** 29, 303 (1912).

4 July 1912

Near Corning, New York State, United States of America (Delaware, Lackawanna & Western)

39 killed, 86 injured

A double-headed excursion train to Niagara Falls on Independence Day was stopped by a stalled freight ahead, and the leading locomotive on the passenger train was detached to run forward to assist. The train was protected by automatic block signals, and a flagman went back half a mile, although he did not put down any detonators. In spite of these precautions, the excursion was struck in the rear by a following express which had continued at 65mph through the thin fog. Some of the passengers escaped because they had alighted and were strolling round the fields alongside the line. The steel car, next to the rear of the excursion train, was pushed into the preceding wooden sleeping-car, *Esthonia*, demolishing two-thirds of it.

Reed, pp73, 79. Shaw, p240. RG **17** 50 (1912).

5 July 1912
Ligonier, Pennsylvania, United States of America (Ligonier Valley)

22 killed

This collision occurred on one of the many 'Short Lines' which have been such a feature of the North American railway scene. The Ligonier Valley Railroad consisted of an eleven-mile 'main' line, with several short spurs serving the coal mines in Westmoreland County, but it also operated a busy passenger service. An excursion was being run to take passengers from Ligonier to the local fairground, a mile and a half away. Because there were no facilities to run-round there, the return working was operated with the locomotive propelling the single coach. A train order telling the conductor of the excursion to wait for a coal train to pass was either not delivered or not obeyed. When the collision occurred, the coach was crushed like 'a pack of cards' by the two freight locomotives, although three members of their footplate crews also lost their lives. During the line's 35

years of operation no previous fatalities had occurred to either passengers or staff.

Shaw, p136. RG **17** 50 (1912).

During the last three months of 1912, no less than 3,994 collisions were reported on the United States' railways, which caused 227 deaths, with 4,010 people being injured.

RG **19** 161 (1913).

30 April 1913
Boregaun, India (East Indian)

40+ killed

A local train from Nagpur to Bhuswal ran at approximately 30mph into the rear of a goods train which had been stopped by signals. Its front six vehicles were smashed and everyone travelling in them was either killed or injured. The railway's English interlocking inspector and his wife were travelling in a coach ahead of the brake van of the goods train, but were unharmed, although two of their servants were killed.

11 May 1913
Drama, Bulgaria

150 killed, 200 injured

A coupling on a 30-wagon Bulgarian military train broke, and 25 of them ran backwards towards Buk, where they collided with 28 wagons also full of soldiers.

RG **18** 620 (1913).

23 May 1913
Between Poroi and Andjista, Bulgaria

Number of casualties not reported.

Two locomotives were destroyed in a collision, the stationmaster responsible for the accident being shot by the order of the Inspector of Bulgarian Railways.

RG **18** 682 (1913).

2 September 1913

Wallingford, Connecticut, United States of America (New York, New Haven & Hartford)

26 killed

The heavy holiday traffic returning to New York overnight coincided with thick fog, and five trains were running in close succession along the double-track main line. This was provided with automatic block signals of the 'banjo' type, which were only capable of providing two aspects, and they were in the process of being replaced with semaphores. Leading the procession of trains was a local, which called at Wallingford, and this stop caused the two sections of the 'Bar Harbor Express' behind it to come to a stand. The second section was duly protected at the rear by a flagman, and, when it moved off, it failed to pick him up. A second stop was made to do this, and as he walked back towards his train he heard the first section of the 'White Mountain Express' approaching through the fog at far too high a speed for the prevailing conditions. He rushed towards it, but was unsuccessful in signalling it to stop in time. The oncoming locomotive split open the two rear Pullmans, and finished up embedded half-way through the one in front of them. The accident was seen by the crew of a trolley car on the parallel track, and their vehicle was brought into use as an ambulance.

This accident caused considerable public concern. The US Congress allocated $25,000 for the Inter-State Commerce Commission (ICC) to conduct an investigation, and the preliminary inquiry produced the information that the driver of the colliding train had worked for 159 hours during the previous week, with only nine hours rest. This was because there were not enough capable drivers. The *Railway Gazette* was critical about the way the US authorities were tackling the bad accident record, as the proposal to reconstitute Block Signal & Train Control Board would only cover four per cent of avoidable accidents.

Shaw, p243. RG **19** 319, 420 (1913).

Mid-September 1913

Villeneuve-Loubet, France

20 killed, 40 injured

An electrically-hauled train of three, well-loaded coaches became derailed on a viaduct in the south of France. The coupling broke and the leading carriage twisted sideways. It smashed through the parapet, and landed 40 feet below in the ravine. Only the power unit remained on the rails. The derailment was blamed on 'the imperfect working of the magnetic brake because of a storm', the same reason being given for at least one other disaster. As the braking system at that time was most likely to have been rheostatic rather than regenerative, this explanation appears to be one that became fashionable in media parlance, but had no basis in fact.

RG **19** 349 (1913).

4 November 1913

Mélun, France (Paris, Lyon & Méditerranée)

39 killed

At Mélun there was a loop used by southbound trains on the far side of the northbound line. As the 8.40pm mail from Paris was taking the junction into it at just over 50mph, it was struck by a northbound express from Marseilles. Considerable damage was caused to the leading vehicles of both trains, and fire broke out in the wreckage, which prevented rescue work for some time. Amongst those killed were 15 postal workers, and the accident scene was strewn with letters and parcels. The driver of the mail train had missed two signals while he was attending to his locomotive. The Minister of Public Works urged the railways to install some form of automatic train control, and abolish the use of gas-lighting in coaches.

A lot of ideas were put forward in the press to avoid similar accidents, one of them being that a pilot driver should ride in a special cab on the front of the locomotive, noting the times at which various signals were passed, and what their aspects were.

RG **19** 517, 545, 552, 574 (1913).

6 December 1913

Costesti, Roumania

100 killed

The fatalities were reported to have occurred in a collision.

Shaw index.

2 April 1914

Near Tanjong-Prioh, Dutch East Indies

20 killed, 50 injured

The morning train collided with a buffalo and left the track on a bridge, which then collapsed as a result of the derailment. The locomotive and the first five coaches fell into the river. All those killed were 'natives', the Europeans travelling in the rear coaches escaping unhurt. There is some confusion about the exact location of the accident. In 1924 there were two places on the railway system in Sumatra called Tandjoeng and Tandjoeng Balai, while the present-day map shows Tandjung Pernik near Batavia on the island of Java.

RG **20** 500 (1914).

5 August 1914

Tipton Ford, Montana, United States of America
(Missouri & North Arkansas train on Kansas City Southern tracks)

47 killed, 25 injured

This was the first major accident in the United States which involved a petrol-electric railcar or 'Doodlebug'. The 70 ft long steel vehicle belonging to the Missouri & North Arkansas weighed 42 tons, which was equal to 47 American short tons. It left Joplin at 5.30pm for Harrison, with all seats taken and some standing passengers. That railway had 'running powers' or 'trackage rights' over the Kansas City Southern, and the railcar was issued with a train order instructing it to wait at Tipton Ford to cross a conventional 7-coach southbound train, but failed to do so. A mile further on the two trains met at a closing speed of about 70mph, which caused the length of the railcar to be telescoped by 20 feet. It was also driven back 651 feet, and the wreckage then burst into flames.

It is interesting to note that Shaw refers to the 42 ton railcar as a 'light' vehicle, with far less resistance to collisions than a conventional train, with its steam locomotive, tender and baggage car at the front to provide valuable protection. For decades now, far lighter railcars than this have been in regular operation on many railways of the world, using the same tracks as locomotive-hauled trains. Our Department of Transport will not, however, permit the use of light-rail units, such as the Tyne & Wear 'Metrocars', or those for the Manchester 'Metrolink', to operate on lines carrying conventional trains.

Some of the early petrol-driven railcars were fairly robust, at least when a collision took place between a pair of them. Two 70ft McKeen steel gasolene motor cars collided on a sharp curve in early 1912 at a closing speed of 75–80mph. There was no loss of life, and neither was even derailed. The front-ends appeared to have acted as 'crumple zones' in best 1990s' automobile practice.

Shaw, p138. RG **16** 91 (1912).

15 September 1914

Lebanon, Missouri, United States of America
(St Louis & San Francisco ('Frisco))

27 killed

The accident was due to a flood washing out part of the track.

December 1914

Kalish, Poland

(400) killed, (500) injured

A crowded troop train from Prussia collided with a train returning from the Russian Front with wounded officers, after the points had been moved at the last moment. More than 20 coaches were smashed. The pointsman, station-master and other officials were arrested on a charge of treason.

RG **22** 21 (1915).

1915–1919

22 May 1915

Quintinshill, near Gretna Junction, Scotland
(Caledonian)

277 killed, 246 injured

This double collision caused the greatest number of fatalities of any railway accident in Great Britain, and the high death-toll was due to wartime conditions. The two night expresses from Euston to Scotland were running late, and just after 6am a local train from Carlisle was sent off in advance of the first of them. The intention was for this to be held at the block post at Quintinshill, ten miles further north. There were loops here on both the up and down sides, but the latter was occupied with a northbound freight. Accordingly the local was stopped and reversed over the cross-over to stand on the down line. An unofficial shift-relief arrangement had been adopted by two of the signalmen working the box, and, on occasions such as this, the one taking over for the day shift travelled from Gretna Junction on the local. To avoid the irregularity being detected, the train movements after 6am were written on a separate piece of paper, rather than in the train register.

After the arrival of the local, an up train of coal empties was sent forward to Quintinshill, and, as Carlisle could not deal with it, the signalman was instructed to put it in the up loop. Then, just before the belated relief arrived, he accepted the first of the down expresses.

While the two signalmen were having a brief conversation, a message was received that a troop special was on its way from Larbert to Liverpool.

The day-shift signalman then began copying the details from the piece of paper into the register, while his mate, now off duty, sat in the back of the box, reading a newspaper. Also in the box were the brakesmen of the goods trains in the two loops, while the fireman from the local arrived to report the presence of his train as required by Rule 55. He made the appropriate entry in the register, using a pen provided by the day-shift signalman, and then went back to his locomotive, 65 yards away. However, he did not check whether collars had been put on the appropriate signal levers to prevent them being moved accidentally. For reasons unknown, one of the signalmen gave 'Train out of Section' for the up goods without sending the 'Blocking Back' signal as he should have done because the local was occupying the up line. The signals were then cleared for the down express and the troop special in the opposite direction.

The latter collided violently with the local, which reduced the length of the heavily-loaded train of 15 coaches from 213 yards to only 67 by the force of the impact. Before anyone could take protective action, the double-headed down express charged into the wreckage. Fire broke out, and burnt for the best part of 24 hours. It consumed not only many of the bodies of the soldiers, but also their regimental records, so the exact number of fatalities was never known. Both signalmen were convicted of man-slaughter and given prison sentences.

In 1994 it was announced that a memorial to those killed was to be built at the nearby Gretna Tourist Centre.

Hamilton, p62, *p92/93*. Nock, p107, *p160/161*. Rolt, p207, *p132/133*. Schneider, p160, *p98*. RG **22** 544, 558, 584, 633, 657 (1915), **23** 286, 307, 310, 495 (1915). RM **139** *vi* (April 1993).

19 October 1915

St Cyr Defavières, (Paris, Lyon & Méditerranée)

'Heavy loss of life'

Several coaches of a train were derailed and fell off a bridge into a deep ravine alongside the railway between Roanne and Lyon.

RG **23** 415 (1915).

30 January 1916

Between Köln and Duisburg, Germany

Officially only 2 killed

An express collided with a hospital train full of wounded returning from the Front, the locomotive of the former climbing on top of the coaches of the other train. The official death toll was given as two, but this was contradicted by eye-witnesses arriving in Amsterdam. Later that year there were reports of a Red Cross train full of wounded colliding with a goods train on the line from France to Charleroi. The number of casualties was not known, but several local civilians who were working on the goods train were killed.

RG **24** 175 (1916), 25 442 (1916).

29 March 1916

Amherst, Ohio, United States of America (New York Central)

26 killed

Two portions of a Chicago–Pittsburgh overnight express collided after the first section had been stopped at a signal. This had gone back to danger because the signalman had failed to pull the lever fully and latch it. When the locomotive whistled for the road it was pulled again, but the train had difficulty getting away. Before it had gone more than a few coach-lengths, it was struck in the rear by the second section, travelling at about 50mph. Some of the wreckage spread on to the westbound track, where, 30 seconds later, it was hit by the 'Twentieth Century Limited', also running at about 50mph. None of the passengers in the NYC's famous named train was killed. It was a foggy night, but the driver of the second section of the train from Chicago claimed to have seen his signals at clear, although his fireman had become completely disoriented in the poor visibility. The inspector concluded that the signals had been against the second section, and the report referred to the fact that the driver concerned had been disciplined five times in 16 years for over-running signals.

Shaw, p450. RG **25** 337 (1916).

12 August 1916

Brookdale, Pennsylvania, United States of America (Southern Cambria)

26 killed

A collision on this interurban line was caused by a runaway train.

1 December 1916

Herczechalen, Hungary

66 killed, 150 injured

A fast train from Vienna to Budapest, carrying a large number of people, mainly soldiers, who had attended the funeral of Emperor Franz Joseph, was in collision with a local. One of them overran signals, possibly because the inferior oil then being used in the signal lamps was producing a poor light. Amongst those killed was the Austrian civilian governor of Serbia.

RG **25** 641 (1916).

19 December 1916

There were three fatal train accidents in England on this particular night, all caused by drivers failing to observe signals. Two of them involved three trains which had left Euston for the north within three hours of each other. At Wigan the 11.15pm from Euston collided with the previous 10pm departure from London, and at Kirtlebridge, just over the border into Scotland, the down Postal ran into a goods train. The Board of Trade issued the three Accident Reports on the same day in March 1917, their quick appearance in print being standard at that time.

RG **26** 316 (1917).

7 January 1917

Ciurea, Roumania

374 killed, 756 injured

An over-crowded train with some 2,000 passengers aboard collided with one from the military headquarters near Ciurea, eight miles from Jassy, and was then derailed. The casualty total came from official sources, one of the injured being the French attaché.

RG **26** 121 (1917).

17 January 1917

Massy Plaiseau, France

10 killed, 30 injured

A British troop train with 40 'carriages', filled with soldiers returning from leave, split in two a few miles south of Paris. This happened on a descending gradient, and the second half then caught up and collided with the vehicles in front, two of the 'coaches' being telescoped. The injured were taken to hospitals at Versailles, and the coolness and discipline of the troops was praised by the French officials. From the number of vehicles in the train, plus the fact that the break-away section was not immediately brought to a halt by an automatic brake, one would infer that the vehicles were the notorious vans, branded 'Hommes 36-40, Chevaux 8', which were widely used in France at this time for conveying troops. By contrast, in 1914 the Great Indian Peninsula Railway started building bogie 'Military Cars', with running-gear and other operating equipment which was standard with their contemporary carriage stock. Each of these saloon-type vehicles had seats for 66, and these could be converted to provide the same number of sleeping spaces for overnight travel.

RG **26** 91, 120 (1917).

In Britain, troops travelled in ordinary coaching stock, but it could be of the non-corridor variety, and this resulted in a somewhat unusual accident at Bere Ferrers later that year, on 24 September 1917. A party of New Zealand troops was travelling up-country from Plymouth on the London & South Western Railway. Orders had been given that, at Exeter, the first stop, two soldiers per compartment were to alight and go to the guards van to draw rations for their companions. Unfortunately the train was stopped by signals at Bere Ferrers, and the troops, no doubt feeling hungry, thought they were at Exeter and started to get out in the dark. They alighted on to the track on the 'six-foot' side, using the doors through which they had boarded the train. Almost immediately a Waterloo–Plymouth express passed at speed, killing ten of them. At the coroner's court the jury returned a verdict of Accidental Death some weeks later.

RG **27** 387 (1917).

These New Zealand troops were undoubtedly unlucky, but a larger number of Scots ones were killed in a train accident at the end of 1918 in Belgium through foolhardiness. They were riding on the *roofs* of the coaches between Namur and Liège, when they were swept off by scaffolding in a tunnel, 17 of them being killed.

RG **30** 34 (1919).

19 January 1917
Sagor, Salonika, Greece

40 killed

A mail train was struck by a landslide on the line between Laibach and Agram, part of it being buried, while the other section fell into the River Save.

19 January 1917
Trifail, Styria

40 killed

The mail train from Trieste to Vienna was cut in two by a falling rock near Trifail, and the train sent to the rescue ran into the debris, causing more fatalities.

RG **26** 118 (1917).

27 February 1917
Mount Union, Pennsylvania, United States of America
(Pennsylvania)

20 killed

The failure by the crew to protect the rear of a stalled passenger train caused it to be hit by the following fast freight even though the line was equipped with modern signalling. Although of all-steel construction, the Pullman car *Bellwood* was completely telescoped by the next vehicle, *Bruceville*, and all its occupants were killed. In the subsequent investigations it was discovered that the driver had only had five hours sleep after being on duty for $15\frac{1}{2}$ hours. Since 30 July 1913 there had been four serious rear-end collisions on the Pennsylvanian Railroad caused by non-observance of signals.

Reed, p80. RG **27** 160, 256 (1917), **28** 285 (1918).

23 July 1917
India

20 killed

A passenger train was held up by a break in the line, and a messenger sent to get assistance. While he was away it proved possible to repair the damage, and the train continued. However, it was driven with such 'recklessness' that it collided with the train coming the other way with the repair gang.

In the year which ended on 31 March 1918, 54 passengers were killed on the Indian Railways, which was considered a bad year, even though the passenger total had been 430 million. During the same period, no less than 1,350 trespassers were killed. Two years later the country's railway accident record was to change dramatically for the worse.

RG **30** 743 (1919).

7 August 1917
Arguata Scrivia, Italy

34 killed, (100) injured

An express from Genoa to Milan was derailed in the station, three carriages being overturned.

13 August 1917

Russia

60 killed, 150 injured

A collision took place between a passenger train and a 'luggage' train on the line from Moscow to Petrograd. (This city was later to be known as Leningrad, but it has now reverted to its original name of St Petersburg.)

28 September 1917

Kellyville, Oklahoma, United States of America (St Louis & San Francisco ('Frisco))

23 killed

The head on collision occurred because one of the crews had failed to obey their train order.

2 November 1917

Caucasus, Russia (Vladikavkas)

25 killed, 70 severely injured

A head-on collision occurred between an express and a military train, the majority of those killed being soldiers.

RG **27** 522 (1917).

12 December 1917

Modane, France (Paris, Lyon & Méditerranée)

543 killed

At the time it took place, this railway accident produced the largest confirmed death-toll of any in the world. Its cause and severity were both directly due to wartime conditions, but it was not in any way caused by enemy action, so is included in this chronology.

Two trains of Italian stock were carrying a total of over 1000 French soldiers going on Christmas leave from the Italian front via the Mont Cenis route. After reaching France through the tunnel, because of the wartime shortage of motive power they were combined at Modane into a single train of 19 coaches. A 4-6-0 was provided to haul it, and the driver initially refused to take it down the 1 in 33 gradient because its maximum permissible load was limited to 144 tons, while the train weighed 526 – three times that amount. To make it worse, only the first three coaches had air brakes, the others being provided with hand-operated ones.

The military officers brought undue pressure on the driver, threatening him with a court martial if he refused to work the train, so he set off very slowly. In spite of applying the hand-brakes as hard as possible, which enabled him to descend the first bank at 6mph, the train soon started to run away. As speed picked up, sparks from the red-hot wheels and blocks began to set fire to the floors of the wooden vehicles. Beyond La Praz, where the line crossed the River Arc on a reverse curve, the locomotive broke away from the train after its bogie had become derailed. The leading vehicle was then derailed against a high retaining wall on the outside of a sharp curve, and the remainder of the train piled up behind it. Fire broke out, adding to the death toll, while the military authorities were reported to have driven back some of the volunteer rescuers. However, amongst the items being taken home illegally by the troops as souvenirs there were live shells and grenades, so it was perhaps safer to keep everyone away until they had exploded in the heat. At La Praz, the signalman, seeing the runaway pass him, contacted the next station at St Michel de Maurienne in time to prevent an ambulance train leaving, which might have collided with the wreckage of the troop train. The driver of the latter was arrested, but subsequently found not guilty by a court martial.

The news of the accident was suppressed by military censorship, and the full details were first published by Schneider & Masé in *Railway Accidents of Great Britain and Europe* as late as 1970.

Shaw, p410. Schneider, p223.

(December 1917)
Shepherdsville, Kentucky, United States of America (Louisville & Nashville)

67 killed, 50 injured

A collision occurred between a passenger train and a local one.

RG **27** 720 (1917).

8 January 1918
Between Kaiserlautern and Homburg, Germany

30+ killed, 100+ injured

A collision occurred between two trains, one of them carrying troops going on leave.

RG **28** 112 (1918).

16 January 1918
Kirn, Germany

25 killed, 25 injured

Heavy rain caused a dam to fail, and the resulting flood in the River Nahe washed away part of a railway embankment. As a result the locomotive, a goods wagon and three passenger coaches of an early morning leave train fell into the water. Recovery of the bodies was slow, only ten having been found several days later.

RG **28** 112 (1918).

16 January 1918
Bohmte, Germany (Nahe)

33 killed, 110 injured

The collision occurred in the station on the line between Bremen and Osnabrück during a snowstorm, the casualties all being soldiers.

18 January 1918
Argeningkem, East Prussia, Germany

23 killed, 50 injured

A leave train was in collision with a passenger one near Argeningkem, south of Tilsit. This was the fourth serious accident to occur on the German railways within the space of a month.

7 February 1918
Between Jezupol and Wodniki, Ukraine, Russia

Unknown

A crowded train from Stanislav to Lemberg caught fire at midnight, and was brought to a stand on a bridge across the River Dneister. Many of the passengers who jumped from the burning coaches were drowned.

22 June 1918
Ivanhoe, Indiana, United States of America (Michigan Central)

59–68 killed, 115 injured

The second section of the Hagenbeck Wallace circus train, en route to Hammond, Indiana, was stopped by a hot box. Although it was protected by automatic block signals, the flagman went back to protect its rear. Following it was an empty troop train formed from 24 steel Pullmans, the driver of which had dozed off after being awake for nearly 24 hours. He had also just eaten a heavy meal and was taking kidney pills which made him drowsy. The fireman was a new employee who had not worked over the line many times. They missed the caution and stop signals, as well as the vigorously waved lantern of the flagman, who finally threw a lighted fusee into the cab of the locomotive as it passed him. The heavy Pullmans ploughed into the rear of the stopped train, and fire broke out. Amongst the dead were many of the circus stars. The driver and fireman were both tried for manslaughter, but acquitted.

Shaw, p245. RG **29** 58 (1918).

(29 June 1918)

Between Mircesti and Roman, Roumania

45 killed

The date of this collision between an express and a goods train may not be quite correct, as the press report was lacking in details.

9 July 1918

Nashville, Tennessee, United States of America
(Nashville, Chattanooga & St Louis)

101 killed

A double-track section on this railroad stretched for $2\frac{1}{2}$ miles between Nashville station and Shops, and on this length the Memphis to Atlanta express was booked to pass local train No. 4 every day. Under the train order system, if the trains failed to meet as laid down, the 'inferior' local had to wait at Shops until it appeared, unless it had been issued with a train order to the contrary. On this occasion, for reasons

unknown, it continued on to the single line ahead, and collided with the express at a closing speed of approximately 100mph. Both locomotives were written off, with all their crews being killed, but the majority of the fatalities occurred in the second and third cars of the local, which were telescoped. This train was packed with negro workmen making their way to the local powder factory. The final death-toll was given by the Interstate Commerce Commission as 101, including 14 crew members, although other conflicting figures appeared in the press.

This was the worst railway accident in the United States, but the reason for it was never satisfactorily established. One theory was that the driver of the local mistook a shunting locomotive and some cars on the double line for the express, although neither its number, nor its formation, tallied with those of the 'superior' train. A contributory factor was that the normal practice of stopping at the end of a twin-track section to consult the train register had lapsed. As with a number of contemporary railway accidents in Europe, although they were not directly caused by the hostilities, wartime conditions nevertheless contributed to the number of casualties.

Shaw, p126.

16 July 1918

Theillay, near Vierzon, France (Paris-Orléans)

22 killed, 76 injured

The accident resulted from a derailment.

31 July 1918

Between Schneidemuhl and Landsberg, Prussia, Germany

30 killed

Two trains were involved in a collision during the final months of World War I.

The *Vossische Zeitung* reported that large crowds had attempted to rob the casualties, and had only been stopped when soldiers and police intervened, arresting several railway officials in the act. In *The Times* this was reported under the heading 'Prussian Ghouls', and described as 'characteristic tokens of German *Kultur*' – a typical example of wartime propaganda.

(Late August) 1918

Near Uggowitz, Austria

20 killed, 80 injured

A collision occurred on the Villach–Pemtaffl line between two trains taking soldiers on leave. The press report specifically mentioned that some officers were among those killed.

RG **29** 246 (1918).

11 September 1918

Near Schneidenmuhl, Prussia, Germany

35 killed, 17 injured

A children's excursion was in collision with a goods train, all the fatalities being young passengers, except for two railwaymen.

13 September 1918

Weesp, Netherlands (Hollandsche IJzeren Spoorwegmaatschappij)

41 killed, 42 seriously injured

An eleven-coach express was derailed when the 7-metre high embankment on the approach to the bridge across the Merwede Canal collapsed. There had been heavy falls of rain during the previous weeks, and, as the train passed, the vibration fluidised the sand of the embankment. In the light of later know-ledge the slope was too steep and a layer of clay prevented the water draining away. The wooden coaches suffered badly after falling down the embankment after the derailed locomotive had hit the steel girders of the bridge. There was a doctor on the train, who was immediately able to assist the injured, and an infantry unit on manoeuvres reached the site in ten minutes to help with the rescue work. Ships on the canal were used to transfer the injured to hospital. The railway company were held to be responsible and had to pay 1.4 million guilders compensation to passengers.

There was an interesting outcome from this accident. The engineer from Delft who investigated the cause of the accident founded a laboratory for the study of soil mechanics at the Technical High School there in 1934. Now part of the university, it is still consulted by the Dutch Railways when new lines are being constructed.

19 September 1918

Pacy Tunnel, near Tonnerre, France (Paris, Lyon, & Méditerranée)

(30) killed, (100) injured

Three coaches were telescoped when two halves of a train or two separate trains collided in the tunnel. The press reports of this accident said that the collision took place between two trains after three coaches at the rear of one of them had broken loose when the 'chains' parted.

RG **29** 347 (1918).

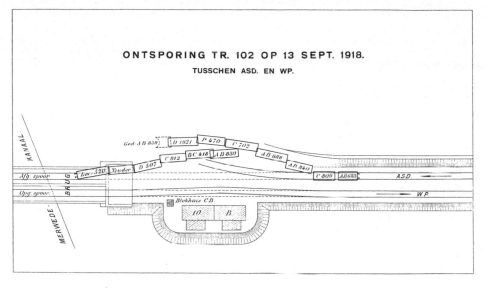

Weesp, 13 September 1918

A plan of the positions of the locomotive and coaches after the deruilment at Weesp in the Netherlands on 13 September 1918. (Boomsma Collection)

22 September 1918
Germany

30 killed, 59 injured, 30 of them seriously

A train from Leipzig ran into the back of one from Berlin, telescoping or damaging the rear four coaches.

RG **29** 347 (1918).

12 October 1918
Selerra, Spain

67 killed, 25 seriously injured

Two passenger trains collided after points had been set wrongly.

RG **29** 423 (1918).

1 November 1918
Near Norrköpping, Sweden

(300) killed

A Malmö–Stockholm train was derailed, the locomotive and coaches falling down an embankment after several days of heavy rain. Seven of the ten coaches were smashed and set on fire by the gas escaping from their reservoirs. Included in the large number of passengers were 50 children returning from the provinces to Stockholm.

RG **29** 371, 395 (1918).

1 November 1918
New York City, United States of America
(Brooklyn Rapid Transit)

97 killed

During a wildcat strike by members of the Brotherhood of Locomotive Engineers & Firemen, seeking recognition from the company, staff from other grades were driving the trains. After an evening train for Brighton Beach had been held up by being misrouted at a junction, the driver attempted to make up lost time. He was unfamiliar with the route, and, in spite of two warning signs, drove the train too fast over a curve with a 6-mph restriction. This was where the line had recently been diverted from running on the surface into a tunnel. The second and subsequent cars were derailed, being scraped along the abutment in which were embedded heavy iron uprights. These ripped the relatively flimsy vehicles apart. The third coach, in which 60 fatalities occurred, was reduced to matchwood. The driver, conductor and guard were all charged with manslaughter, and the mayor, who was a member of the striking union, also got several of the company's senior officials similarly indited. On the grounds of popular prejudice the trials had to be moved out of the city. All the cases finally collapsed, but the last person involved was not acquitted until April 1920.

Shaw, p388. RG **29** 538 (1918).

6 November 1918

Between Steinbruch and Rakos, Hungary

60 killed, 180 injured

A troop train was derailed by a broken axle near Budapest.

7 December 1918

Lothiers, France
(Paris-Orléans)

68 killed, 151 injured

A leave train was involved in a collision in the station.

12 January 1919

South Byron, New York, United States of America
(New York Central)

22 killed

A rear-end collision occurred after the driver of a train had passed a signal at danger. A similar accident on 9 June 1920, which resulted in a further 14 deaths, prompted the state regulatory body to set up an inquiry into the use of Automatic Train Control.

RG **33** 390 (1920).

22 January 1919

Mauvages, France (Est)

20 killed, 40 injured

The collision took place between Neufchateau and Toul.

(16 February 1919)

Kambove, Belgian Congo

(27 killed)

A train was standing in the station overnight when one of its wagons, containing several tons of explosive, blew up. Everyone in the train was killed, the only European involved being a Belgian non-commissioned officer. Afterwards no trace could be found of the ganger's cottage which used to stand nearby.

RG **30** 348 (1919).

17 April 1919

Crissé, Sarthe, France
(Former Ouest section of État)

33 killed

After a French leave train had stopped because the locomotive had broken down, it was hit from the rear by another travelling to Brest, which was loaded with returning United States servicemen. The guard had gone back and laid detonators, but the second train was running fast downhill, and could not stop. Of the first 23 bodies recovered, 16 were American soldiers.

19 June 1919

Between Firozabad and Makkhanpur, India (East Indian)

(100–300) killed

Down Goods No. 127 left Firozabad with the wrong token for the single line ahead, and collided head-on with up passenger train No. 7 travelling towards Calcutta. Fifteen passengers and the four enginemen were killed in the collision, and approximately 40 people injured. Fire then broke out, destroying six of the ten passenger coaches. This caused a considerable additional loss of life, it being estimated that between 100 and 300 died in the conflagration. There was a remarkable number of similarities to the causes of the collision 18 months later at Abermule on the Cambrian Railways in Mid-Wales.

RG **32** 62 (1920).

29 June 1919

Near Rohtak, Punjab, India

35 killed, 46 injured

A mail train from Delhi collided with a goods train. Two of the fatalities were Indian railwaymen, and three European passengers were among those injured.

RG **31** 132 (1919).

5 October 1919

Mexico

60 killed

A train from Laredo in Texas, USA, was derailed on its way to Mexico City.

RG **31** 470 (1919).

25 October 1919

Kranowitz, Silesia, Germany

25 killed

A collision between a passenger and a goods train occurred in the station at Kranowitz, which was later to become part of Poland. The wreckage then caught fire. Most of those killed were reported to be smugglers taking spirits across the frontier, either in specially-shaped tins on their persons, or hidden in loaves of bread. In their attempts to get rid of the evidence they were said to have poured the alcohol on the floor, which would have added to the flames.

RG **31** 573 (1919).

1 November 1919

Vigerslev, Sjælland, Denmark (DSB)

40 killed

A collision occurred between two passenger trains at night outside Vigerslev station, between Copenhagen and Roskilde. An up train for the capital stopped because a small boy had fallen out. It then set back for about a quarter of a mile to pick him up, but was not protected in the rear by detonators or handlamps. While this was happening, the signalman reversed the junction ahead for a special train carrying a large fire brigade which was being sent to a major conflagration in the Roskilde district. This was routed from the down goods line to the down main, crossing the up line in the process. Having done this, it stopped alongside the stationary passenger train, the glare from its headlamps masking the latter's tail-lamps. To permit this unauthorised movement, the signal interlocking had been irregularly released, which also freed the electric locking of the box in the rear. This enabled the following up express to be sent on from the Roskilde direction without reference to the signalman at Vigerslev. Hauled by an 'Atlantic', the express charged into the stationary passenger train, pushing five of its coaches down the embankment and then landing in the middle of them.

RG **32** 119 (1920).

3 November 1919

Pont-sur-Yonne, France
(Paris, Lyon & Méditerranée)

26 killed, (42–60) injured

The 'Simplon Express' was held up by signals at Pont-sur-Yonne just before 11pm, and, while it was standing, was hit by the following Paris–Geneva express. The latter had overrun signals, possibly because the exhaust from the steam locomotive was beating down and obscuring the driver's vision. Considerable damage was done to both trains, and there were differing reports about the number of fatalities, the PLM referring to 18 deaths in its statement.

RG **31** 613 (1919).

According to a report in *The Times* a few

weeks earlier, there were 31 railway accidents in France during the first three months of 1919, causing 115 deaths and 363 cases of serious injury. Even in one of the winning countries, the aftermath of four years' conflict had seriously eroded the safety standards of its railways.

On 4 September 15 had been killed and 40 injured on the morning express from Gare d'Orsay to Toulouse. It had come to a stand because of bad coal between Castennau d'Estretefonds and St Jory, and was hit by the following Bordeaux–Cette train. A few days after the Pont-sur-Yonne disaster a train from Juvisy to Paris was stationary for some time, and fearful for their safety, some of the passengers got out. They were run down by another train, four being killed and one injured.

RG **31** 336 (1919).

10 December 1919

Asia Minor

35 killed and injured

A Kassaba passenger train was in collision with one from the Ottoman Railway at a junction.

RG **32** 34 (1920).

20 December 1919

Between Onawa and Benson, Maine, United States of America
(Canadian Pacific)

23 killed, 35 injured

Early in the morning, an eastbound freight train collided with the fourth section of train No. 39 from St John, New Brunswick to Western Canada, badly damaging the locomotive and two leading coaches. The westbound train was conveying passengers who had landed from RMS *Empress of France* the previous day, some of them being immigrants and others returning servicemen. The first sections of the train had seriously delayed the freight, which had taken twelve hours to cover the 91 miles from Megantic. The crew were becoming concerned about reaching Brownville Junction, 27 miles further east, before they ran foul of the 16-hour duty limit. At Morkill, where they were stopped to cross the third section of No. 39, they were handed a copy of a new train order, giving them instructions about the additional fourth section, which was running eight hours behind the usual time of the main train. The crew misread the order as applying to the *third* section, and set off eastwards again before it had passed.

The passenger train had 300 immigrants aboard, who had crossed the Atlantic in steerage class, and, once again as a result of a railway accident, many of them never reached their destinations in the New World. Relief trains were sent to the site of the collision from both directions, and the bodies of the dead were laid out on the snow-covered sides of the embankment. To reach Montreal from the port of St John on the west coast of the Bay of Fundy, the Canadian Pacific Railway's line runs through Maine in the United States. Since the passengers were immigrants from Europe, the accident was an international one in more senses than one.

Shaw, p129. RG **32** 25 (1920).

1920–1924

12 April 1920

New York, United States of America (New York Elevated (Sixth Avenue Line))

1 killed, 12 injured

During the morning rush-hour, an express came into converging collision with an empty-stock train at a cross-over, and one car fell into the street below. The 'Elevated' was a remarkable line, their trains, in the main, being operated 'on sight' without signals. To reduce the chance of any derailed vehicle falling into the street, continuous balks of timber, 6in × 8in (150 × 200mm), were mounted outside each of the running rails, and normally proved remarkably successful at the low speeds prevailing.

RG **32** 573, 600, 709 (1920).

There was another accident on 25 June 1923, when two wooden cars fell 66 feet into the street. One of them, which landed on its side, was badly flattened.

RG **39** 144 (1923).

24 April 1920

Mewa Newada, India (Oudh & Rohilkhand)

45 killed, 55 injured

Goods train No. 159 was held for about an hour at the outer signal at Mewa Newada. Just after this had been lowered, and the train had started to move forward, it was hit in the rear by the 'Allahabad Delra Dun Express' travelling at about 35mph, which had also been issued with a similarly-numbered train order. Fire broke out from the gas cylinders in the coaches of the express, but several of the vehicles were manually pushed clear on the initiative of the Deputy Inspector General of the Government Railway Police, who was travelling in the train. As a result of the official inquiry into the accident, the Assistant Stationmaster at Mewa Newada was prosecuted. Reports spoke of some of the injured complaining that the police had 'callously looted the train', but one wonders if they were merely recovering the valuables from the site before anyone could steal them.

RG **32** 680, 710, 911 (1920).

Bodies line the track after the collision at Bullo Pill, in West Wales, on 5 November 1868. An up broad-gauge cattle train from Carmarthen stopped in the section, which was still operated on the 'Time Interval' system. Rob Roy on the up Mail from New Milford ran into its rear, causing the death of 36 animals whose carcasses remain on the lineside. According to differing reports, 3–8 men in the rear van were also killed, some of them possibly being drovers.

(GWR Museum, Swindon)

Above *On 4 October 1894, in thick fog at Castle Hills, just north of Northallerton, a double-headed Edinburgh–King's Cross express ran past signals and hit a mineral train. The only fatality was the driver of the leading locomotive, but two of the passengers were severely injured, and a further 17 less seriously so.* (National Railway Museum)

Below and opposite top *The so-called "Flying Welshman" was derailed on straight and level track between Llanelly and Loughor on 3 October 1904, causing three fatalities and 18 serious injuries. Because of its heavy load of nine vehicles, the 10.35am from Milford Haven had stopped at Llanelly to attach a 0-6-0 saddle-tank as pilot to assist the 'Bulldog' 4-4-0 Montreal. The derailment started with the saddle-tank, but the reason for this was never positively determined, although the inspecting officer considered it unwise for such a locomotive to be used at speeds of over 50mph. The severe damage to the wooden-bodied vehicles at the front of the train is very obvious.* (GWR Museum, Swindon)

Below *The aftermath of an accident on the North Eastern Railway near Darlington on 24 October 1905, involving two 0-6-0s of very different types. The 'long-boiler' design, further away, is No.1219, but some earth obscures the numberplate of the other locomotive. This illustration is from a commercial postcard, date-stamped 21 July 1906, which was used to arrange a 'date' for two young people.* (Author's Collection)

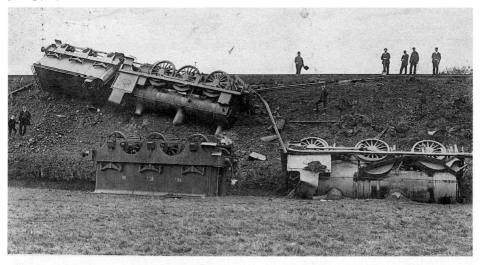

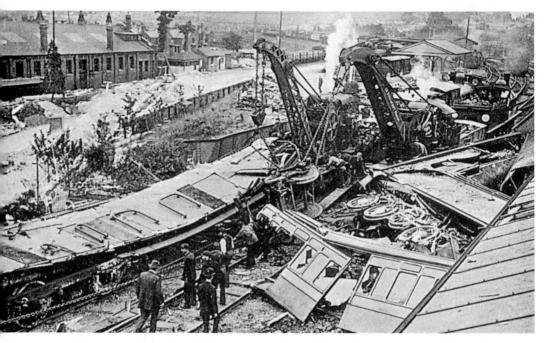

Above *A general view of the wreckage of the Salisbury disaster of 1 July 1906, looking in the direction of Waterloo. The boat-train's locomotive and tender can be seen, jack-knifed, on its side, in line with the right-hand crane.* (Author's Collection)

Below *Clearing up after the Salisbury disaster, seen from the London end of the station. The leading wheel of the boat-train locomotive is just visible above the crane's tool-wagon.* (Author's Collection)

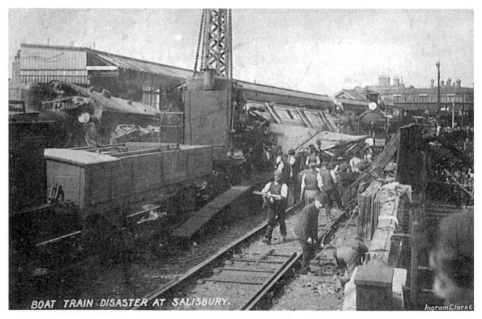

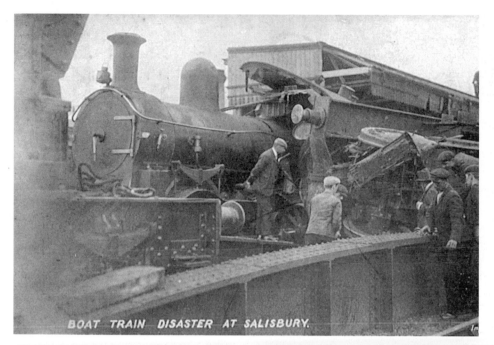

BOAT TRAIN DISASTER AT SALISBURY.

Above *A closer view of the front of the boat-train locomotive at Salisbury, and the one on the milk-train which it hit.*

(Author's Collection)

RAILWAY SMASH · GRANTHAM 19·9·06

Right *Another of the well-known major railway accidents of the Edwardian era took place on 19 September 1906. The down East Coast Mail failed to stop at Grantham, and was derailed at high-speed on the turn-out beyond, which was set for the Nottingham branch. The driver and fireman were among the 14 killed, and the reason for the failure to stop was never determined. The writing on the underframe in the foreground was presumably for the benefit of photographers.*

(National Railway Museum)

Above *The Shrewsbury derailment of 15 October 1907 resulted from another unexplained failure by a driver to reduce speed for a well-known restriction at night. This time the LNWR
'Experiment' 4-6-0* Stephenson *did not reduce speed as it ran down the steep bank from Hadnall
into Shrewsbury, where there is a sharp curve over the junction at the entrance to the station.
Eighteen people were killed, including the footplate crew and three Post Office sorters. The newspapers made great play of the fact that the railways were apparently using an 'experimental' locomotive in regular service! The official report concluded that the driver might have dozed off, which
caused considerable protest from other drivers.*   (Stephenson Locomotive Society)

Opposite *Telescoping was one of the greatest causes of death and injury in the days of wooden-
bodied coaches. The first illustration shows a typical example after two electric trains had collided
at West Hampstead on 26 October 1907. In thick fog the train on the left hit the back of the other one,
which was standing in the platform.*

*To prevent this problem, Robinson on the Great Central fitted some of his coaches with corrugated
metal devices on their ends, which would prevent one underframe lifting over the other during a
collision. These were never widely adopted, but another device, which was introduced at much the
same time, was far more effective in preventing telescoping. This was the Buckeye coupling, and the
collision at Doncaster on 9 August 1947 illustrated what it could achieve. The lower illustration
shows how the coupling between two coaches held, even though they were both twisted on to their
sides. Interestingly, in the 1990s, the 'Networker' suburban electrics have been provided with a
modern version of the Robinson device, but the corrugations are hidden inside the lightweight
covers on their 'dumb' buffers.*   (Both National Railway Museum)

Two scenes showing the wreckage of the derailment near Weesp in the Netherlands on 13 September 1918. The embankment gave way as the train was passing over it, and much of the wreckage rolled down the 20-feet drop. In the illustration above, a ship can be seen on the canal in the background, loading casualties to take them to hospital, while in the other, Prince Hendrik is looking at the locomotive which hit the bridge structure after its derailment. (Boomsma Collection)

3 May 1920

Les Laumes-Alesia, France (Paris, Lyon & Méditerranée)

2 killed

A strike on the French Railways had started on 30 April, but was not universally supported. The number of services running was increased by the employment of volunteers, although suburban double-deck trains arrived in Gare St Lazare, Paris, with passengers standing on the footboards and roofs of the lower deck. A special 'Riviera Express' left Nice at 1530 on Sunday 2 May, but ran off the lines at Les Laumes-Alesia, near Dijon, in the early hours of the following morning. The two fatalities were the regular driver and a volunteer student from an engineering college, who was being taught to drive.

RG **32** 710 (1920).

17 May 1920

Jakhwada, India

23 killed, 27 injured

A passenger train leaving Bombay collided with a goods wagon, the casualties all being 'third-class passengers'.

RG **32** 812 (1920).

20 May 1920

Neon Daroston, Spain

40 killed

A head-on collision took place between a passenger and goods train, the front portions of each being completely wrecked and the remainder derailed.

RG **32** 811 (1920).

16 July 1920

Between Barcelona and Tortosa, Spain

20 killed

An express collided with a goods train.

RG **33** 142 (1920).

7 October 1920

Arkonam, India (Madras-Bangalore)

13 killed, 15 injured

The 'Madras-Bangalore Mail' was derailed by disgruntled platelayers, who removed a rail from the track. Sixty coolies were subsequently arrested on suspicion of complicity.

RG **33** 525, 558 (1920).

8 October 1920

Venice, Italy (Italian State)

25 killed, 20 injured

Shortly after midnight, the Venice–Milan express was brought to a stand on the bridge connecting Venice with Mestre on the mainland, where it was hit from the rear by a fast train from Trieste. The signals had not been restored to danger behind it. Work at 'establishments' in the area was temporarily stopped as a sign of mourning.

RG **33** 525 (1920).

9 October 1920

Houilles, Paris, France (Ouest)

47 killed

An unfitted goods train from Mantes to Paris became divided, and the driver brought the front portion to a stand at the suburban station of Houilles. On the falling gradient the wagons that had broken away ran into the back of the stationary train, the resultant wreckage fouling the other line. A down suburban passenger train could not stop clear of the obstruction, and many of its coaches, as well as the signal box, were destroyed. The French Minister of Public Works subsequently undertook to have continuous brakes installed on all French goods wagons, in conformity with the clause in the Treaty of Versailles which stipulated that all European railways should do this as soon as possible.

October 1920

Pogranitchnava, Russia

(100) killed

The mail train from Vladivostok to Kharbin was wrecked.

RG **33** 590 (1920).

27 October 1920

Lufany, Transylvania, Roumania

(50) killed (200+) injured

The *Daily Express* reported that two passenger trains were in collision as a result of 'a mistake by an unskilled railwayman'.

RG **33** 627 (1920).

14 December 1920

Bommidi, India (South India)

30 killed, 35 injured

A collision occurred between a mail train and a goods train, all the casualties being Indians.

RG **33** 836 (1920).

January 1921

Near Luga, Russia

68 killed

A consignment of 'benzine' (probably petrol) was being conveyed on a mixed train from Novgorod, 117 miles south of Petrograd (later Leningrad, and now St Petersburg), to be bartered for grain. It blew up while the train was travelling at speed, wrecking it and setting the vehicles on fire.

RG **34** 79 (1921).

27 February 1921

Porter, Indiana, United States of America (Michigan Central and New York Central)

37 killed

A feature of North American railway practice has been the widespread use of flat crossings between the tracks of two different companies. At Porter, Indiana, the Michigan Central (MC) and New York Central (NYC) had such a crossing, the rails intersecting at an angle of approximately 45 degrees. Both lines consisted of multiple tracks, and the approach on all sides was virtually straight. The crossing was fully protected with signals, interlocked with derailers. On the day of the accident, in the darkness the NYC's 'Interstate Express' triggered the track-circuit controlling its warning bell in the signal-box, and the route was cleared for it. The MC's 'Canadian', approaching in the other direction, got the distant signal 'on', but failed to slow for either it or the permanent restriction of 40mph over the crossing. As he approached it, the driver thought the three-position, upper-quadrant, home signal was at clear, and opened up again. The locomotive hit the derailer 311 feet from the crossing, but, by a freak set of conditions, it was rerailed by the 'Vee' of some trailing points further on. After breaking free from its train, it finished up 400 feet beyond the crossing, but its derailed coaches came to a stop with one of them on the intersection itself. Almost immediately the NYC express hit the vehicle, hurling it 75 feet and reducing it to matchwood. Thirty-five Michigan Central passengers were killed, as well as the crew of the New York Central locomotive. The two railways also had another flat crossing between their two tracks, in Chicago, and there had been a collision on this in 1853, causing 21 fatalities.

Shaw, p107.

25 June 1921
Beaucourt Hamel, France (Nord)

25 killed, 60 injured

A luggage van on the rear of an express from Lille to Paris became derailed at 60mph as it crossed a small concrete bridge over the River Ancre, and then dragged the three passenger coaches ahead of it off the track. After continuing in this fashion for some distance, the coupling at the front of the derailed vehicles broke, and they plunged down an embankment. The inquiry concluded that the van became derailed because the light vehicle was marshalled at the back of the fast train, although a slight track defect contributed. It was also possible that the rails might have buckled due to the heat. The instability of such vehicles on the end of passenger trains was the cause of derailments in other countries. The Great Western Railway carried out some tests with a specially-instrumented horsebox in 1943, which resulted in these vehicles being subjected to very severe speed restrictions.

25 June 1921
Amroha, India (Oudh & Rohilkhand)

42 killed

Less than an hour after a goods train had passed, floods caused a 150-yard breach on the Delhi–Moradabad branch. The locomotive and the two leading third-class coaches of an early morning passenger train plunged into the gap and disappeared under the water.

25 July 1921
Between Tawwi and Peinzalok, Burma

104 killed, 48 injured

The Rangoon–Mandalay Mail collided with a goods train at night, at a point about 100 miles from Rangoon. Both locomotives, and four bogie carriages from the mail train, were overturned.

RG **35** 270, 304 (1921).

27 August 1921
Near Rome, Italy (Italian State)

29 killed, over 100 injured

A passenger train bringing visitors back to Rome from Ladispoli, the popular resort near Civita Vecchia, collided with a shunting locomotive.

10 September 1921
Les Eschets (Ain), France (Paris, Lyon & Méditerranée)

38 killed

During World War I one of the tracks between Bourg-en-Brasse and Lyon had been lifted for use elsewhere in the country. Crossing loops were left at the intermediate stations, the approaches to which were limited to a maximum speed of 20km/h (12mph). After the war, traffic on the line increased, and initially there were no supplies of steel available to replace the second track, but the necessary authority was given at the end of August 1921. Before any work could be undertaken, a serious accident occurred to an express from Strasbourg to Lyon, crowded with French soldiers on leave from the newly-freed Alsace-Lorraine and the Rhineland. It took the turnout into the loop at Les Eschets too fast, three of its wooden coaches being demolished in the subsequent derailment.

5 October 1921

Batignolles Tunnel, Gare St Lazare, Paris, France
(Former Ouest section of État)

28 killed

The 1,000-yard Batignolles Tunnel, situated just outside St Lazare station in Paris, had long been a bottleneck, and plans to open it up had been delayed by the war. On the evening of 5 October 1921 the 5.48pm for Versailles came to a stand in the tunnel, and, as a result of an irregularity in block working, was hit in the rear by the 5.52pm to Issy-les-Molineaux. Fire broke out, and it was thought that the number of fatalities may have been higher than that given, because some bodies may have been consumed in the blaze.

This collision, occurring in the capital, brought to a head the poor contemporary safety record of the French railways, 43 accidents having occurred to date that year, killing 140 people and injuring no less than 542. As a result, a number of measures to improve safety were put in hand. The railway companies were instructed to abolish gas lighting, while the installation of the automatic warning system over the

whole country continued. In Paris, the work to open up Batignolles Tunnel was accelerated. The two signalmen responsible for the collision received prison sentences of six and four months.

The last stone of the tunnel was not removed until September 1926.

RG **35** 554, 581, 677 (1921), **45** 355 (1926).

19 November 1921

India

64 killed

The ventilation equipment of one of the vans used to transport prisoners by rail in India was choked by paint. As a result, 64 Moplah prisoners were asphyxiated.

RG **36** 237 (1922).

5 December 1921

Woodmont, Pennsylvania, United States of America
(Philadelphia & Reading)

27 killed

Two local passenger trains collided head-on after one of them had disregarded signals. A fire in the wreckage added to the fatalities.

27 June 1922

Berlin, Germany (Berlin Metropolitan)

29 killed, 60 injured

Following the Rathenau funeral ceremony outside the Reichstag building in central Berlin, particularly large crowds were travelling on the railway system. On one train going towards the northern part of the city, passengers were standing all the way along the footboards of the coaches. As it passed a train in the opposite direction, a swinging door on the 'six-foot' side swept scores of people off the train, many of them falling on the tracks and being run over.

RG **36** 1052 (1922).

11 July 1922
Paredes, near Palencia, Spain

32 killed, 19 seriously injured

The 'Asturias Mail' collided head-on in the station with an express from Galicia. In addition to both sets of enginemen, many first-class passengers in the mail train were killed. Considerable telescoping of the vehicles took place, and the last of the bodies were not removed until 17 hours after the accident took place.

RG **37** 108 (1922).

1 August 1922
Near Mielan, France (Midi)

40 killed

A collision occurred between two trains carrying pilgrims from Moulins to Lourdes. The first train stalled on a steep bank in the Gers Hills, and then ran backwards, colliding with the second train. A relief train was sent from Auch with medical staff and the Prefect for Gers, and the injured were removed in military ambulances to hospital at Tarbes. The driver of the runway train had complained about the air compressor at Agen, and it got worse after that point. The lack of air prevented the use of the sander during the climb, causing the train to come to a halt, but the main braking system would also appear not to have been working properly, as the train should have been able to stand safely on the gradient.

RG **37** 179, 245 (1922).

5 August 1922
Sulphur Springs, Missouri, United States of America (Missouri Pacific)

34 killed, 175 injured

A local train from Hoxie to St Louis, heavily laden with Saturday-night crowds going to the big city, was running about two hours late. Its crew were aware of a following express, but were given verbal instructions at Riverside to continue to Wickes, seven miles further on, and shunt for it there. As the line was equipped with automatic block signals there was no need for a train order confirming this. Just after the local had stopped at a water tank, $3\frac{1}{2}$ miles beyond Riverside, it was hit from the rear by the express travelling at about 40mph. The last two cars of the standing train were demolished and the wreckage hurled into a creek, while the next two vehicles were also badly damaged. 32 passengers on the local were killed, plus one trespasser, but the only fatality on the express was the driver. His death made it impossible to discover why he had passed two stop and one caution signal at full speed, or why had he not seen the local ahead of him at a range of nearly 300 yards.

Shaw, p247.

13 December 1922
Humbel, Texas, United States of America (Southern Pacific)

22 killed

A passenger train came into glancing collision with a light engine which had fouled the main line.

14 January 1923

Anuradhapura, Ceylon

39 killed

The 'Jaffa Mail' was wrecked as a result of the track being washed away during a severe storm in northern Ceylon. The locomotive and tender, the TPO, brake van and one coach came off the line at the approach to a bridge and were submerged in the rapidly-rising flood waters. A special train conveying a number of senior railway officials was sent to investigate its disappearance, the accident having taken place on the edge of the jungle, a long way from any other means of communication or access.

RG **38** 102 (1923).

26 January 1923

Between Madawachchi and Anuradhapura, Ceylon

Casualties unknown

A second railway disaster in less than two weeks occurred when the mail train from Talaimannar was derailed because of a washout.

RG **38** 258 (1923).

18 February 1923

France (Est)

27 killed

A Paris–Strasbourg train was involved in a collision.

2 July 1923

Vinty-Leanca, Wallachia, Roumania

63 killed, over 100 injured

As a result of a shunter's error, the Bucharest–Jassy Mail was diverted into a siding, where it came into collision with a stationary goods train. Three passenger coaches were telescoped. The accident happened between Buzeu and Ploesti, the injured being removed to hospitals in the latter by special train.

RG **39** 144 (1923).

31 July 1923

Kriensen, Germany

47 killed

The night express from Hamburg had been supplemented by an earlier relief train, to accommodate the large numbers of Bavarian holidaymakers returning home before railway fares trebled. At Kriensen, between Hildesheim and Göttingham, the first train came to a stand because of locomotive trouble. While it was waiting for a fresh engine, it was struck in the rear by the main train. The three rear coaches of the relief were telescoped and the wreckage piled in a heap as high as the station roof, which was set on fire. The driver of the second train had not seen the distant signal for Kriensen, because something had blown into his eye, and did not treat it as being at caution.

1 September 1923

Japan

130 killed, 91 injured

A large area of Honshu, the main island of Japan, was devastated by a major earthquake just before mid-day, with thousands being killed, either by the shock wave or the resulting fire which destroyed much of Tokyo. Initial reports indicated that several trains had been wrecked, with considerable loss of life. The collapse of the tunnel at Sasako was said to have killed 600, while 300 were stated to have drowned when a passenger train was hurled into the sea near Atai. Fortunately the number of fatalities on trains directly due to the earthquake was a lot less. Six passenger trains were involved, and the same number of freight trains, only a single fatality occurring on the latter, although 129 were killed on the passenger ones. 73 other railway employees died elsewhere, and over 10,000 were made homeless. Considerable damage was done to the railway infrastructure and rolling stock. 33 locomotives, 486 passenger carriages, 1,249 freight vehicles and 31 electric cars were put out of action.

RG **39** 319, 659 (1923), **40** 102 (1924).

8 September 1923
Omsk, Russia

82 killed, 150 injured

An express train was derailed.

RG **39** 350 (1923).

27 September 1923
Lockett, Wyoming, United States of America
(Chicago, Burlington & Quincy)

31 killed, 3 injured

The railway line crossed Cole Creek on a pile-driven trestle, 111 feet long, about a quarter of a mile before the stream joined the North Platte River. Normally there was very little water flowing under it, the annual rainfall in the area averaging only twelve inches. In 1923 there were five inches in September alone, of which nearly three fell during the two days before the accident. The danger to the trestle was appreciated, and it had been inspected an hour before it collapsed as a train was crossing it. The locomotive and the first five coaches were swept away, being discovered subsequently almost covered with sand, probably coming from a bar across the creek. This was believed to have given way suddenly, the crest of the resulting surge of water engulfing the trestle just as the train reached it.

Reed, p98. Shaw, p305.

14 March 1924
Bareilly, India (Oudh & Rohilkhand)

18+ killed

A train was blown off a bridge during a cyclone, five of its third-class coaches finishing upside down in the river. At the time of the report 18 bodies had been recovered, but others were feared to be trapped in the two coaches which were, at that time, still submerged.

In the year ending in March 1924, 2,818 people were killed on the railways of India. Of these, 2,029 were trespassers, but the total included 372 passengers and 417 employees. With the rising accident rate on Indian railways, some of the companies began 'Safety First' campaigns. In a leaflet produced by the Great India Peninsula Railway in mid-1926, it was stated that 3,447 people were injured in the year up to March 1924, in addition to those killed. The leaflet asked, 'Must this Sacrifice Continue?'

RG **41** 719 (1924).

24 April 1924
Bellinzona, Switzerland
(Swiss Federal)

21 killed

In the early hours of the morning, a Basel–Milan express collided in the station with one travelling in the opposite direction, both of them being double-headed. Unfortunately there was an old German coach in the northbound train, fitted with gas lighting. It caught fire immediately after the accident and all those travelling in it were killed. The fire spread to an adjoining Italian vehicle, but most of its passengers were rescued. People of eight different nationalities were on the train, and one of those killed was a former German cabinet minister. The accident was caused by the southbound train over-running signals. Unfortunately the points had been wrongly set at the south end of the station, as a freight train was expected in ahead of the passenger express, and was due to be crossed over the southbound line into the goods yard. This had routed the northbound train on to the 'wrong' line, where it was hit by the other one. As a result of the fire, the Swiss banned all gas-lit coaches from their railways from the beginning of August that year.

2 May 1924

Between Odessa and Moscow, Russia

Casualties not reported

The brand-new 'Lenin Express' on its first run to Moscow was derailed. Four coaches were overturned and the remainder destroyed after falling down an embankment. According to passengers there were many killed and injured. No mention of the accident appeared in the Russian press, and sabotage was thought to have been responsible.

RG **40** 794 (1924).

19 August 1924

Paporah Bridge, French West Africa (Theis-Kayes)

29 killed

The bridge collapsed in the floods as the train was crossing it. With the exception of the French head district official, the dead were all Africans.

29 August 1924

Montgomery, India (North Western State)

107 killed, 104 injured

Two passenger trains collided at Montgomery, approximately 60 miles from Lahore. The assistant stationmaster at one of the adjoining stations was subsequently arrested on a charge of criminal negligence. *The Times* reassured its readers that there were no Europeans amongst the casualties.

October 1924

On Moscow–Ivanove– Vasenensk line, Russia

(177) killed

Some petrol wagons were attached to a passenger train and caught fire, virtually the whole of it being destroyed. Only 27 of the 200 aboard were said to have survived, and details were hushed-up by the Soviet authorities.

RG **41** 495 (1924).

1925–1929

13 January 1925

Herne, Westphalia, Germany (DR)

32 killed, 57 injured

A local passenger train, carrying workers for the Ruhr, was running slightly late, and, while waiting to leave Herne station, it was struck from the rear by a Berlin–Köln express running five minutes early. The majority of the casualties occurred in the four *fourth-class* coaches at the rear of the local, which were badly damaged, the roof of the second from the rear being driven right through the vehicle in front of it. None of the passengers in the express was hurt. The driver of the express had left Dortmund, 13 miles away, in clear weather, and had suddenly run into a bank of fog. This disorientated him, and he only realised he had reached Herne when he saw the station platforms. At almost exactly the same time a similar accident occurred at Hattingen, another station not very far away in the Ruhr, but there the casualty list was less, three being killed and twelve injured.

RG **42** 91 (1925).

9 April 1925

Las Planas, Barcelona, Spain

25 killed, 46 seriously injured

A collision occurred on the electrified line running inland to Tarrasa, at the entrance to the last tunnel at Sierra, where there is a very sharp curve. The derailed coaches were crushed against the sides of the tunnel.

RG **42** 544 (1925).

1 May 1925

Between Swaroschin and Preassisch Stargard, Poland

26 killed, 12 seriously injured

The accident occurred in the early hours of the morning to a Königsberg–Berlin express in the Polish Corridor between East Prussia and the rest of Germany. A number of trains made this journey every day, being worked through by Polish crews with the doors locked. The express was derailed on a sharp curve, the locomotive and the first six vehicles falling down a 25ft embankment. Most of the fatalities occurred in the leading first-class coach, which was telescoped by the one behind it. With the exception of one Polish customs officer, all those killed were Germans. The Polish locomotive crew managed to jump clear and then ran away, but the passengers in the undamaged coaches were kept locked in for a further two hours, although the injured Germans were taken to a Polish hospital in Dirschau.

After the accident a political dispute about it broke out between Poland and Germany. The latter's engineers in Danzig claimed that the derailment had been caused by subsidence after heavy rain, the line not having been kept in good condition by the Poles. They, on the other hand, considered that the accident was due to sabotage, perhaps by Germans wishing to discredit the Poles, and offered a reward of 50,000 zlotys for the discovery of the culprits. The matter was finally referred to the commission dealing with disputes between the two countries, and their judgement after the inquiry rivalled that of Solomon. They ruled that the derailment was not due to subsidence, while saying that the burden of *proving* sabotage lay with the Poles.

RG **42** 659 (1925).

16 June 1925

Hackettstown, New Jersey, United States of America (Lackawanna)

45 killed

A heavy downpour had washed a considerable amount of spoil along a dirt road and on to a level crossing, and this derailed a special train from Chicago. It was heading for the piers at Holboken, where the passengers, a party of German-Americans, were going to join the SS *Republic* for a visit to their native country. The leading bogie of the locomotive was derailed, and initially bumped along the sleepers without causing any further trouble. Fifty yards further on there was a disused siding, and the turnout forced the bogie to one side, causing the locomotive and four coaches to fall twelve feet down the embankment. The first coach finished up lying on its side on top of the locomotive, whose crew and many passengers

were scalded to death by the water from the boiler. The survivors continued their journey and joined the ship for Europe.

Shaw, 313. RG **44** 777 (1926).

27 October 1925

Victoria, Mississippi, United States of America (St Louis & San Francisco ('Frisco))

21 killed

The derailment was caused by a broken rail. (For reasons unknown, Shaw in his index states that this accident occurred on the same day of October *in 1905*.)

14 March 1926

Varillá River, Costa Rica (United Fruit Company)

238 killed, 93 injured

A Sunday excursion from Cartago to San José had been chartered on behalf of a home for the country's aged inhabitants. It was overcrowded and three coaches were derailed crossing a river. They fell down the embankment, one of them plunging 50 feet into the water. Medical relief was organised quickly, and a special train with doctors and nurses aboard was sent from Port Limon by the railway's owners. Nearly all the passengers were farmers or labourers, and whole families perished in the accident.

24 May 1926

Munich East, Germany (DR)

33 killed, (100 injured)

An excursion train standing in the station was hit by another one which had failed to stop clear of it. The last two coaches of the stationary train were telescoped, and it was very difficult to rescue those trapped in the wreckage. The bodies of many of those killed could not be positively identified. Ten months later the driver of the incoming train was convicted of causing the accident through carelessness, and sent to prison for five months.

9 June 1926

Salt River, South Africa (SAR)

17 killed, 40–50 injured

Two miles outside Cape Town the rear portion of a train was derailed, and two of the coaches hit an overbridge. At the time it was reported that the train had become divided and had consequently been derailed. For many years this was a frequent reporting convention, the implication being that, if a train splits, there is a risk of the rear portion coming off the tracks simply because it is no longer coupled up. A much more valid reason than this is needed technically, and frequently the derailment has happened first and the resulting snatch has caused the train to split. In this case it was subsequently found that a screw coupling had become wedged between the check-rail and the running rail, and this had derailed four of the train's eight coaches. On this occasion the split might therefore have occurred first, but there was a specific cause for the derailment, which might not have been connected with the breakaway.

RG **44** 772 (1926), **45** 105 (1926).

3 July 1926

Achères, France (Est)

20 killed, 98 injured

At Ambassadeurs Junction in the Forest of Achères, Pacific No. 231-603 on the 7.50pm train from Le Havre to Paris failed to observe a 30-km/h speed restriction over the turnout into a loop. This diversion was required to permit some emergency engineering work on the main line. The train approached the restriction at nearly 60mph, the locomotive and leading coaches being derailed and badly damaged. The driver was among those killed.

RG **45** 37, 53 (1926).

19 August 1926

Between Leiferde and Meinersen, Germany (DR)

21 killed

An express from Berlin to Köln was derailed in the early hours of the morning some 25 miles east of Hannover while travelling at approximately 50mph. The locomotive fell down the embankment on to its right-hand side, and was followed by the first seven vehicles of the train. A sleeping car and the third-class coach behind it were telescoped. The accident occurred on a long straight stretch of one of the country's most important main lines, which was well maintained, but the cause of the derailment was quickly determined as being due to sabotage. One rail had been loosened, and the coach-screws were found in the ballast, while the fish-plate bolts had been placed on the sleepers. A reward of DM25,000 (£1,250) was offered for information leading to the arrest of those responsible. By the beginning of September police in Berlin had arrested two young men who had planned to derail the train and then rob the mail van, but, overcome by the severity of the accident, they had run away. The two responsible were sentenced to death on 4 November, while another man was given two years in prison for aiding and abetting them.

RG **45** 266, 363, 402, 404, 598, (1926).

A few days after this accident the police spotted two men placing an obstruction on the line near Halle, and fired on them. The men fired back before fleeing into the nearby woods.

RG **45** 408 (1926).

In 1926 there were 2,947 accidents on the German railways, which caused the deaths of 174 passengers and 318 staff. Of these accidents, 470 were derailments, which accounted for 66 of the passenger fatalities, and 834 injuries.

RG **46** 128 (1927).

1 September 1926

Between Anetlla and Ampolla, Spain

25 killed, 50 injured

The Barcelona–Valencia Mail was derailed when it ran into a landslide caused by heavy rain. A third-class coach was telescoped.

RG **45** 292 (1926).

5 September 1926

Waco, Colorado, United States of America (Denver & Rio Grande Western)

23 killed, 50+ seriously injured

The 'Scenic Limited' passenger train was derailed by excessive speed on a curve. The locomotive and six of the 14 coaches fell into the Aranksas River.

RG **45** 316 (1926).

13 September 1926

Murrulla, New South Wales, Australia (New South Wales State)

27 killed, 46 injured

An unusual collision which occurred between Murrurundi and Wingen on the North-West Line became the worst railway disaster to have occurred in New South Wales up to that time. Just before midnight a goods train was being shunted clear of the main line to let the Maree to Sydney Mail pass. Five wagons loaded with wool broke away and ran at high speed down the incline towards the express, which was climbing the bank at approximately 30mph. Hitting the front of the locomotive, the wagons somersaulted over it and the first coach, landing on the roof of the second, where most of the casualties occurred. The wool caught fire but the flames were prevented from spreading to the passenger coaches. The coroner later committed the driver and guard of the freight train for trial.

RG **45** 354, 779 (1926).

23 September 1926

Between Akinakano and Umitashi, Japan

28 killed, 40 injured

At 3.30am the Tokyo–Shimoneseki express was derailed near Hiroshima after the track had subsided following heavy rain. Four coaches were badly damaged.

8 December 1926

Machungho, Manchuria (South Manchunian)

25 killed, 54 seriously injured

A collision occurred between a passenger train and a goods one.

RG **45** 709 (1926).

11 December 1926

Near Tiehlong, Manchuria (South Manchunian)

25 killed, 54 seriously injured

Another collision occurred, similar to that three days earlier.

RG **45** 772 (1926).

23 December 1926

Rockmart, Georgia, United States of America
(Southern)

20 killed

The head-on collision took place between two passenger trains in a driving rainstorm. It was caused by one of the crews misunderstanding their train order.

RG **45** 802 (1926).

7 July 1927

Near Alpacatal, Argentina (Buenos Aires & Pacific)

28 killed

A double-headed special was taking military cadets from Mendoza to the capital for the unveiling of a monument to General Mitre on Independence Day. It collided with an ordinary passenger train 15 miles from the Mendoza–San Luis provincial boundary. Nearly all the casualties were on the special, and the fatalities included three drivers and a locomotive inspector. The latter, as well as one of the drivers, was English.

RG **47** 249 (1927).

27 July 1927

Heidelberg, Cape Province, South Africa

29 killed, 54 injured

A crossing loop had recently been opened at Mapleton and the driver of a goods train going south from Roodekop only had the staff from Glenroy to Mapleton. Instead of stopping there for the northbound Durban–Johannesburg passenger train to pass, he continued on and collided with it. The accident occurred in the evening, and the intense cold of the southern-hemisphere winter, plus the driving rain, caused some of the injured to die of exposure before they could be taken to hospital.

RG **47** 334 (1927).

25 August 1927

Montamert, France

16–20 killed

Following a violent snowstorm in the afternoon, many of the tourists in the Mer de Glace area flocked to the rack railway to return the three miles down to Chamonix. Leaving the summit there was a fairly level stretch before the steep descent began. The normal drill was for the driver to accelerate and then put the locomotive in reverse, so it braked the train on the rack. The driver of the third train that afternoon stopped on the first section to pick up some local guides, and forgot the locomotive was still in forward gear. When he restarted, speed quickly reached 10km/h (6mph), at which point the brakes were automatically applied. They came on rather fiercely, which made the guard on the first coach, who was still closing the doors, fall off. (That was an operation he should have done before the train started.) The driver became disorientated and continued to accelerate, and the first coach left the rails, pulling the locomotive off with it, together with a section of the rack. This happened by a large viaduct near Montamert Hotel, and this part of the train fell 45 feet into a deep ravine. The guard on the second coach was able to apply the brake, and the passengers from it assisted guides in the rescue work. The line, although situated in France, was largely financed by Swiss interests.

RG **47** 392 (1927).

22 January 1928

Between Hayagat and Kishanpur, India

30+ killed

A locomotive separated from its coaches, and the two sections came together again with considerable force. The first two coaches were derailed and fell down an embankment.

RG **48** 393 (1928).

28 January 1928

Kyauktaga, Burma

54 killed, 30+ injured

The Mail, en route from Mandalay to Rangoon, was derailed at a bridge between Yindsikkon and Kyauktaga, the locomotive and four coaches falling 50 feet into the river. The railway agent went to inspect the site and returned with the information that the accident had been caused by deliberate tampering with the line, four fishplates having been removed. Dacoits were suspected as being responsible, and it was thought that they had intended to derail and rob the previous goods train, but, because of its slow speed, it was not derailed. In May an Indian was sentenced to death for wrecking the train, but his conviction was subsequently quashed in the High Court.

RG **48** 152, 393 (1928).

12 March 1928

Near Kalatura, Ceylon

25 killed, 41 injured

An express from Galle to Colombo was in collision with an ordinary passenger train, 28 miles south of Colombo. The driver of the latter was held responsible for this accident, and there was contributory negligence by the guard. The officer in charge of the station at Kala-

tura was also found not to have been 'fully alive to his responsibilities'.

RG **48** 384 (1928), **49** 173, 229 (1928).

10 June 1928

Siegelsdorf, Germany (DR)

22 killed

Shortly after 2am a Munich–Frankfurt express was derailed, the locomotive falling down an embankment and over-turning, with the first coach on top of it. Three more coaches followed.

RG **48** 828 (1928).

27 June 1928

Darlington, England (London & North Eastern)

25 killed, 48 injured

Late at night a passed fireman carrying out some shunting with a parcels train passed a signal at danger at Bank Top station, Darlington. A return excursion from Scarborough to Newcastle on the down main line outside the station hit his train at about 45mph. Its driver's action, on seeing the other train ahead, was too late to reduce speed, the two locomotives meeting head on. Many of the casualties occurred in five compartments of the excursion, which were penetrated by the underframe of the next coach. The majority of those killed were women, and no less than 14 came from the Mother's Union in one of the Durham mining communities. The passed fireman had never before shunted at Darlington, and was not familiar with all the signalling arrangements there. He had only driven one through train to York, although he had fired over the route many times. The shunter had seen him passing the signal at danger, and tried to attract his attention by applying the brake-setter in the third coach. Initially he was afraid of putting it on hard, 'in case he might divide the train'. This is one of the myths which is part of the folklore of train operation, as, in steam days, no locomotive had a high enough tractive effort to break a coupling, even if the train brake was hard on, as long as there was no snatching.

Hamilton, p90. Rolt, p241. RG **49** 5, *30*, 31, 92, 128 (1928), **50** 5, 26 (1929).

8 July 1928
Belur, India

25 killed, 60+ seriously injured

The train was derailed seven miles from Calcutta because a pair of fishplates had been removed from the track. The locomotive plunged down the embankment and finished up partly buried in mud. The guard walked back for two miles to telephone, while the passengers formed rescue parties. It was later claimed in the local press that the railways had murdered some of the injured, and done away with the bodies to avoid having to pay compensation.

This was a very bad period for sabotage on the Indian railways, the Belur disaster being the eighth attempt in ten months, including the one at Kyauktaga in Burma. On 12 July the 'Calcutta—Gaya Mail' was derailed after one rail had been removed and the other twisted out of alignment. It was believed that the 'Punjab Mail' had been the target, but it had passed safely two hours earlier. There were two more derailing attempts on 4 and 5 October, one of which was noticed in time, and on 25th the special train conveying the Governor of Bombay also had a narrow escape. Another derailment occurred on 13 December. A reward of 10,000 Rupees for information leading to the arrest and conviction of the offenders was offered, and this was later increased to 30,000.

RG **49** 229, 260 (1928).

Later still a goods train carrying the pay clerk and his assistant on the Hindubagh—Kila Saifulla section of the North West Railway's strategic lines was attacked by a 'gang of tribal marauders.' They shot the clerk dead and wounded his peon. The driver set the train back for a mile or so, but as the Dacoits were still in pursuit, he returned all the way to Hindubagh.

RG **49** 447 (1929).

13 August 1928
New York City, United States of America (New York Elevated)

A few injured

A collision occurred on the New York Elevated railway, followed by a fire. No one was seriously injured, but several hundred passengers had to be rescued by ladders.

RG **49** *214*, 229 (1928).

10 September 1928
Saitz, near Lundenberg, Czechoslovakia (Czechoslovakian State)

21 killed

A Paris—Bucharest express hit a goods train near the Austrian frontier. 29 injured people were taken to hospital at Brno.

RG **49** 340 (1928).

26 October 1928
Resca, Roumania

34 killed

A fast Bucharest train was diverted on to a line occupied by the 'Simplon Orient Express', and a bad collision took place, virtually all the damage being on the 'internal' train. Two of its coaches were badly telescoped, and almost everyone travelling in them was killed.

It was alleged that the station staff did little to render assistance, and a passenger had to telegraph to the neighbouring stations for help. As a result of the inquiry, the station pointsman was dismissed, and the traffic agent suspended for two months. The driver of the Bucharest train was also suspended for a similar period and barred from promotion for a year, such a combination of actions making it difficult to assess the cause of the accident. The *Railway Gazette* refers to the accident taking place near Slatina.

RG **49** 567 (1928).

During 1929 there were 325 collisions in Roumania, 1,555 trains were derailed, and 1,895 other accidents occurred. No less than 500 people were killed on the railways.

RG **52** 178 (1930).

23 September 1929

Zuevka, between Kursk and Kharkoff, Russia

30 + killed

A passenger train from Moscow to Siberia was derailed and six of its coaches wrecked, 50 miles from Viatka.

RG **51** 490 (1929).

1930–1934

7 April 1930

Near Oira, Kyushu, Japan

17 killed, two seriously injured

Some dynamite in the locomotive coal exploded, perhaps having come from the colliery after a blasting misfire. The explosion wrecked the locomotive and several coaches, and ignited a forest fire which burned all night.

RC **52** 576 (1930).

16 April 1930

Domodedovo, near Moscow, Russia

45 killed, 23 seriously injured

Some methylated spirits was spilled in one of the coaches and accidentally ignited by a dropped match. The vehicle then caught fire. News of the accident was not released for about two months.

RG **52** 934 (1939).

20 May 1930

Chernaya, Russia

28 killed, 29 severely injured

A passenger train and a goods train were in collision on the Moscow–Kazan line.

RG **52** 833 (1930).

29 June 1930

Near Leningrad, Russia

22 killed, 28 severely injured

A passenger train from Itkutsk to Leningrad was derailed as a result of a signalman's error.

RG **53** 42 (1930).

16 July 1930

Between Petrova and Viseul Bistra, Roumania

22 killed

A collision took place between a passenger and a goods train.

RG **53** 138 (1930).

27 December 1930

China (Peking—Mukden)

80 killed

A train was deliberately wrecked on a branch line in south-west Manchuria. The boiler of the locomotive burst and many of the passengers were burnt to death. Twenty of the survivors were carried off for ransom after the bandits who caused the accident had pillaged the train.

(20 April 1931)

China

30+ killed, 20–30 seriously injured

A stretch of embankment which had been undermined by heavy rain collapsed as a train from Humchun to Kowloon was passing over it, the vehicles falling 30 feet into a ravine.

RG **54** 657 (1931).

29 April 1931

Benha, Egypt

48 killed

A bad fire occurred on a crowded train from Alexandria to Cairo during the Bairam holiday. As it was approaching Benha station, it was seen that the last coach was on fire, and the blaze quickly spread to the two adjoining third-class carriages. The driver failed to realise that anything was wrong, and many of the passengers were killed or injured when they jumped out. By the time the train had stopped, the blaze was too fierce for those from the station to carry out any rescue work, and the fire in the three vehicles had to be allowed to burn itself out. The coaches were old ones which had been used because of the large numbers travelling during the holiday. After an initial theory that the fire was due to an overheated axlebox, it was later considered to have been caused by a passenger.

13 September 1931

Biatorbagy, Hungary

25 killed

The international express for Genoa, Paris and Ostend, which had left Budapest for Vienna on the previous day, was blown up as it crossed a viaduct near Biatorbagy station. All but two of the eleven coaches, as well as the locomotive, fell approximately 100 feet. It was quickly determined that the accident had been caused by an explosion, and a scrap of paper found nearby had the following written on it: 'Brother Proletarians. If the capitalist state cannot provide work, we shall get it ourselves. We have plenty of petrol and explosives.' The railway offered a reward for information leading to the arrest of anyone responsible. Although suspicion initially fell on some local workmen, investigations soon showed they were not responsible. A month after the disaster a man was apprehended in Austria, and was tried on a charge of attempting to wreck two trains in that country. His behaviour during the case indicated that he had a severe mental illness, but he was sentenced to three years' imprisonment. The Hungarian authorities had already applied for his extradition, and sentenced him to death *in absentia*, while he was incarcerated in Austria. In 1938 his sentence was changed to life imprisonment by the Regent of Hungary.

RG **55** 376, 379 (1931).

(End of September 1931)

South-west of Leningrad, Russia

Heavy loss of life

A troop train blew up during army manoeuvres, the locomotive and twelve wagons being completely destroyed.

RG **55** 444 (1931).

2 January 1932
Kossino, Russia

68 killed, 130 injured

A double collision occurred ten miles from Moscow on the line to Kazan. A suburban train had stopped, and was hit from the rear by one from Moscow, travelling at about 40mph. A train of empty wagons then collided with the wreckage, while a fourth train was only just stopped clear of the site. An official announcement blamed the staff concerned for gross violations of discipline and regulations, there having been sufficient time between the collisions to have protected the line. The eleven surviving railwaymen were sent for trial on charges of criminally neglecting their duties.

RG **56** 125 (1932).

During the previous year, new rules for discipline had been introduced in Russia, the *railway* authorities being able to impose summary punishments of up to ten years in prison for breaches of discipline. If there was 'malice aforethought', the sentence could be death and confiscation of all possessions. No one was allowed to leave the railways, and anyone who had recently moved away had to return and remain attached until the end of the Five Year Plan. Any slowness in loading or dispatching goods was punishable with ten years in prison.

RG **54** 170 (1931).

17 July 1932
Leeudoorn Stad, South-West Transvaal, South Africa

5 killed, 7 injured

Over 300 tons of dynamite on a train blew up near Leeudoorn Stad. Explosions spread along the 52 wagons, and 250 yards of permanent way were torn up, leaving two craters 40 feet deep.

RG **57** 187 (1932).

14 September 1932
Turenne, Algeria

120 killed, 150 injured

A troop train with two officers, 27 NCOs and 481 men of the French Foreign Legion was derailed by track subsidence while it was travelling from Sidi-bel-Abbès to Tiemçen. The accident took place just after the train had emerged from a tunnel and was negotiating a curve 240 feet above the bottom of a ravine, the permanent way subsiding after heavy rain. Only the guard's van remained on the rails, the locomotive and 32 coaches falling into the defile. A shepherd witnessed the accident, and ran $2\frac{1}{2}$ miles through rough country to raise the alarm in Turenne. The Inspector-General of the Legion personally directed the rescue work, which had to be conducted from the railway, as that was the only means of reaching the isolated site, and searchlights were used during the night. There were no heavy cranes available, and conditions were made worse by the hot sirocco wind, which necessitated bodies having to be covered with quicklime as soon as they were recovered. Most of the *legionnaires* killed were given a public military funeral at their headquarters in Sidi-bel-Abbès, after a requiem mass had been celebrated by the Bishop of Oran.

RG **57** 355 (1932).

16 October 1932
Lublino, Russia

36 killed

The 'Black Sea Express' was wrecked on the outskirts of Moscow. The stationmaster at Lublino was considered to have been responsible, and, within a month, he had been executed for 'negligence and giving confused information'. As with Admiral Byng, this was clearly an example *'pour encourager les autres'* !

17 March 1933

Between Chengchitun and Ssupingkai, Manchuria

50 killed, 70 injured

A freight train collided with the rear of a passenger train, which had been stopped by 'a dislocation of the rails'. Manchuria was then the Japanese puppet state of Manchukuo, and, at about that time, there were several other incidents involving trains in that country and China which are referred to in the chapter on Wars & Revolutions.

24 October 1933

Between St Elier and Conches-en-Ouche, France (Former Ouest section of État)

36 killed, 68 injured

An express from Cherbourg to Paris was derailed at approximately 65mph on the approach to a bridge over the River Iton. The locomotive, its tender, a brake van and four coaches fell into the stream below. The first three coaches were wooden ones and telescoped badly. Although a permanent-way gang was engaged in some track repairs, the derailment occurred before the train had reached that point.

RG **59** 579, 612 (1933).

23 December 1933

Lagny–Pomponne, France (Est)

230 killed, 300 injured

In thick fog just before Christmas, a rear-end collision proved to be the worst peacetime accident on the French railways. Express No. 55 for Nancy did not leave Gare de l'Est until 7.25pm, two hours late, and was further delayed before being stopped by signals at Pomponne, approximately a mile before Lagny. As it was moving off again, it was hit by the Paris–Strasbourg express (No. 25bis), which was an hour late. Running at 60mph, the 'Mountain' 4-8-2 ploughed its way through nearly the whole length of the Nancy train, which was packed with families laden with Christmas presents, students and servicemen, as well as some Members of Parliament. Virtually all the casualties occurred in that train, only the bogies, with their twisted axles, remaining as identifiable items from five of its coaches. On the other hand, there were no fatalities in the steel vehicles of the Strasbourg express, providing a clear indication of the superior strength of that sort of coach. Some of its rear vehicles remained on the line, which enabled them later to be used to take the survivors back to Paris.

In the fog and hard frost, the task of rescue was very difficult, and bonfires were made from the wreckage to give light and provide warmth for the injured in fields alongside the line. The driver and fireman of the Strasbourg train were arrested, the former being made to stand beside his locomotive between two policemen for several hours while the bodies of the dead were carried past him to be laid out in rows in a field. The locomotive involved was always known afterwards to railwaymen as *'la charcutière'* (the butcheress).

This accident caused a lot of concern in France, and it was rarely out of the news throughout 1934. The trial of those claimed to be responsible did not start until December that year, and the judgement was delivered in January 1935. The driver had been tried on a charge of 'Homicide caused by want of caution', but was acquitted, and the charges against a number of the company's officials were dropped. The *Railway Gazette* remarked that, 'We cannot escape the probability that the Strasbourg express, which was admittedly being driven at a high rate of speed in bad weather, ran past at least one stop, and two warning, signals without the driver being aware of it'. There had been some doubt about the working of the automatic signals, and whether the automatic warning system had been affected by the frost. The French equipment, widely installed after World War I, relied on contact being made between some metal brushes on the locomotive and the ramp or 'crocodile' between the rails. This contact provided the warning signal, so was not fail-safe like the GWR's Automatic Train Control. The railway's own immediate investigation was that the equipment had been working, but it considered that the driver's inattention for 40 seconds was no more than imprudence.

Schneider, p74, p116. RG **59** 953, 972 (1933), **60** 5, 7, 20, 24, 65, 93, 253, 491, 565, 707, 1039 (1934), **61** 939, (1934), **62** 58, 184, 216 (1935).

8 January 1934
Kyoto, Japan

(70) killed, 60–70 injured

A huge crowd thronged the station to say goodbye to a party of naval recruits leaving for Kure. Some were swept over the edge of the platform and crushed by others falling on top of them.

RG **60** 256 (1934).

18 February 1934
Populonia, Italy

34 killed

A petrol-engined railcar travelling at 75mph collided with a special steam train three miles from Populonia, on the single line between Capglia and Piombino. Fire broke out and 34 of the 48 people travelling in the railcar died.

RG **60** 311 (1934).

4 March 1934
Near Moscow, Russia

19 killed, 52 injured

Two of the coaches of a train standing in a station five miles from Moscow were badly damaged when an incoming train hit it. Subsequently the driver and fireman of this train were condemned to death, and three other staff were given prison sentences.

RG **60** 507 (1934).

12 March 1934
Tavatui, Russia

33 killed, 68 injured

A local passenger train in the Urals ran past signals and collided with a goods train which was carrying out some shunting in the station. The trial of the officials involved began on 19 March.

RG **60** 559 (1934).

16 March 1934
San Salvador, South America

250+ killed, (1,000) injured

Seven tons of dynamite on a train exploded. The resulting flames spread to a petrol warehouse and devastated hundreds of houses in the neighbourhood.

RG **59** 559 (1934).

1935–1939

6 January 1935

Porbelo, USSR

23 killed, 56 badly injured

In the intensely-cold weather, some of the rails near Porbelo had fractured, but this was noticed in time to halt a Leningrad–Teflis express clear of the affected track. While it was standing, it was hit from the rear by an express from Leningrad to Moscow, which had run past signals at danger. Several coaches in both trains were telescoped, and the wreckage caught fire. There were suggestions that the cold had affected the signals, but this was later discounted. The stationmaster and six other railwaymen were subsequently found guilty of criminal negligence, and sent to prison for periods of three to ten years.

RG **62** 64, 216 (1935).

A few months later the Commissar for Railroads in the USSR reported that there had been 62,000 railway accidents in the previous year, causing death to hundreds of people. No less than 7,000 locomotives had been put out of action.

RG **62** 623 (1935).

16 October 1935

Rio de Janeiro, Brazil (Central)

20 killed, over 100 injured

The collision occurred in the city's suburbs, when an express hit a stationary passenger train.

24 December 1935

Gross-Herringen, Thuringen, Germany (DR)

33 killed, 27 seriously injured

As a local train from Erfurt to Leipzig was leaving the junction station at Gross-Herringen and was crossing the main line to reach the loop, it collided with a double-headed Berlin–Basel express. Hit from the side, seven of the coaches in the local were telescoped and wrecked, the body of one finishing up on top of a locomotive from the express. The accident occurred on a bridge over the River Saale, and it was initially reported that one coach had fallen into the water. However this was only a large piece of wreckage, although several bodies were also recovered from the river, and seven people were reported missing, so the death toll may have been higher than that given. A goods van was also left hanging precariously half-off the bridge. The all-steel coaches of the express were not badly damaged, and none of the passengers in them was seriously injured. A telegram of sympathy was sent by the German Chancellor, Adolf Hitler, to the local governor. The accident was caused by the express running past signals, the leading driver having missed two sets of them. The one on the train locomotive had just applied the brakes after he had seen the second signal at danger.

RG **64** 35 (1936).

16 April 1936

Tadakuma, Kyushu, Japan (Sumitomo Minc)

52 killed, 2 missing, 28 injured

Workers in this mine were transported on a railway with a 1 in 9 cable-worked incline. A train of nine vehicles was half-way up it when the cable broke, and it crashed to the bottom. Only a few of those on it were able to jump out. Safety brakes were fitted, and had been tested two months earlier, but they failed to hold it.

RG **64** 1080 (1936).

22 June 1936

Karymskaya, USSR

51 killed, 52 injured

News of this major disaster only became known in mid-July, when the Soviet authorities announced that 13 people were being tried in Chita, Siberia, for their part in causing it. A train had been allowed to leave the station before the line ahead was clear, and caused a rear-end collision. After the 'trial' the station-master was sentenced to death, and eight others were given prison sentences of three to ten years. It was stated that there had been 86 other accidents so far that year at Karymskaya.

RG **65** 161 (1936).

For the next half-century, the Russian authorities suppressed news of virtually every sort of disaster in their country, including railway accidents, unless there were unusual circumstances, such as the presence of foreign nationals, which prevented them from being concealed. In the light of the information given by the Commissar of Railroads, referred to in the report of the accident at Porbelo on 6 January 1935, the Russian safety record at that time certainly did not reflect much credit on the regime. The methods adopted to deal with this would, however, certainly not have met with international approval if the report after another Siberian accident in March 1937 was correct. On that occasion it was stated that the 72 railway employees held responsible had been executed. One's mind boggles at trying to imagine the circumstances whereby that number of individuals could have actually had a hand in causing an accident. The statement added that 3,000 officials of the Soviet Railway Commissariat were under arrest on other charges, which would indicate that one of the purges, for which the Soviet system was notorious, was at that time being directed at those who worked on the railways.

RG **67** 300 (1937).

The policy of secrecy about accidents was not to be reversed until *Glasnost* came in under Gorbachev's leadership in the 1980s. As recounted in the report of the accident at Kamensk-Shakhtinsky on 7 August 1987, the process could actually be seen happening during the investigations into the cause of that disaster.

1 October 1936

Lamberg, Poland

20 Killed, 150 injured

A passenger train from Berlin to Piala in East Prussia collided with a goods train in the Polish Corridor.

RG **65** 594 (1936).

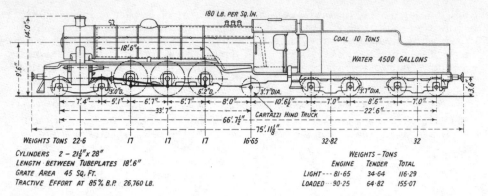

Bihta, 17 July 1937

Diagram of the Indian standard Class XB medium-weight Pacifics, like the one involved in the derailment at Bihta on 17 July 1937. (Railway Gazette)

10 October 1936
Columbia

30 killed, 40 injured

The accident occurred when troops were travelling on a special train to round up some bandits. Two coaches at the rear broke loose and ran away before overturning. It was suspected that the coupling had been broken intentionally.

16 January 1937

Sheklung, China
(Canton–Kowloon, Chinese section)

112 killed, 40 injured

Fire broke out in the third-class coaches of a Hong Kong–Canton express, which were not fitted with communication cords, or continuous brakes. It was a considerable time before the driver became aware of the problem and stopped, by which time many passengers had leapt out of the three coaches involved in the blaze. The fire was believed to have been caused when a passenger ignited a celluloid toy, large numbers of which had recently been on sale.

RG **66** 316 (1937).

17 July 1937
Bihta, India

107 killed, (65) injured

The Punjab–Howrah express was derailed as it was entering the station at Bihta, approximately 15 miles from Patna. Like the locomotive, the first coach was not badly damaged, but the next four were telescoped. Initially the cause was suspected as being sabotage, but this was quickly disproved, and a major investigation, including various tests, was carried out on the stability of the Class XB 'Pacific' locomotives. During these some trains were derailed at different speeds, and a whole train was also wrecked, the passenger load being represented by sandbags. The conclusion from these tests was that the track at Bihta had been distorted by the locomotive, the XBs being particularly prone to do this when running at speed. This was one of the accidents which raised a lot of interest world-wide, and the investigations were followed by a judicial inquiry. A commission of eminent railway engineers and others from Europe was then set up, to examine the design and purchase of these particular locomotives, and delivered its report two years later. The conclusion was that the class was sensitive to poor maintenance and defective track, and it was also recommended that speed recorders should be fitted to all express locomotives to help enforce strict compliance with restrictions.

RG **67** 168, 469, 491, (1937), **68** *116*, 824, 921, 986 (1937), **69** 442, *462*, 636 (1938), **70** 12, (1939).

The deputy traffic controller at Bihta when the accident occurred was tried for failing to put a temporary speed-restriction on the stretch of track after a previous driver had reported a 'double lurch' while travelling over it. He was found guilty, but later released pending an appeal.

RG **69** 623 (1938).

29 July 1937

Villeneuve-St Georges, France (Paris, Lyon & Méditerranée)

29 killed

Train No. 107, leaving Paris for St Etienne, Vichy and Nimes, via Corbeil at 10.35pm was derailed at the junction points as they moved under it at a speed of 50mph. Fire broke out in the wreckage, but was quickly extinguished. The fourth vehicle, a wooden third-class coach, was badly telescoped. The junction at Villeneuve-St Georges is eight miles from the Gare de Lyon in Paris, and was equipped with power signalling. The route for this train had mistakenly been set via Melun, because the staff on duty thought that it was, on this occasion, following Train No. 511, which left Paris 15 minutes later for Vallorbe and Switzerland. It was considered somewhat surprising that the points could be reversed so quickly after the signal protecting them had been put to danger. Such power-signalling systems usually have a time-delay to prevent that happening.

RG **67** 242, *250* (1937).

4 December 1937

Valencia, Spain

20 killed

A ten-coach steam train from the Central of Aragon line hit a two-car electric outside the station.

RG **67** 1039 (1937).

10 December 1937

Castlecary, Scotland (London & North Eastern)

35 killed, 179 injured

As darkness descended that evening, it was snowing hard in Scotland, and trouble was building up on the former North British main line between Edinburgh and Glasgow. Snow blocked some points at Gartshore, and, while they were being cleared, several trains were halted in successive block sections, the last being a goods at Dullatur, immediately west of Castlecary. This was being followed by a Dundee to Glasgow express, hauled by one of the Class D29 4-4-0s, the driver of which ran past the Castlecary signals in the snow. Although the signalman there held a red light out of the window of his box, he thought it had not been seen, and sent the 'Train Running Away' bell code to Dullatur. The driver, however, had seen the warning and stopped, but the signalman did not realise this, although the track-circuit indicator in his box showed it had come to a stand. The shock of the run-past upset his powers of judgment, and he then accepted the following express from Edinburgh, hauled by the Gresley Pacific No. 2744 *Grand Parade*. The driver of this locomotive was convinced that he saw the Castlecary distant at clear, and continued at full speed. There was some argument about the position of the arm of the Castlecary distant signal, but no positive conclusion about this emerged from the Ministry of Transport inquiry. The drivers of the D29 and A3 both

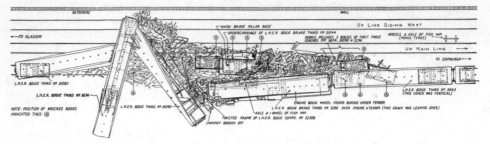

Castlecary, 10 December 1937

Plan of the debris covering the Pacific Grand Parade *after the collision at Castlecary in Scotland on 10 December 1937.* (Railway Gazette)

failed to see the home signal in the snow.

The 'Pacific' hit the rear of the train from Dundee at 60mph, and it finished up embedded in the side of the cutting 100 yards further on. Its momentum pushed the standing train forward 50 yards, demolishing the six-wheeled fish van at the rear, as well as the two coaches ahead of it. These were of contemporary British construction, with wooden-framed bodies on steel underframes, and the metal-work of one of them was folded virtually in two. Somewhat surprisingly the official report went out of its way to say that there would not have been much advantage had the coaches been of all-steel construction, as the energy of the colliding train would still have had to be dissipated somehow. The evidence from the French collision at Lagny-Pomponne in 1933 provided a very clear indication of the superior 'survivability' of all-steel coaches. This has also been extensively demonstrated in this country since British Railways' adoption of this type of construction from 1951 onwards. There have been many instances when their superior strength has markedly reduced the casualty list in several very severe accidents.

The driver of *Grand Parade* was charged with culpable homicide, but he was formally found 'Not guilty' when this was withdrawn in the course of the trial. In later years he became one of the Top Link drivers on the East Coast Route, working such trains as the non-stop 'Capitals Limited'.

Hamilton, *p92/93*, 108. Nock, p150. Rolt, p223.

3 January 1938
Near Shinchow, China

100 + killed and injured

A Canton–Hankow train was derailed when the roadbed subsided in Kwantung province.

RG **68** 36 (1938).

3 January 1938
China

42 killed

A train from Canton to Wuchung ran into debris in a tunnel which had been damaged by Japanese bombs.

RG **68** 36 (1938).

16 January 1938
Milepost 74, China (Kowloon Canton, Chinese Section)

87 killed, 30 injured

A fire broke out in the second coach (No. 92) of an express, arson being suspected. The first four vehicles were detached, and moved clear of the rest of the train, and the leading coach was then also hauled out of the way. Photographs taken of the incident show how rapidly the fire spread. All the casualties occurred in coach No. 92, although those either side of it were also gutted. As a result of this accident it was decided to fit emergency brake cocks under glass covers in place of the chain alarms, and provide sliding doors rather than the hinged variety.

RG **69** 443 (1938).

(29 March) 1938
Valencia, Spain

39 killed

In the part of Spain in the hands of the Republicans, an electric train hit a lorry carrying petrol on a level-crossing near Valencia. Immediately after the collision the whole train caught fire, making rescue difficult, although a number of the passengers saved were only suffering from slight burns.

4 April 1938
Between Plumtree and Tsessebe, Southern Rhodesia

26 killed, 22 injured

An express from Bulawayo to Johannesburg and Cape Town collided head-on with a goods train in a cutting near the border between Southern Rhodesia and Bechuanaland. Several of those killed were the spare crews who travelled in the trainmen's cabooses on the 484-mile stretch from Bulawayo and Mafeking. Some of the passenger coaches remained on the rails and the uninjured passengers and staff were able to render first-aid. Rescue work was hampered by the location of the accident, and there were no good roads nearby. The line was blocked for over 48 hours before the cutting could be widened to get the wreckage clear. At the subsequent inquest it emerged that telegraph arrangements were made for the trains to cross at Ramaquabane siding, but the orders given to the goods train driver stipulated it would take place at Vakaranga. Because the freight was running early, the normal crossing point at Tsessebe had been changed.

RG **68** 732, 977 (1938).

19 June 1938
Miles City, Montana, United States of America (Milwaukee)

47 killed

A bridge across Custer Creek collapsed as the westbound 'Olympian' crossed it just after midnight. This was a long structure, consisting of seven spans, built across a tributary of the Yellowstone River, which was normally dry for nine months of the year. Heavy flash-floods were known to occur in the area however, and the bridge had been designed to withstand them when it was built in 1913. On the night concerned, heavy rain had been reported in the hills to the north, and the bridge had been inspected just over two hours before the accident took place. At that time the water was only six or seven feet deep, well below the 16ft clearance. During the intervening period a cloudburst caused a 20ft wall of water to sweep down the creek, which displaced one of the main piers. As the eleven-coach express crossed it, the bridge collapsed. The locomotive and the first five coaches reached the far side, but two tourist sleeping cars fell into the water and were completely submerged. The last four cars were not derailed, and were later able to continue their journey over the tracks of the Northern Pacific. Some of the bodies of those drowned were recovered from the Yellowstone River, 50 miles away, and there may have been more killed than the total given above.

Shaw, p306.

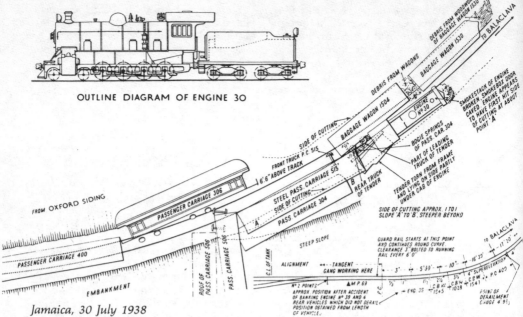

Jamaica, 30 July 1938

Plan of the positions of the locomotive and some of the coaches after the derailment near Balaclava in Jamaica on 30 July 1938. A diagram of the locomotive involved is included. (Railway Gazette)

30 July 1938

Balaclava, Jamaica

32 killed 71 injured

A passenger train from Kingston to Montego Bay was being banked up a steep gradient when the leading locomotive was derailed on a sharp curve. The report said that the crew of the banker was not aware of this, and continued to push the rear of the train forward, the coaches finishing up piled on top of one another, but shutting the regulator would have had little effect on the magnitude of the pile-up. There was initially a suggestion that the derailment was due to sabotage, but this was quickly discounted, it being determined that the train was doing 35mph instead of the 25 allowed. At first it was feared that a party of 40 Girl Guides had also been killed, but they were later found to have alighted at the previous stop. This was the first fatal accident to occur on the country's railway.

RG **69** 261, 623 (1938), **71** 110, *111* (1939).

21 August 1938

Vadamadura, India (South India)

33 killed, 93 injured

A passenger train was derailed after a flood had weakened a bridge. It was crowded with Muslim pilgrims and a large wedding party. The locomotive finished up half-buried in mud, with the first coach and a mail van on top of it. The replacement of a bridge in the nearby road by a culvert had caused the flow pattern of the river to breach the railway embankment. The nearby villagers knew of the damage two hours before the train was derailed, but did nothing to warn anyone of the danger.

RG **69** 487 (1938), **70** 853 (1939).

25 September 1938
Martorell, Spain

68 killed, (300) injured

Two well-loaded trains collided head-on in Republican Spain, 15 miles west of Barcelona. A scheduled working from the coast hit a special from Vilafrance del Panades in a blinding rainstorm. The initial inquiry into the accident was told that the electrical disturbances which accompanied it had interfered with the working of the signals and points. However it was also suspected that the staff at Mortorell had given the all-clear to the slow train before the other had left the single-line section. The death toll given was that mentioned in the early reports, and it was feared that it might rise.

RG **69** 575 (1938).

19 December 1938
Between João Ayres and Sitio, Brazil (Central of Brazil)

42 killed, 70+ injured

A goods train and a passenger one collided head-on, the first three coaches of the latter being reduced to a mass of splintered wreckage. Two of the coaches were filled with Bahian emigrants and another with Boy Scouts. The driver of the previous freight had left his line-clear ticket at João Ayres and the passenger train picked it up by mistake.

RG **70** 215 (1939).

24 December 1938
Etulia, Roumania

93 killed, 147 injured

Two passenger trains collided on a single line after a misunderstanding between the stationmasters at three successive stations about where they were to cross. One of the trains was a local one, but the other was carrying soldiers going on Christmas leave, the fatalities including a general and two colonels. Both locomotives and seven coaches were destroyed in the collision, which took place in a blizzard, and this also held up the dispatch of the two rescue trains for several hours. The severe weather also delayed the news reaching Bucharest, the first vague reports not being received until late in the afternoon of Christmas Day, and another 24 hours were to elapse before the first official communication arrived from Galatz. An inquiry was held after the president of the railways and two government ministers had visited the site, where they had ordered the dismissal of the three stationmasters and an inspector. The official at Galatz had arranged for the trains to cross at Frecatzei rather than Etulia, as usual, but his colleague at the former station was unaware of the change, and let one of the trains depart according to the normal arrangements.

12 January 1939
Hazaribagh, Bihar, India (East Indian)

21 killed, 71 injured

The 'Dehra Dun Express' from Howrah was derailed in the early morning, five of its coaches overturning and catching fire. The accident was caused by 'malicious interference' to the track, two previous accidents having been caused by sabotage on that railway in 1938. Rails had been moved out of position, but the locomotive crossed the 36ft gap and rerailed itself. However, the resulting damage to the track prevented the coaches from doing the same, and they were derailed. A judicial inquiry was ordered into the accident. A sum of 5,000 rupees (£375) was initially offered for information leading to the apprehension of those involved, but no one was charged, even after the reward had been increased to 25,000 rupees (£1,875). A

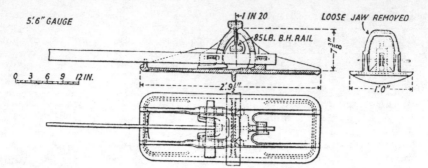

Diagram of the Denham & Olphert plate sleeper used on the East India Railway which was tampered with to cause the derailment of the Dehra Dun Express on 12 January 1939. In tropical countries it is often not possible to use wooden sleepers because of attack by insects. (Railway Gazette)

number of further sabotage attacks on the railway was made in the next two months, and at the inquiry it was stated that there had been 131 incidents of wrecking or attempted wrecking during the previous ten years, but in only 34 of these had railway employees been involved.

RG **70** 116, 157, 214, 236, 237, 332, 726 (1939)

11 February 1939
San Gervasio, Spain

53 killed, (100) injured

A crowded workman's train running downhill from Tarrasa collided with a stationary wagon near Sarriá Tunnel, and then ran into the rear of another train at San Gervasio, close to Barcelona. The leading train had left Tarrasa 20 minutes earlier, and most of the victims were in the central vehicle of the three.

RG **70** 284 (1939).

13 April 1939
Mexico

26 + killed

A collision occurred between trains from Guadalajara and Laredo 180 miles

west of Mexico City, twelve coaches carrying a large number of American tourists being telescoped and destroyed. *The Times* correspondent referred to the accident being the 'worst in a series that has occurred almost weekly during recent months, while the railways have been in the hands of a workers' management committee'. The railways had been expropriated two years earlier, and handed over to the employees twelve months later, the accidents being officially attributed to neglect by the staff and the poor condition of the equipment. Experts had stated that an expenditure of $40,000,000 was necessary to restore the railways to proper working conditions.

17 April 1939
Najdia, India (East Bengal)

35 killed, 31 injured

The 'Dacca Mail' collided with the 'North Bengal Express' in the station, 66 miles from Calcutta. Two members of the Bengal Legislative Assembly were among those killed.

RG **70** 672 (1939).

12 August 1939

Carlin, Nevada, United States of America (Union Pacific train on Southern Pacific tracks)

24 killed, 115 injured

The Union Pacific Railroad's stream-lined express, 'City of San Francisco', hauled by three diesel-electric locomotives, was derailed at 60mph 16 miles west of Carlin as a result of sabotage, a rail having been deliberately misplaced on the outside of a curve. Some of the derailed vehicles then collided violently with the steelwork of a Warren-truss underbridge, located 170 feet beyond the point where the vehicles came off the track. The structure, 120 feet long, was demolished, and several of the coaches finished up on the bed of the Humboldt River, more than 30 feet below the track. The kitchen-diner took the brunt of this collision, together with the three coaches immediately behind it, and were themselves the most severely damaged. The leading locomotive did not leave the track, nor did the last two of the 14 coaches. Of the 24 deaths, 15 of them were dining-car staff, and another 16 railway employees were among the injured. This was the first major wreck involving one of the American light-weight streamlined trains, and there was considerable interest in how well the aluminum-alloy vehicles stood up to the impacts. In those days the cars were not of welded construction, and in places the metal sheeting tore loose from the rivets. While the Bureau of Safety's report discussed the cause of the accident at length, there was some regret that they had not studied the effect of the impacts on the vehicles with the same degree of thoroughness. The streamliner was booked to cover the 2,263 miles from Chicago to Oakland in 39¾ hours, an overall average of 57mph, inclusive of many intermediate stops. Although the train was owned by the Union Pacific and operated over its line, the tracks of the Chicago & North Western and the Southern Pacific were also used.

RG **71** 264, Diesel Supplement 133, *145*, **72** 523 (1940).

2 September 1939

Les Aubrais, France (SNCF)

35 killed, 77 injured

A collision took place.

8 October 1939

Gesundbrunnen, Berlin, Germany (DR)

20 killed

During the first winter of World War II, no less than seven serious railway accidents took place in Germany, all of them collisions. This period was known as the 'Phoney War', and one of our schoolboy jokes at that time was that the slogan of the German Railways was 'Travel by train and see the *Next* World!' This accident was a collision between an express from Sassnitz, the port for the train-ferry from Trellenborg in Sweden, and another passenger train in Stargard station. Under wartime conditions few details of these accidents reached Britain.

RG **71** 502 (1939).

21 October 1939

Between Santa Lucrecia and Matias Romero, Mexico

40 killed

A freight train from Vera Cruz to the Pacific Coast was derailed, and two of its petrol tanks caught fire. The casualties occurred among workers and their families travelling in the goods wagons.

RG **71** 566 (1939).

26 October 1939

St Valentin, Austria (then part of Germany)

At least 20 killed, 30 seriously injured

The bare information about this unspecified accident reached England from Copenhagen in Denmark. It occurred near Linz in Austria, which had been annexed by the Germans a few years previously.

RG **71** 594 (1939).

30 October 1939

Lambrate, near Milan, Italy (Italian State)

(20) killed

An express from Venice collided with an electric train from Milan to Rome. Italy had not at that time entered the war, and in July that year a demonstration run with one of their 'ETR200' streamlined electric units had established a world record by averaging over 100mph start-to-stop between Florence and Milan.

RG **71** 594 (1939).

12 November 1939

Rosengrund, Upper Silesia, Germany (DR)

43 killed, 60 injured

A mistake by the signalman at Rosengrund caused two crowded local trains to collide between there and Langliebeni, on the single-line branch between Cosel and Bauerwitz.

RG **71** 658 (1939).

1 December 1939

Sibiu, Roumania

20 killed, 16 seriously injured

A special train, carrying materials and railway workers for a new line between Marsa ad Avric, ran away down an incline and crashed near Sibiu in central Roumania.

RG **71** 754 (1939).

22 December 1939

Genthin, Germany (DR)

196 killed, 108 injured

At 1am an express from Berlin to Köln was standing in Genthin station, 57 miles west of the capital, on the line through Magdeburg and Hannover, when it was hit from the rear at 60mph by the following train to Saarbrücken. At the block post four miles before Genthin the second train failed to slow for the distant and stop signals, and the signalman telephoned a warning down the line. At Gethin East the signalman ran out with a red lamp, but this was seen by the fireman of the first train. He got his driver to stop, and the Saarbrücken one ran into its rear. Both trains were crowded, and figures given for the death toll rose from 70, to 132, and finally 196, which made the accident the worst ever to happen in Germany. The use of wooden coaches, brought back into service to handle the wartime traffic, added to the casualties.

RG **71** 855 (1939), **72** 372 (1940).

22 December 1939

Between Marksdorf and Kluftern, Germany (DR)

101 killed, 28 injured

This collision occurred in the evening after the accident at Genthin. A special passenger train hit a goods train on the single line between Friedrichshafen and Radolfzell which runs round the north end of Bodensee (Lake Constance). It was a foggy evening, and the passenger train was incorrectly allowed to leave a crossing station because the two stationmasters failed to comply with the block telegraph rules. Both were arrested.

RG **71** 855 (1939), **72** 372 (1940).

This was the last of the seven major collisions which took place in Germany during the first three months of World War II. Those not recorded separately were the one at Spandau on 20 November, killing nine, and that at Neider Wöllstadt six days later, which caused 15 fatalities. There was also a head-on collision near Hagen in Westphalia, on 12 December, when 15 died. All told 311 people were killed in the accidents, none of which was stated to have been the result of sabotage. The high numbers of casualties were officially ascribed to the crowds travelling, and the use of old coaches brought out of reserve.

RG **71** 690, 722, 823 (1939).

30 December 1939

Torre Annunziata, Italy

29 killed

The Calabria express was scheduled to overtake a troop train at Torre Annunziata, near Naples, but this could not be done because the points there were frozen. It was decided to send the latter on ahead, but, as it was leaving, the express, which had run through signals, hit it from the rear. Unofficial figures put the number of fatalities at 40.

RG **72** 33 (1940).

1940–1944

29 January 1940
Osaka, Japan
176 killed, 669 injured

In the Osaka suburban area, an over-crowded petrol-engined railcar or tram turned over after a collision, and caught fire. Those aboard were workers from various heavy industries in the area.

RG **72** 166 (1940).

(Late February 1940)
Near Queretaro City, Mexico
20 killed

An express travelling to the border with the United States collided with a goods train six miles from Queretaro City, approximately 120 miles north-west of Mexico City.

RG **72** 322 (1940).

4 March 1940
Yamagati Prefecture, Japan (Japanese Imperial)
37 killed

An avalanche destroyed a bridge located between two tunnels. The loco-motive and part of its train emerging from one of them fell 75 feet into the river bed.

RG **72** 362 (1940).

5 March 1940
Iitala, Finland
21 killed

Three months after the war with Russia had started, a train was taking evacuees to neutral Sweden. North of Tampere, on the Helsinki–Tornio line, it came into head-on collision with a southbound train, which had over-run signals in a blizzard. Fire broke out, and those killed comprised 16 children, two mothers and all three leaders of the group. One family in Stockholm awaiting the arrival of three children had to be told that all of them had died.

RG **72** 349 (1940).

17 March 1940
Between Zaluka and Ozaij, Yugoslavia
20 killed

A train on the line from Kalrovacz and Ljubljana was derailed by a landslide.

RG **72** 486 (1940).

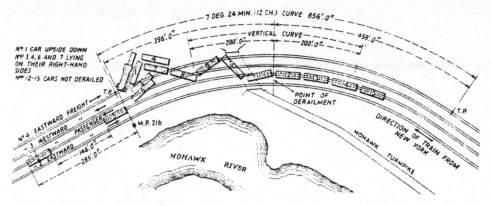

Little Falls, 14 April 1940
  Diagram of where the locomotive and coaches finished up after the derailment at Little Falls on 14 April 1940. (Railway Gazette)

19 April 1940

Near Little Falls, New York State, United States of America (New York Central)

30 killed, 100 injured

The 'Lake Shore Limited' was running 21 minutes late when the Road Foreman of Locomotives joined the 73-year old driver on the footplate of the 'Hudson' 4-6-4 at Albany, but no time had been made up on the 75mph stretch to Little Falls. At this point, the New York Central, keeping to its famous 'Water-Level' route, had to share the narrow valley with the river, a canal, a highway and another railway. As a result, at Gulf Curve, the sharpest anywhere on the system, there was a permanent speed restriction of 45mph. This was protected by two fixed signals, both provided with automatic train control equipment, but the driver cancelled the warnings he received, and only braked at the last minute. The whole train overturned, and the locomotive and first three coaches were badly crushed where they hit the solid masonry abutment of a road over-bridge. As with many other accidents involving excessive speeds, no satisfactory explanation was forthcoming for the failure to brake in time. The elderly driver was killed, and the foreman was too badly injured to recall the circumstances that led to the crash. This was another of the railway disasters which caused considerable international interest, references being made in the British technical press for over a year.

Reed, p34, 40. Shaw, p299. RG **72** 740 (1940), **73** 153 (1940), **74** 387 (1941).

5 May 1940

Between Epineuil-le-Fleuriel and Vallon, France (SNCF)

33 killed, 46 seriously injured

Torrential rain had caused the river to rise 15 feet above normal, and the rapid flow of water had weakened the foundations of the bridge, which failed when the Paris–Montluçon express was crossing it at 1am.

18 May 1940

Morgny, France (SNCF)

53 killed, 128 injured

The disaster resulted from a collision.

31 July 1940

Cuyahoga Falls, near Cleveland, Ohio, United States of America

41 killed

As a result of failure to obey the instructions on a train order, a double-headed, steam-hauled freight with 74 cars collided head-on with a petrol-driven railcar on a single-track stretch, at a closing speed of approximately 75mph. The railcar was pushed back 400 feet, petrol was spilt, and it caught fire. The crew of the railcar had failed to take the siding as laid down in their train order, and all three of them jumped when they saw the freight ahead. Each of them was seriously injured, but all the passengers died.

RG **73** 158, *281* (1940).

5 August 1940

Jairampur, India (East Bengal)

34 killed, 90 injured

The down 'Dacca Mail' was derailed 80 miles from Calcutta after a rail had been removed from the track. The loco-motive, together with some of the coaches, rolled down the 15ft embank-ment, finishing up half-buried in the mud. All the victims were Indians. The locomotive was one of the 4-4-2s used on the 'Darjeeling Mail' from 1911, when it was booked at 60mph between Dum Dum Junction and Ranaghat.

RG **73** 158, *431, 435* (1940).

4 November 1940

Norton Fitzwarren, England (Great Western)

27 killed, 75 injured

The 13-coach Paddington to Penzance sleeping-car train, with some 900 people aboard, was running over an hour late at Taunton, and the signalman decided to let the following newspaper train overtake it on the stretch of quad-ruple track before Norton Fitzwarren. On a dark night, with the 'Black Out' in force, the driver of the passenger train, whose home had recently been damaged during the 'Blitz' on London, failed to note that he was on the relief line. This finished at Norton Fitzwarren where he should have waited for the other train, but he misread the signals, and therefore cancelled the warnings he received from the Automatic Train Con-trol. It was not until the second train started to pass him on his right that he realised what was happening. By this time it was too late to stop, and the locomotive ran through the buffer-stops into soft earth, with its coaches spread-eagling themselves behind. Something flew through the window of the news-paper train, and hit the guard, who got his driver to stop for an examination. It was not discovered until later that the exterior of some of their coaches had been scored by the ballast thrown up by the derailed sleeping-car train, and it turned out that a rivet-head from the locomotive's bogie had hit the guard. A second collision had thus only been avoided by seconds, as the fourth coach of the derailed express finished up foul of the main line.

Hamilton, p92/93, 117. Nock, p162. Rolt, p248. Schneider, p102.

14 November 1940

Diegem, Belgium

21 killed

A train from Tirlmont collided with a standing train at Diegem, five miles from Brussels.

RG **73** 555 (1940).

19 November 1940
Malvik, Norway

22 killed

A collision took place between a passenger train and a goods one ten miles east of Trondheim. Sabotage was suspected.

RG **73** 582 (1940).

(December 1940)
Near Iguala, Mexico

71 killed

A repair train was derailed on a curve, and fell over a precipice.

RG **73** 652 (1940).

3 December 1940
Velilla de Ebro, Spain

47 killed, 64+ injured

An express from Barcelona collided with one from Madrid to Barcelona just outside the points of the crossing-loop at Velilla de Elbro, a small station 32 miles east of Zaragoza at 4am. Large fires had to be lit alongside the track to provide light and warmth in the −10°C temperatures. The two trains were due to cross in the loop, but the one from Barcelona over-ran the station and was foul of the single-line stretch ahead.

RG **74** 62 (1940).

6 January 1941
Near Berettya-Ujfalu, Hungary

20 killed

The fatalities occurred to soldiers in a train accident, details of which were not reported in Britain.

RG **74** 79 (1941).

15 February 1941
Zumaya, Spain

20 killed, over 100 injured

A metre-gauge electric train on the line from San Sebastián to Bilbao along the north coast was blown off a bridge, three coaches falling into the river below. It had come to a stand on the structure after the storm had interrupted the power supply. Although Spain's 'Green Coast' is now popular with holidaymakers, ferocious winds can arise with comparatively little warning.

RG **74** 210 (1941).

Trains have also been derailed by winds miles away from the coast. In December 1907 four coaches of a Colorado & Southern train were blown off straight track in open country near Marshall, 24 miles from Denver in the USA, killing one and injuring six of those aboard. In Ireland the West Clare Railway had five 'blow-offs' on its exposed coastal stretch in the years prior to 1909, and in 1916 two metre-gauge trains were blown over on the South India Railway by a cyclone, the locomotives in each case remaining on the rails. (See also the accident on 8 June 1962.)

(Mid-March 1941)
Calera, Chile

20 killed, 60+ injured

No details of this accident were reported in the British press.

RG **74** 354 (1941).

23 April 1941
Near Kampala, Uganda

20 killed

A train was derailed.

RG **74** 510 (1941).

(May 1941)

Kyujo, Japan

200 killed or injured

An express from Keelung collided head-on with a goods train from Takao. A signalling error was thought to have been responsible.

RG **74** 611 (1941).

20 July 1941

Near Como, Italy

30 killed

The coaches of a passenger train taking Italian workers to Germany were hit by something projecting from a passing goods train, as it was crossing a viaduct near Como.

RG **75** 122 (1941).

2 November 1941

Paris, France (SNCF)

21 killed, 7 injured

An express from Orleans collided with a train of empty stock in Austerlitz terminus.

RG **75** 514 (1941).

16 September 1941

Aboshi, Japan (Japanese Imperial)

63 killed, 67 injured, 19 seriously

No. 8 express from Tokyo on the Sanyo line ran into the rear of a stationary train for Kyoto nine miles west of Himeiji. The driver had missed the signals and was detained by the police.

RG **75** 611 (1941).

21 December 1941

Naples, Italy (Vesuvius Railway)

25 killed

No details of this disaster appeared in the British press.

RG **76** 74 (1942).

27 December 1941

Between Frankfurt on Oder and Posen/Poznań, Germany/Poland

38 killed

A Berlin–Warsaw express hit a stationary train in a snowstorm.

RG **76** 74 (1942).

28 December 1941

Between Laventie and La Gorgue, France (SNCF)

56 killed, 40 injured

A collision took place on the line between Nantes and La Roche-sur-Yon.

30 December 1941

Near Hazebrouck (SNCF)

50 killed

A second major railway disaster occurred in France within two days.

RG **76** 74 (1942).

30 December 1941

Eccles, England (London, Midland & Scottish)

23 killed, 56 seriously injured

Just after 8.15 on a dark, extremely-foggy morning, an eight-coach sub-urban train from Rochdale to Penn-ington, hauled by a tank locomotive, over-ran the signals on the four-track section through Eccles station. It col-lided, side-on, with a similar Keynon–Manchester (Exchange) train which was crossing from the Up Slow line to the Up Fast. The signalman erroneously thought there was a fogman at the Down Slow distant signal, and so con-travened the Block Telegraph Regula-tions by allowing the conflicting movement to take place in such bad visibility.

16 May 1942

Between Oderolal and Tando Adam, India

22 killed, 26 injured

The 'Punjab Mail' en route to Lahore was derailed 146 miles from Karachi by Dacoits from a criminal Sind sect, known as Hurs. The locomotive and six coaches came off the track and over-turned. The surviving passengers were attacked with shot-guns and axes, and had their money and valuables stolen. Two state ministers from Sind were on the train, and one of them was killed. There was subsequently more similar trouble in the area, and the driver of another train narrowly averted a second disaster four days later. Armed escorts were carried on passenger trains, while police protection was provided at stations, but the operation of trains during the hours of darkness between Hyderabad and Rett was suspended for some time. The militia were sent in pursuit of the Hurs, these lawless fol-lowers of Pir Fagaro being subsequently killed or arrested.

RG **77** 175 (1942).

In August that year the leaders of the Indian Congress were arrested, and this sparked off widespread riots in the country. Amongst the other damage caused, 258 stations were destroyed and 40 trains derailed.

RG **77** 602 (1942).

27 December 1942

Almonte, Ontario, Canada (Canadian Pacific)

36 killed, more than 200 injured

This serious rear-end collision, in which two coaches were telescoped, was caused by the failure of both crews to follow the rules. The leading train, travelling from Chalk River to Ottawa, was running late because of the heavy wartime and Christmas traffic. When it reached Almonte, its rear end projected nearly 200 feet beyond the station limits, but, in the rain and fog, the crew did not protect it, as laid down in the instructions. The following troop special, in spite of having been held at an earlier station to give the Ottawa train an opportunity to get clear, was making better time than the latter's schedule, which was again contrary to the rules. The scheduled train was just moving off from Almonte, with the signal lowered for it, when the troop train came round the curve. Thinking the clear signal was for them, the driver released the brakes, and was then unable to stop when he sighted the train ahead at short range.

Shaw, p182.

Wartime saw a major increase in traffic on the North American railways. This, coupled with skilled staff being drafted into the armed forces, resulted in a marked rise in the number of accidents. In the United States, during the year ending 30 June 1942, there were 3,682 collisions and 5,837 derailments, mak-ing a total of 9,519 incidents. In the previous twelve months the corres-ponding total had been only 6,471.

RG **78** 499, 532 (1943).

4 January 1943

Between Hannover and Wunstorf, Germany (German State)

20 killed, 20 seriously injured

An express ran into the rear of another train standing at a signal.

3 June 1943

Near Akola, India (Great Indian Peninsula)

50 killed, 100 injured

According to the official statement, the mail train from Bombay to Calcutta collided at full speed with a goods train nine miles from Akola, the dining-car and two coaches being wrecked. A party of British soldiers gave valuable assistance in putting out a fire near the locomotive, and helping the driver to escape. The reason for the collision did not appear in the British papers.

(Mid-July 1943)

Istanbul, Turkey

18 killed, 44 injured

The cable of a funicular broke, and both cars ran away down the gradient to crash into houses alongside the lower terminus in Galata. There were considerable differences between the German version of the casualty list quoted above, and the earlier report from Reuters which said two were killed and 22 injured. Normally arrangements are made with railways of this sort to ensure that special brakes are immediately applied to stop the cars should the main means of haulage break, which often consists of more than one cable, each of which is able to hold the car on its own.

RG **79** 75, 122 (1943).

30 August 1943

Wayland, New York State, United States of America (Lackawanna)

27 killed, 114 injured

The 'Lackawanna Limited', en route from New York to Buffalo and Chicago, came into head-on collision with a freight train. The latter had been standing in a siding for nearly an hour, and was called to move forward to within 350 feet of the points. Unfortunately the driver misunderstood the instructions, and continued past the point where his locomotive fouled the main line. The express had been running at 80mph, but braked slightly approaching Wayland, and the driver then got a restrictive cab-signalling indication. He immediately made an emergency brake application, but this only reduced his speed to 50mph before the collision. Both locomotives and six coaches were badly damaged. A jet of live steam from the freight locomotive scalded some of the passengers in the remains of the third coach. The accident happened at 5.30pm, and rescuers were still searching the wreckage long after dark. Any movement of the freight train within ten minutes of the booked arrival of the express should have required a written train order, and the issuing of that would have also required one to be given to the crew of the express, cautioning them to slow down.

RG **79** 270 (1943), **80** 161 (1944).

6 September 1943

Frankford Junction, Philadelphia, United States of America (Pennsylvania)

79 killed, 103 injured

A hot-box on the dining-car of the advance section of the 'Congressional Limited' caused the journal to shear off as the train was accelerating from the usual slowing through Philadelphia. The main section of this train, which was the fastest and best-known of the Washington–New York expresses, had a 63mph schedule between Washington and New York. This was inclusive of three intermediate stops, one of them at Philadelphia, but the advance section ran non-stop from Washington to Newark. On this occasion the electrically-hauled, 16-coach train weighed over 1,100 (long) tons, and the failure of the axle caused the dining-car to hit a signal gantry, which sliced right through its full length, 'like a giant can-opener'. The following car was also wrecked, and the seven behind it all derailed. Two miles from the point where the accident occurred, the crew of a shunting locomotive had noticed the burning journal, but their telephone call to the signal-box did not enable action to be taken before the axle broke.

The diner was one of the only two cars in the train without roller-bearing axleboxes, having been put into service to deal with the heavy weekend traffic. There was some criticism about the use of such a vehicle, but this was one of the examples quoted by the American Museum of Safety when they awarded the American railways their 'Certificate of Special Commendation' in 1944. One speaker said that much comment of that sort was inspired by owners of patented items, anxious to increase their sales. It was further pointed out that a coach with roller bearings had experienced a similar accident a few months previously, but that derailment did not take place where there was an 'inpenetrable obstacle' on the lineside. Incidentally the caption for a picture of the Philadelphia accident in *The Railway Gazette* said it illustrated a gantry crane being used to clear the wreckage, but it actually showed a gantry for the position-light signals!

Shaw, p319. Reed, p128, 138. RG **79** 304, 581 (1943), **81** 614 (1944).

6 October 1943
Near Chalon-sur-Saône, France (SNCF)

21 killed, (90) injured

An express for Lyon hit a derailed goods train.

RG **79** 636 (1943).

14 November 1943
Villupuram Junction, India (South India)

39 killed, 88 injured

The 'Indo–Ceylon Boat Mail', bound for Madras, was derailed.

RG **79** 674 (1943).

16 December 1943
Rennert, North Carolina, United States of America (Atlantic Coast Line)

74 killed, 54 injured

On a bitterly-cold morning, the 18-car southbound 'Tamiami Champion' ground to a halt at Rennert, and the conductor and trainmen went back to find the cause. They discovered a broken coupling and disconnected brake hose between the second and third cars, and began repairs. The conductor instructed the fireman to 'flag' the northbound line, but he did not take any detonators, and the fusee he was carrying was damaged when he fell in the snow, so could not be used.

The train had actually stopped because the last three cars had been derailed by a broken rail, and two of them were foul of the other track. Most of the passengers in these vehicles, none of whom was more than slightly injured, climbed clear of the coaches. The rear brakesman went back to carry out his protection duties, and gave a white handlamp signal to the crew at the front end of the train, half a mile away. He did not, however, ensure that they knew the rear vehicles were derailed and foul of the northbound track. Forty minutes later the northbound 'Tamiami Champion' appeared travelling at about 85mph, and its crew were only alerted to the danger ahead as they passed the front of the halted train, by a passenger waving one of the tail-lamps from the derailed coaches. It was then too late to stop, and the diesel locomotive hit the first of these vehicles, which was leaning over at an angle of 45 degrees, becoming derailed, together with eight coaches behind it. Most of the fatalities were servicemen, and only one of those killed was travelling on the southbound train. (Some reports refer to the accident taking place at Buie, and differ in detail. This account is based on the summary of the ICC report which appeared in the 1944 Railway Gazette reference given below.)

Shaw, p183. RG **79** 650 (1943), **80** 544 (1944).

As a result of these and other serious railway accidents that took place in 1942 and 1943, the House of Representatives set up a select committee to inquire into the causes. Subsequent information showed that the number of accidents on the American railways had risen from 7,106 in 1940 to 16,061 in 1943, although the number per million locomotive miles only increased from 5.43 to 8.87. Comparisons were made between the numbers killed on the railways from all causes during the two world wars, the figures for some of the years being as follows:

Year	Killed
1917	10,087
1918	9,286
1942	5,337
1943	5,051

In 1944 the American Museum of Safety awarded a 'Certificate of Special Commendation' to the entire United States' railway industry, pointing out that there were only three passenger fatalities for every 10^9 (one billion) passenger train-miles, which was three times as safe as in World War I.

RG **81** 251, 641 (1944), **82** 634 (1945).

In 1943 1,743 people were killed on level-crossings in the United States, and 4,217 injured.

RG **80** 450 (1944).

3 January 1944
Torre, Spain (RENFE)
91 killed

As a result of brake failure, an eleven-coach passenger and mail train collided with a locomotive shunting two wagons in a tunnel near Torre station on the line between Léon and Coruña. The first six coaches caught fire, and a second collision occurred when a coal train ran into the shunting locomotive which had been forced out of the tunnel by the first impact. The middle of the tunnel was still blocked by burning wreckage the following day.

RG **80** 50 (1944).

11 January 1944
Near Arevale, Spain
37 killed

No details of this accident were reported in the English press.

20 January 1944
Porta Westfalica, Germany (DB)
53 killed, 62 injured

An express hit a stationary train in the station, where the line from Hannover to Osnabrück passes through the Weser Gorge.

RG **80** 126 (1944).

2 March 1944

Armi Tunnel, near Balvano, Italy

426 killed, 60 injured

Late at night, a heavy freight train with 47 vehicles behind two 2-8-0 steam locomotives set off fom Balvano for Potenza in southern Italy. Over 600 people climbed aboard to get a free ride. On the steep climb through Armi Tunnel the locomotives stalled, the quality of their coal being poor because of the war. Although they could have backed out, considerable efforts were made to get the train going again. As a result, the restricted space in the bore became filled with smoke and carbon monoxide, which killed all those who were inside the tunnel. The only survivors were from the wagon which was still out in the open air. The brakesman ran back to Balvano to get assistance, arriving just as the stationmaster was about to set off on a locomotive to find out what had happened.

Southern Italy was noted for its black-market activities, and many of the survivors disappeared into the countryside, while a high proportion of those killed had no papers, so were never identified. An investigation was carried out by a board of Allied and Italian officers, and the official report issued by General Clay, the head of the allied military services for the area, said that 426 passengers had been killed by carbon monoxide poisoning as the result of 'an act of God'. Figures given elsewhere differ somewhat. It said the catastrophe was caused by a combination of natural causes, such as a murky atmosphere, lack of wind of sufficient velocity to ventilate the tunnel, and wet rails which ordinarily might have been expected to occur singly and not simultaneously. The board found that no single fact contributed more than another to the catastrophe, which could not be attributed to human negligence nor mechanical failure.

As in World War I at Modane, the disaster was not directly attributable to the hostilities, but wartime conditions did play an important part in causing the accident and were largely responsible for its severity. Understandably, the military authorities' first priority was to get on with the campaign, which was involving vastly more deaths, but one would not expect to get away with such a bland conclusion these days.

RG **80** 267, 351 (1944). Schneider, p284. Shaw, p410.

There was another fire in an Italian railway tunnel on 30 March 1961. This time an electric passenger train was involved, and it caught fire after a short-circuit. Most of the 400 passengers safely were evacuated from the train in the 991-metre Bonassola Tunnel, between there and Framura, but five were killed.

Schneider, *p199*.

6 July 1944

High Cliff, near Jellico, Tennessee, United States of America (Louisville & Nashville)

35 killed, 98 injured

The locomotive and five coaches of a troop train were derailed as it negotiated some reverse curves at 45mph, which was 10mph more than the speed authorised over them. The last of the three sections had a radius of only $7\frac{1}{2}$ chains, and was provided with a check rail. At the point of derailment the track was $\frac{5}{8}$ inch wide to gauge, and, as the locomotive rolled, its inner leading bogie wheel mounted the check rail. The whole of the curving forces were thus being provided by the outer rail, and this finally overturned the locomotive and derailed coaches which fell 50 feet down an embankment into a stream.

RG **81** 223, 569 (1944).

4 August 1944

Stockton, Georgia, United States of America (Atlantic Coast Line)

47 killed, 36 injured

Although the track had been satisfactorily patrolled a year previously by one of the Sperry detector cars, a rail broke as a passenger train was passing over it at high speed. The break occurred under the ninth vehicle, a Pullman sleeping car, which, although derailed, was little damaged and no one in it was injured. The following coach, however, on loan to the railway from another company, and occupied by a Negro track-gang, hit the locomotive of a freight train on the next track. It was sliced in two, from floor-level on one side to the opposite cant-rail, for most of its length, and all the fatalities occurred in this coach.

Shaw, p203. RG **82** 132 (1945).

14 September 1944

Terre Haute, Indiana, United States of America (Chicago & Eastern Illinois)

29 killed, 42 injured

A head-on collision occurred near Terre Haute between a northbound passenger/mail train, and the first portion of the southbound 'Dixie Flyer'. The two trains had been ordered to meet at Atherton, 6½ miles north of their normal crossing point at Dewey, but the express 'failed to take the siding'. The line was equipped with automatic colour-light signalling, and both trains received the correct signal indications as they approached the crossing place. The 'Dixie Flyer' did not slow from 55 to 30mph as it should have done, and hit the other, stationary train at about 35mph. Most of the casualties were members of the armed forces; many of them airmen on leave after being wounded overseas.

RG **81** 232, 294 (1944).

18–19 September 1944

Near Castle Rock, Washington State, United States of America (Northern Pacific)

Two collisions took place on successive days on a section of double-track line used by the Great Northern, the Union Pacific and the Milwaukee Railways, in addition to the Northern Pacific. The first occurred when a Great Northern freight hit one belonging to the owning line as it drew out of a siding without giving sufficient warning for the automatic signalling to stop the approaching train. This accident blocked the eastbound track, and the following day two Great Northern special passenger trains collided as they were preparing to take the wrong line past the wreckage, an operation not allowed for with the automatic signalling system. The second, 13-coach, train was being used by Governor Dewey for his 'Whistle-Stop' presidential campaign, and, although a fusee had been thrown out by the crew of the first one, it did not burn for long enough to prevent a rear-end collision at 25mph. On 20 September a third collision occurred on the Northern Pacific's Hoquiam branch, when two freight trains collided head on at a combined speed of 60mph after a serious blunder by the dispatcher. Four people were killed and 69 injured in the three collisions.

RG **82** 268 (1945).

2 November 1944

Craiova, Roumania

60 killed, 100 injured

There was a collision between a military train and a goods train.

31 December 1944

Bagley, Utah, United States of America
(Southern Pacific)

50 killed

The first section of the 'Pacific Limited' was slowed to a crawl alongside the Great Salt Lake by a freight train ahead which had a hot box. Although the double-track line was protected with automatic signals, the flagman of the express put down two detonators and lit a flare. In spite of this the second section of the train, comprising 20 coaches, approached through the fog at 65mph, and its brakes were only applied twelve seconds before the collision. The driver of the second train, aged 64, was clearly at fault, and he was found to have died from shock or heart failure after making the brake application. He may have been taken ill earlier, as the fireman shouted to him when he saw the second signal at danger, but the driver was sluggish in applying the brakes.

Dealing with the aftermath of this accident was difficult, as it occurred on a stretch of embankment several miles long, crossing the marshes beside the Great Salt Lake. All the rescue work had to be carried out by rail, but the two army hospital cars in the undamaged section of the front train were able to assist the injured.

Shaw, p249.

1945–1949

10 January 1945

Belfast, Northern Ireland (Belfast & County Down)

21 killed, 40+ injured

On a dark, foggy morning, the 7.10am workmen's train from Bangor was stopped by signals at Ballymaccarret Junction on the outskirts of Belfast. It was then hit in the rear by the 7.40am motor train from Holywood, which, although claimed to be travelling at only 8–10mph, badly smashed the rear coach. Some of the wreckage was used to light fires on the lineside to assist the rescue work. The driver of the motor train was later acquitted of manslaughter, and the coroner's jury brought in a verdict that the accident was caused by 'failure of a faulty signal, and fog which obscured the driver's vision'. The official report concluded that the train from Holywood, which had continued under the 'Stop & Proceed' rules, was travelling far too fast. It considered that it was probable that passengers in the crowded first coach were actually standing beside or behind the driver. In a subsequent civil action a judge ruled that the railway company were guilty of negligence in adopting the 'Stop & Proceed' rule, as 'other methods were practicable and could be used'.

RG **82** 54, 144, 407, 607 (1945), **83** 30, 48 (1945), **85** 93, 115, 135 (1946).

11 January 1945

Rozières-sur-Mouzon, France (SNCF)

21 killed, nine injured

A collision occurred on the cross-country line between Nancy and Dijon.

17 January 1945

St Valéry-en-Caux, France (SNCF)

84 killed, 226 injured

In the final months of World War II a train crashed into the buffers of the terminus at St Valéry-en-Caux, at the end of a branch on the Channel coast, west of Dieppe. It finished up in the yard outside the station, and most of the local population assisted with the work of digging victims from the wreckage.

1 February 1945

Cazadero, Mexico

127 killed

Two trains carrying people to a festival at San Juan de Las Lagos were in collision at Cazadere in the province of Queretare. The first was standing in the station when it was hit by the second, all nine coaches being derailed, after which three of them caught fire.

RG **82** 147 (1945).

22 March 1945

Jungshahi, India (North West Railway)

24 killed, 43 injured

A passenger train from Karachi to Rohri was hit in the rear by a goods train.

RG **82** 417 (1945).

13 June 1945

Near Orvieto, Italy

(70) killed

A passenger train carrying British and Italian troops on leave, together with returning deportées from Germany, collided at high speed with a train conveying petrol. As a result of the fire that followed it was not possible to determine the exact death toll, but it included up to 20 British soldiers.

27 July 1945

St Fons, France (SNCF)

(150) killed

A munitions train exploded after coming into collision with a passenger train in a suburb of Lyon. The resulting fire produced continuous explosions, which prevented rescuers from reaching the wreckage. As well as wrecking houses nearby, flying debris set the local gas works on fire.

9 August 1945

Michigan, North Dakota, United States of America (Great Northern)

34 killed, about 50 injured

The first section of the 'Empire Builder' stopped because of a hot-box, and its crew did not protect the rear, as laid down in the rules. As a result the second section collided with it, ploughing through the combined observation and sleeping car.

13 August 1945

Goch, near Kleve, Germany

21 killed

In the early hours of the morning, two leave trains collided head-on on the single line branch from Krefeld which serves the area just inside Germany between the Rhine and Maas rivers. The railway had only been reopened a week earlier, using German signalmen, although the drivers of both trains were Dutch, which makes it a difficult accident to ascribe to a particular country. The coaches in one of the trains were all of steel construction, but a wooden one in the other train was telescoped. With Britons, Belgians, Germans and Poles aboard, there was considerable linguistic chaos during the rescue operations. At least four British soldiers were among those killed.

4 September 1945

Kédange, France (SNCF)

39 killed, 34 injured

A French military train consisted of eight passsenger coaches, separated from 19 petrol tanks by four empty wagons. A mistake by a signalman diverted it into a siding near Thionville, where it collided with a stationary goods train. Fire broke out, and, in spite of the barrier wagons, spread to the passenger vehicles. Six hours after the accident it had still not been brought under control.

9 September 1945

Between Tres Cruces and Iturbe, Jujuy Province, Argentina

40 killed, (60) injured

The 'Pan-American' express from La Paz in Bolivia was derailed on a line that was at a height of 12,000 feet above sea level. The train had been delayed after entering Argentina at La Quiaca, and the driver was trying to make up time, but was travelling at 35–40mph, which was too fast for the sharp curves in the spectacular Humahuaca Valley. Amongst those on the train was the English Deputy Manager of the Antofagasta (Chili) & Bolivia Railway, who was travelling to Buenos Aires en route to England. He was uninjured.

RG **83** 302, *366* (1945).

21 September 1945

Vernaison, France (SNCF)

30 killed, 105 injured

Two trains were in collision.

30 September 1945

Bourne End, England (London, Midland & Scottish)

43 killed, 124 injured

The overnight Perth–Euston sleeping-car express was derailed on a fine sunny morning when it failed to slow for the 20mph restriction over a turnout from the fast to the slow line. Although it could probably have managed to negotiate it safely at a speed of 40mph, the train was doing over 50mph when it took the points. The 'Royal Scot' locomotive finished up at the foot of a 9-feet high embankment, and the leading seven coaches piled up on top of it.

Only the last three of the 15 vehicles in the train remained on the track. The diversion was required because of Sunday engineering work on the up fast line, and reference had been made to this in the railway's 'Fortnightly Notice' issued to the operating staff.

The LMS had been replacing semaphore distant signals with colour lights for some time, and the one protecting this turn-out showed a double-yellow aspect when a train was being diverted on to the slow line. It provided the driver with more than 2,600 yards' warning. A similar accident, fortunately with many fewer casualties, had occurred at Leighton Buzzard in 1931, but that train had run past signals at danger. There was to be another at Goswick in Northumberland two years later (see entry for 26 October 1947), and one at Milton on the Western Region in 1955. While there were other significant factors in these later accidents, the failure of experienced and conscientious drivers to slow for the diversions was to some degree unexplained.

In his report on the Bourne End accident, Lt Col. A. H. L. Mount, the Inspecting Officer, considered that there could be confusion with this particular use of the double-yellow aspect with the one used in full colour-light areas, where it provided an *additional* warning ahead of a single yellow. For this reason he recommended that the use of double-yellow aspects should be confined to colour-light areas, and this has since become standard practice.

Hamilton, *p92/93*, 126. Rolt, p286.

15 November 1945

Fuensanta, Almeira Province, Spain

20 killed

A mail train collided with one conveying fruit.

1 January 1946

Lichfield, England
(London, Midland & Scottish)

20 killed, 22 injured

This accident occurred in the low-level Lichfield (Trent Valley) station on the main West Coast Route. It was freezing hard when a four-coach local evening train from Stafford to Nuneaton was diverted into the platform loop to make its stop. Here it was due to be overtaken by a fish train from Fleetwood to Broad Street in London, these services customarily being given priority over even local passenger trains. When the signalman tried to reverse the points at the north end of the loop to enable the fish train to use the up fast line, some frozen ballast prevented the facing points lock from being fully withdrawn. The lever working the points was then put back to normal, and, as they were still locked, they could not move. Instead, the 10ft long down-rod in the signal box bowed, and the signalman thought he had changed the points, particularly as he was then able to move the facing-point locking lever to 'relock' them. With both these levers fully over in the frame, both distant signals and the starter could then be cleared for the fish train to pass.

A point-detector prevented the home signal for the fast line being pulled off, but the driver of the fish train, seeing all the others set for him, missed the red light from this one. (A number of independent witnesses, as well as the driver, claimed they had seen that signal at clear, but the satisfactory working condition of the detector convinced the inspecting officer that they had been mistaken.) As a result, the fish train was diverted into the platform loop, colliding at 35mph with the rear of the local train, which was pushed forward for about 100 yards. All its coaches were wrecked, but the vehicles in the fish train continued to London later that night.

Hamilton, p92/93, 133. Vaughan, p89, *inc.p.*

4 March 1946

Bhagauli, India

60 killed, 84 injured

A head-on collision took place between the 'Dehra Dun' express and a goods train 48 miles from Lucknow. Both drivers were among those killed. Two upper-class coaches were badly damaged, but most of the casualties occurred in a third-class one which was completely smashed.

RG **84** 377 (1946).

20 March 1946

Near Aracaju, Brazil

185 killed

The press reported the 'wreck' of a train, presumably the result of a derailment.

25 April 1946

Naperville, Illinois, United States of America
(Burlington)

45 killed, 36 injured

In the early afternoon the conductor of the westbound 'Advance Flyer' saw an object flung out from under his train, and signalled to the driver, who stopped at Naperville, the next station. Although they were on a stretch of line with automatic colour-light signalling, the fireman went back to protect its rear. He had gone less than 300 yards when he saw the following train, the 'Exposition Flyer' approaching at speed. Although it slowed from an estimated 80mph, it was still doing 45mph when it hit the rear of the train in front. The leading diesel locomotive forced itself three-quarters of the way through the last coach, but the one ahead of it was not badly damaged. In front of that, however, was a lightweight dining car, the body of which was crumpled into a

U-shape. The signalling was in order, and tests subsequently showed the overtaking train could have been stopped safely had the 68-year-old driver braked in time, there being no evidence on the locomotive of any emergency application having been made. The 'approach' indication was shown by Signal 227.1, which was visible from no less than 5,000 feet away, and this was followed by a 'stop-then-proceed' indication at Signal 228.1. The driver was subsequently charged with manslaughter, but the county grand jury refused to indite him, because of 'insufficient evidence'.

Shaw, p250. RG **84** 630 (1946), **85** 320 (1946).

28 July 1946

Bhatni Junction, India (Oudh Tirhut State)

223 killed

An Allahabad train ran into the rear of one for Katihar. The guard's van and two coaches were destroyed.

RG **85** 320 (1946).

23 September 1946

Between Dighwara and Barra Gopal, India (Oudh Tirhut State)

27 killed, 70 injured

The 'Lucknow Express' was derailed some 185 miles from Gorakhpur. The driver escaped.

RG **85** 689 (1946).

4 October 1946

Ongole, India (M&SM)

36 killed, 81 injured

The Madras to Calcutta mail train collided with a goods train at Ongole, 76 miles from Bezwada. A former premier of the state of Orissa escaped unhurt.

RG **85** 689 (1946).

12 November 1946

Revigny, France (SNCF)

31 killed

In thick fog a goods train over-ran two colour-light signals and collided at 30–40mph with a local train standing in the station at Revigny, near Bar-le-Duc. The rear three coaches were telescoped. All the victims were local people, some of whom were waiting on the platform. About half of the casualties were school-children. The locomotive of the goods train was of North American origin, and had passed two signals at danger.

RG **85** 595 (1946).

12 December 1946

Savigny-sur-Orge, France (SNCF)

31 killed, 50 injured

A collision occurred.

18 February 1947

Gallitzin, Pennsylvania, United States of America (Pennsylvania)

24 killed

The two of the company's famous Pacific locomotives on the 'Red Arrow' express left the track on a sharp curve, dragging seven of the train's 14 coaches down a 90ft embankment into Gumtree Hollow. The driver of the leading locomotive, who was the only member of the two footplate crews to survive, claimed that, although they were running an hour late, they were not exceeding the 30mph restriction. He claimed that the regulator became unlatched while he was looking out of the cab window, and moved to the half-open position. It would be surprising if he had not realised this immediately from the changed exhaust note, and it would, in any case, take quite a while to accelerate to a dangerous speed. Neither locomotive was equipped with a speedometer, but investigations by the Interstate Commerce Commission showed that the overturning speed of the locomotives on that curve was 65mph. There were also 'compression burns' on the outside rails. Because of their concern about the sharpness of the curve, the railway had installed a speed recorder on it, triggered by a pair of sensors, but on this occasion the train never reached the second one. As with the similar installation in this country at Durham, while it would pinpoint any *minor* infringement, this type of instrument would not provide information if the speed was so great that the train was derailed.

Shaw, p301. RG **86** 301, 673 (1947).

25 February 1947
Japan (Japanese National)
184 killed, 800 injured

Another of Japan's post-World War II railway disasters resulted when a passenger train was derailed about 40 miles west of Tokyo, and fell down a low embankment.

RG **86** 226 (1947).

17 May 1947
Between Kamalasagar and Nayanpur, India (Bengal Assam)
36 killed, 58 injured

The locomotive and nine bogies of the Surma express on the metre-gauge

Laksham–Comilla–Akhura section of the railway were derailed, and rolled down an embankment.

RG **86** 612 (1947), **90** 400 (1949).

15 June 1947
La Cruz, Corrientes Province, Argentina (Argentine North Eastern)
20 killed

An international train on this British-owned railway was en route from Buenos Aires to Ascunsion in Paraguay when it hit a cow, derailed and overturned. It was one of the few railway accidents to counter George Stephenson's famous statement in Parliamentary committee, that such a collision would be 'so much the worse for the coo'. In July 1984 a similar accident at Polmont in Scotland also caused a bad derailment, 13 being killed on that occasion.

23 July 1947
China
27 killed, twelve seriously injured

A passenger train from Shanghai to Tientsen struck a mine planted by Communist guerillas, 67 miles east of its destination.

23 August 1947
Velten, Berlin, Germany
24 killed, 35 injured

Petrol leaking from a can on the luggage rack was ignited by a passenger's cigarette, and the flames then spread to a package containing films, probably nitrate-based. A ticket collector stopped the train, but the passengers panicked and rushed to the only exit, which was at one end of the coach. A returning prisoner-of-war fell, which caused the other passengers to stumble over him, blocking the only escape route.

1 September 1947

Dugald, Manitoba, Canada (Canadian National)

31 killed, 85 injured

A westbound extra train (No. 6001) had its orders changed, so its booked crossing point with one in the opposite direction (No. 4) was moved 16 miles onwards from Dugald to Vivian. Under the complexities of the train-order system, No. 4 was the 'superior' train, for two reasons: it was an eastbound one, and had been mentioned first in the train order. The westbound train should therefore have taken the 'siding' at Dugald, which involved the crew getting out and resetting the points. Instead of doing this it continued along the main line and collided, at a speed of 30mph, with the other train standing in the station. Even as late as 1947, the Canadian National was still operating some wooden coaches, and a third of its passenger stock was gas-lit. Nine of the vehicles in Train No. 6001 suffered from both these disadvantages, and fires started along its length after the collision.

Shaw, p139. RG **87** 581 (1947).

24 October 1947

South Croydon, England (Southern)

32 killed, 183 injured or shocked

In dense fog, two electric multiple-units collided during the morning rush-hour near South Croydon Junction, on the 'Brighton Line'. A train from Tattenham Corner to London Bridge was incorrectly given a clear road, and collided at 40–45mph with the rear of one from Haywards Heath, which had reached about 15–20mph after a signal check.

Although there had been plans to provide colour-light signalling on this busy route in 1940, the work had been held up because of the war, and the line was still worked with semaphore signals and Sykes' Lock-and-Block. This involved the use of plungers, which interlocked the block instruments with the signal levers. The starting signal in one box was only freed when the signalman in the one ahead had accepted a train by pressing his plunger. Having been pulled, this lever could not be replaced until the train had actuated a treadle on the track in advance of the signal. In this way a cyclic system was set up, physically linking the movements of the trains with the block instruments and the signal levers. With any such arrangement, means had to be provided to 'free' it if something unusual happened, or one of the components failed to work. With the Sykes' Lock-and-Block there was a release key in each signal box, but, as any irregular use could defeat the interlocks, very stringent rules were laid down for its operation.

On this occasion the signalman at Purley Oaks forgot the Haywards Heath train, which, because of the fog, he was unable to see while it was standing in the station for 6–7 minutes. When he got an inquiry from the signalman at the box in the rear about the delay, the Purley Oaks man assumed that his instruments had failed, and irregularly used the release key. He was then able to accept the train from Tattenham Corner under clear signals, and it collided with the train in front. Although 183 passengers suffered injury or complained of shock, only 58 were taken to hospital and, of these, 41 were detained. Thus under a quarter of them could be said to have suffered 'serious' injuries.

Hamilton, p92/93, 139. Nock, p160/161, 184. Rolt, p278. Schneider, p155.

A considerable number of less serious collisions has occurred as a result of the irregular use of such a release mechanism, examples being the one at Waterloo East in September 1913, and that between Cannon Street and London Bridge fourteen months later.

RG **19** 486 (1913), **22** 19 (1915).

means that the driver has to slow down sufficiently to be able to stop there should it not clear.

Hamilton, p145.

26 October 1947
Goswick, England
(London & North Eastern)

28 killed, 94 injured

Early on a Sunday afternoon the 11.15am express from Edinburgh to King's Cross was derailed when it failed to slow sufficiently for the diversion from the Up Main to the Up Independent line at Goswick, in Northumberland, just south of the Berwick. In many ways this was a repeat of the Bourne End accident just over two years before. Although the diversion was not included in the 'Fortnightly Notices', details were posted at the signing-on points, but none of the train-crew had seen them. The driver, who had an unauthorised passenger on the footplate, failed to observe the distant signal for Goswick, which was properly held at caution. At this time the Pacific No. 66 *Merry Hampton* still had right-hand drive, and, having missed the signal, the driver failed to cross to the other side, or ask the fireman about it. The home signal was probably 'off' when he saw it, although the signalman threw it back in his face when he realised the train was not slowing down for the turn-out. The Up Main starter had been held at danger by a collar on the lever all the time the track ahead was occupied by engineeering work, and this locked the distant at caution.

The MoT report recommended that, for all unbooked diversions of trains over low-speed junctions, the stop signal protecting it should be kept at danger until the signalman was sure the train was under control. In today's colour-light era, nearly all low-speed diversions are protected with what is known as 'Approach Control'. Track circuits ensure that the stop signal for the junction will not clear until the train is comparatively close to it, which

3 December 1947
Near Arras, France
(SNCF)

21 killed

After earlier widespread industrial action, a general railway strike was declared in France on 25 November. There were several incidents of sabotage, which culminated in the unbolting of 30 metres of rail on the main line between Paris and Lille, derailing the night mail from Paris to Turcoing. The saboteurs ensured that the track-circuits had not been affected, so the signals remained clear, giving the driver no warning. A number of other incidents were reported on the same day, at Étampes, Epônes, Le Mans, Livren, Melun and Sorgues, but none had such serious consequences.

22 December 1947
Near Neuweid, Germany
(French Zone)

42 killed, 116 injured

A collision occurred between trains from Munich and Freiburg to Dortmund.

Ritznau p250.

17 February 1948
Thumeries, France

22 killed, 30 injured

A goods train collided head-on with a local passenger train as it was leaving the small station on an independent local railway between Douai and Lille.

In the press report next day it was mentioned that several of the injured were in a critical condition, so the death toll may have increased.

RG **88** 262, 298 (1948).

22 February 1948

Wädenswil, Switzerland (Schweizerische Südostbahn)

21 killed

The main line of this private railway, from Rapperswil to Arth-Goldau, is very steeply inclined, with gradients as steep as one in 20. On a Sunday evening a through train, hauled by a Ce6/8 'Crocodile', was returning from Sattel to Zürich with skiers, and ran away down the bank approaching Samstagern. At Burghalden it ran past signals, where the driver indicated that the staff should send a warning to Wädenswil, and this was done. Unfortunately both tracks there were occupied, so the runaway was diverted into a dead-end siding, which finished against some offices that were extensively damaged in the result-ant crash. The accident was caused by the driver not moving his controller to the resistance braking position, so that his movement of the handle applied power rather than slowing the train down.

Schneider, *p182*.

21 March 1948

Spoleto, Italy

4 killed, 60 injured

Two coaches of a passenger train ascending a steep incline on a line north-east of Rome were telescoped after a passenger had pulled the communica-tion cord. The report stated that the accident ocurred because the banking locomotive failed to stop, but this is another of the popular falacious causes of accidents. The rear-ends of coaching stock must be strong enough to take the thrusts of a banker that is properly buffered-up, and there is no way the coaches would be crushed if the train-engine stopped. What almost certainly happened in this instance was that the banker was not coupled to the train, and had become separated from it at the time the brakes were suddenly applied, perhaps because it had lost adhesion. The crew of the assisting locomotive might then have been unable to stop in time, or may not have been keeping a proper lookout. Because such a sudden impact could cause a serious accident, the bankers used between Glasgow Queen Street and Cowlairs, for ex-ample, were provided with 'Slip Coup-lings' which kept them attached to the coaches as far as the summit of the bank, where they could release themselves without the train having to stop.

RG **88** 418 (1948).

17 April 1948

Winsford, England (British Railways, London Midland Region)

24 killed, 18 seriously injured

An evening express from Glasgow to Euston was stopped north of Winsford station by a soldier going on leave pulling the communication cord in one of the toilets. This was to enable him to get home much quicker than continuing to Crewe and catching a train back. The signalman at Winsford station box thought he had seen the train pass, and irregularly cleared his block instru-ments. He was then able to accept the following Pacific-hauled postal train from Glasgow, which collided with the rear of the passenger train after it had been standing for about 17 minutes. The passenger guard was slow in protecting the rear of this train, and had only gone about 400 yards when he saw the postal one approaching. His red hand-lamp warning enabled the driver to reduce speed slightly, but the rear coach of the passenger train was destroyed, plus half of the one in front of it.

As was the case immediately after the accident, some people still consider that the cause of this particular accident was the soldier's irresponsible action in pulling the communication cord. In his report, the inspecting officer, Lt Col. G. R. S. Wilson, put the position quite clearly:

> The chain of events which lead to this collision was initiated by the stoppage of the passenger train in mid-section: such an unexpected stoppage may be brought about in a number of ways and on this occasion it was due to the irresponsible action of a passenger who pulled the communication chain without good cause. The standing train, however, should have been protected by the Block, and the irregular admission of the postal train to the occupied section arose from a grave breach of Regulations by Signalman [X], who gave 'Train Out of Section' to Winsford Junction for the passenger train, although it had not passed his box. Responsibility for the collision therefore rests with him.

When assessing responsibility in any such case, it is vital to consider who it was who failed to carry out the particular rule which *directly* caused the accident. In this instance it was not the guard who was slow going back to protect the rear of his stopped train, although he might have *prevented* it occurring had he been quicker.

In this country these rules for protecting the rear of a train were of the 'belt & braces' sort, but conditions have been very different in other parts of the world, particularly North America. There it is still often the case that rear-end protection, with detonators or fusees, is the only way that a following train can be stopped from colliding with one that has stopped or is running slowly for any reason.

Hamilton, p92/93, 150. Schneider, p202.

15 May 1948

Dhanbad, India (East India)

31 killed, 101 injured, 19 seriously

The 'Dehra Dun Express' from Howra was derailed on a 40ft high embankment near Dhanbad, 160 miles from Calcutta, on the Grand Chord line of the East India Railway. Sabotage was suspected.

RG **88** 681 (1948).

14 September 1948

Near Taejon, South Korea

40 killed, nearly 60 injured

A passenger train collided with the rear of another about 15 miles north of Taejon. Most of the casualties were members of the United States forces serving with the United Nations in the country.

28 October 1948

Near Ankara, Turkey

100 killed, 150 injured

A special train heading for the capital was derailed near the end of its journey. It was carrying members of the Peoples' Party on their way to attend the twentieth anniversary celebrations of the formation of the Turkish Republic by Kemal Ataturk.

RG **89** 534 (1948).

23 November 1948

Jullundur Cantonment, India (Eastern Punjab)

21 killed, 106 injured

As a refugee special was being backed into the station, a trunk and the bedding of one of those riding on the roof of the sixth coach fell onto the track. The coach became derailed and damage was also caused to the next one.

RG **90** 400 (1949).

The railways in the sub-continent were used extensively to transfer refugees in both directions between India and Pakistan after partition. Although there were accidents like this one and that on 17 May 1948, the operations were, in the main, carried out peacefully. On 12 January 1948, however, there had been a serious clash at Gujerat, where Indian military personnel were escorting non-Moslem refugees from Mari Indus in Pakistan to Karnal in India. When the train arrived in the station, a crowd of Moslem refugees, who had been living on the platform for several days, tried to force their way on to it. Finding themselves outnumbered, one of the Indian military escorts threw a hand-grenade, which caused several casualties. The explosion attracted a number of tribesmen on their way to Jammu, who then joined in the attack. When order was finally restored by Pakistan troops, it was estimated that the non-Muslim refugees and their escorts had suffered 1,000 casualties.

RG **88** 186 (1948).

24 November 1948

Sambhu, India (Eastern Punjab)

171 killed, 300 injured

A train from Ambala Cantonment, with Moslem refugees for Pakistan, crashed into the dead-end at Sambhu station, eleven miles after starting its journey.

RG **88** 262 (1948), **90** 400 (1949).

13 February 1949

Near Mons La Nueva, Catalonia, Spain (RENFE)

28 killed, 24 injured

A Barcelona–Madrid express was derailed, and three of its coaches rolled down a 130ft embankment into a dry river bed.

18 February 1949

Pont d'Atelier, Haute-Saône, France

43 killed

A Nancy–Dijon express collided with a light engine. The first two wooden coaches were crushed between the luggage van and the following postal van, both of which were of steel construction. The driver of the express, although suffering from a head injury and half-blinded by steam, made his way along the line, to lay detonators and warn the crossing-keeper. He then collapsed, and died shortly afterwards.

28 April 1949

Near Johannesburg, South Africa (SAR)

70 killed, 166 injured

Three electric trains were in collision on the Midway–Langlaate line, near Johannesburg. The first had been halted by signals, and the second stopped behind it. A third train then collided with the second, forcing it into the leading one.

RG **90** 605 (1949).

22 October 1949

Nowy Dwor, Poland

Over 200 killed

A Danzig–Warsaw express was derailed on a curve, the locomotive and several coaches overturning. Although there was an official statement about the numbers killed, following typical communist practice, no other details were given.

15 November 1949

Near Waterval Boven, Transvaal, South Africa (SAR)

55 killed, 100 + injured

A double-headed train was derailed, and seven of its coaches plunged 70 feet from a bridge into the Elands River. Six other coaches overturned. The train was taking some 500 Africans to Portuguese East Africa, many of them at the end of their service contracts with Witwatersrand mines. Some passengers were trapped under water and drowned, while others fell to their deaths from one coach which finished up hanging from the bridge. Three Dakotas from the South African Air Force operated an ambulance shuttle from the site to hospitals in Pretoria. As in the accident on 28 April, the train crew members who were killed were all Europeans.

RG **91** 613 (1949).

1950–1954

29 January 1950
Sirhind, Punjab, India
63 killed

There was a collision between a mail train and a goods train, the press reports stating that approximately half the fatalities were Indian soldiers.

RG **92** 165 (1950).

17 February 1950
Rockville Center, Long Island, New York State, United States of America (Long Island)
31 killed

Major engineeering work was being carried out at Rockville Center to separate the levels of the up and down tracks, and the only way to accommodate the existing ones in the meanwhile was to gauntlet them for two miles. The installation was protected by automatic signals at both ends, the operator at Rockville Center allocating priority to opposing trains. Late in the evening the 10.31pm from Babylon to New York was given the road, but, just as it was leaving the gauntletted section, it collided with a down train. This was heavily loaded with returning theatregoers, and had run past the protecting signals at the other end of the section. The two trains met at an angle with a closing speed of about 50mph, and the left-hand sides of each were badly damaged. In their right-hand corner cabs of the multiple-unit commuter stock both drivers survived. At his trial the driver who ran past the signals admitted seeing them and hearing the cab signalling buzzer, but said he had suffered a momentary blackout because of his high blood-pressure. The jury accepted this statement and he was acquitted.

Shaw, p355.

6 April 1950
Brazil (Leopoldina)
110 killed, over 300 injured

After three days of heavy rain, a bridge across the Tangua River, 50 miles north of Rio de Janeiro, collapsed as an excursion train to Victoria was crossing it at night. The locomotive, a baggage car and five passenger coaches fell into the water. One of the coaches was carried into mid-stream by the current, but the others remained near the bank. Rescue efforts were hampered by the torrential rain, and the collapse of one of the main road bridges because of flooding delayed the arrival of medical assistance. The state government decreed three days of official mourning.

RG **92** 435 (1950).

12 April 1950

Near Bitroi, India (Oudh Tirhut)

36 killed, 101 injured

The down 'Kumaon Express' was derailed just before Tarara Bridge. The locomotive and first coach got across, but the rest of the train fell into the river. The cost of the accident was stated to have been nearly £33,000, and it was caused by someone tampering with the track.

RG **96** 60 (1952).

7 May 1950

Jasidih, Bihar, India (East India)

92 killed, 67 seriously injured

The Calcutta–Delhi 'Punjab Mail' was derailed just before reaching the abutment of the Tamakhan bridge, and the locomotive and three of the six coaches which came off the track fell down the embankment. One rail had been removed from the track, and 15 people were committed to the sessions court for alleged complicity in the act of sabotage. A week before the accident, the Minister of State for the Railways had said there were 91 cases of attempted sabotage on the Indian Railways during the previous six months. Leaflets issued by one of the political parties – by inference the Communist Party – had been calling for acts of this sort to create chaos in the country.

RG **92** 494 (1950), **96** 60 (1952).

12 July 1950

Between Zwickau and Aue, Saxony, East Germany

20 killed, 50+ injured

A collision occurred between a workers' train and a stationary goods train.

13 August 1950

Banares, India (East India)

29 killed, 113 injured

A goods train was derailed on a bridge near Benares, and was then hit by the Delhi–Calcutta 'Toofan Express.' The express locomotive and three coaches of its train fell down the embankment into four feet of flood-water. The initial derailment occurred because the track had been sabotaged, a joint being opened and the rail slewed out of line. This had occurred in spite of the State Police patrols along this stretch of line. Three of the five most serious accidents which occurred on the Indian railways during the year 1950/51 had thus been caused by sabotage.

RG **93** 190 (1950), **92** 60 (1952).

3 September 1950

Gurdaspur, India (East Punjab)

20 killed

The Delhi-bound 'Kashmir Mail' was derailed near Gurdaspur, on the Amritsar–Pathankot line. The locomotive and three coaches plunged down an embankment after the train had been derailed on a bridge across a ravine.

RG **93** 316 (1950).

6 September 1950

Pantojo, Brazil

36 killed

A train was derailed and overturned on the Sorocabana line.

9 September 1950

Bhairabazar, Pakistan

(50) killed

The locomotive and the leading three coaches of the Dacca–Chittagon express were derailed near Bhairabazar in East Bengal. The train was approaching a river bridge, and the derailed vehicles finished up in ten feet of water. The police announced that they had recovered some fishplates and bolts which had been removed about 40 feet before the bridge by saboteurs.

11 September 1950

Coshocton, Ohio, United States of America
(Pennsylvania)

33 killed

A 20-car troop train, taking members of the National Guard to training camp, was hit by the following express, 'The Spirit of St Louis.' The special was having trouble with its brakes and had previously delayed the express behind it. Near Coshocton it had to stop, and the flagman went back to protect the rear, after throwing off a lighted fusee before they came to a stand. The line was automaticaly signalled, but the express checked for the warning and then increased speed again, running past the flagman. The 56-year-old driver and his fireman were unable to give any reason for failing to stop, other than the slight fog.

Shaw, p251. RG **93** 375 (1950).

21 November 1950

Between Canoe River and Cedarside, Canada
(Canadian National)

21 killed

A head-on collision took place between a westbound troop train (Extra No. 3538 West) and a passenger train (No. 2), because of an error by the operator at Red Pass, wrongly identifying the point where the trains should cross. It is worth going into this in some detail, as it gives an insight into the North American train-order system. The telephoned instructions from the dispatcher at Kamloops were 'Passenger Extra 3538 West to meet No. 2 Engine 6004 at Cedarside and No. 4 Engine 6057 Gosnell'. The operator at Red Pass repeated the message back correctly, but when he issued it to the conductor of the troop train its wording was significantly different. It read 'Passenger Extra West 3538 meet No. 2 Engine 6004 and No. 4 Engine 6057 Gosnell'. As a result of the vital omission it had become what was known as a 'Lap' order, and thus potentially fatal.

From Red Pass it is 35 miles to Cedarside and a further 25 on to Gosnell. The dispatcher had intended the troop train to wait at Cedarside for the first section of the westbound express to turn up. The crews were to identify each other's trains by the numbers of the locomotives, in case there were any other rakes of stock or locomotives about. As a result of the faulty order, the troop train's crew were not expecting to make the meet until Gosnell, and went straight through Cedarside. On a sharp curve in the mountainous section between these two points, the trains collided head-on, both locomotive crews being killed, in addition to 17 soldiers in the sleeping cars of the troop train.

Shaw, p149.

22 November 1950

Richmond Hill, Long Island, New York State, United States of America (Long Island)

79 killed, 352 injured

In the dark, a 12-car electric multiple-unit from Penn Station for Hampstead reduced speed for an adverse signal near Jamaica, but, when it cleared, the motorman was unable to release the brake. They ground to a stop, and the conductor got out to protect the rear of the train. They were in a colour-light area, but the most restrictive signal on open track was 'Stop & Proceed', which meant the motorman, after halting, had not to exceed 15mph until he saw the next clear signal. It was not therefore necessary for the rear brakesman of the train in front to go back very far. Shortly after leaving the train he heard the driver get ready to move off, so got back into it. However, the train failed to move, and he suddenly saw a train approaching from behind at high speed. He could do nothing more than wave his red lantern at it before it ploughed into the rear of the standing train, pushing it forward 75 feet.

The colliding train was a similar twelve-coach set, and had duly received a 'Stop & Proceed' aspect, which the motorman had obeyed. For reasons never positively determined, after some distance the speed had picked up to 35mph, which was held until emergency braking was applied just before the crash. The driver was one of the fatalities, and it was assumed that he might have seen the signal clear for the stopped train, and had thought it applied to him, rather than the train in front. The 'Stop & Proceed' rule has been used in this country, particularly on the London Underground, where, however, it is reinforced by a train-stop. This automatically applies the brake, which the driver has to reset, but, even so there have been several cases in recent years where the train has subsequently gone too fast and collided with a stationary one in front. While the Railway Inspectorate would like to stop the procedure, London Underground's view is that, with adequate training of drivers, it is safe, and its use is necessary to keep trains moving on their heavily used lines.

Shaw, p357. RG **93** 485 (1950).

6 February 1951

Woodbridge, New Jersey, United States of America (Pennsylvania)

84 killed

In the early afternoon a 25mph restriction came into force on a stretch of line west of Woodbridge station, where the track had been slewed to permit work to take place on the New Jersey Turnpike. A steam-hauled commuter train, 'The Broker' approached the restriction too fast. Although the locomotive took the first half of the reverse-curve without coming off the track, as at Goswick and Bourne End its weight was thrown onto the wrong rail for the rest of the curve, and it toppled over on to its right-hand side. It remained on top of the embankment, but the first seven all-steel coaches behind it were also derailed. Four were spread-eagled across the tracks, the last of them being torn open on one side for its full length. The sixth finished up spanning the gap between the abutments of an underbridge, the girders of which had collapsed. Because of a strike on the Jersey Central the train was carrying more passengers than usual, which added to the death toll.

Although the driver had seen the notice posted in the bulletin board at his Jersey City depot, he failed to slow down from about 50mph, although he claimed to have obeyed the 25mph restriction. Evidence at the inquiry, however, indicated that he might not have realised exactly where the restriction was. The route between Jersey City and Bay Head used two different railways. As far as Perth Amboy, the journey was on Pennsylvania tracks, where   temporary   speed-restriction signs were not marked, whereas on the longer stretch over the New York & Long Branch they were. The driver talked about 'looking ahead for the warning signals', and, as it was his first journey since the restriction had been imposed, he may have been lulled into a false security. The lack of consistency with any rules that have to be obeyed by a particular individual is always a potential danger, especially when they concern the vital question of speed limits. The official inquiry by the New Jersey Board of Public Utility Commissioners put the full blame on the driver, who was doing 60–65mph instead of the 25 permitted.

Reed, *p52*. Shaw, p359. RG **95** 28 (1951).

24 April 1951
Yokohama, Japan (JNR)
106 killed

During some repairs to the overhead electric wires, the pantograph of an electric multiple-unit became entangled in a length of dangling wire as it entered the Sakuragicho terminus at Yokohama. An attempt to free it was made by lowering and raising the pantograph several times, but this caused an arc between the wire and the power-car, which continued long enough to set fire to the first two coaches. Nearly everyone in these two vehicles was burnt to death, three United States' servicemen being among the fatalities. The roofs of the coaches consisted of canvas-covered wooden planking, which had been tarred and then sanded. With an all-metal vehicle any contact with the overhead wires shorts them to earth, immediately causing the circuit-breakers to trip at the sub-station. This discharges the voltage, and any temporary arc is extinguished.

After the fire had started, it was not possible to open the doors of the coaches involved, because they were operated electrically, and the power had been switched off. There were some safety releases, but the method of operating them was not displayed to the public, in case they were misused. After this accident they were clearly marked, but, as described later, some passengers who had left a derailed train in May 1962 were killed when a second collision caused the coaches to tip over on top of them.

Shaw, p412. RG **94** 514 (1951).

7 June 1951
Novaiguassu, Brazil (Estrada de Ferro Central do Brasil)
51 killed, 100+ injured

An electric suburban train collided with a petrol tanker on a level-crossing in Rio de Janeiro, and the whole of the six-coach train caught fire. Everyone in the leading coach died, either from the collision or the fire.

RG **94** 683 (1951).

18 August 1951
Szekesfehervar, Hungary (MÁV)
150+ killed

A signalwoman who had just completed her training allowed an express to leave the station too early, and it collided with another passenger train. The news of the accident was included in a subsequent article in *The Times* referring to the current problems on the railways of Hungary caused by the heavy traffic and lack of resources.

24 August 1951
Sary-sur-Sud, France (SNCF)
21 killed, (35) injured

A signalman's mistake resulted in a Frankfurt–Paris express being stopped in Sary-sur-Neid station, near Metz, where it was hit from the rear by a

Basle–Calais express. The luggage van at the rear of the Paris train virtually disintegrated, and the next two vehicles finished up on top of each other. Several United States' servicemen were among those killed or injured, and some French troops were also injured. Teams of French and US forces assisted the Metz fire brigade in the rescue work. The American army authorities at Fontainbleu sent some military police to the scene to check on the casualties, and rescue the supplies for units in the region which were aboard the trains.

RG **95** 250 (1951).

25 September 1951
Langenwang, Austria (ÖBB)

22 killed, 40+ injured

Shortly after midnight the Vienna–Rome express collided with a goods train in Langenwang station on the Vienna–Semmering–Klagenfurt line in Styria. At the time it was approaching Murzzuschlag, a Vienna–Graz goods train was being shunted out of its way at the far end of the station. Instead of keeping all the signals at danger, the station supervisor cleared those at the entry to the station, thereby reducing the safety overlap. The driver of the express failed to stop, only making an emergency brake application when he saw the supervisor's frantic hand signals. All the fatalities were among a party of Italian railwaymen who had been the guests of their Austrian colleagues.

Schneider, p91. RG **95** 380, 535 (1951).

5 October 1951
Montenegro, Caldas Province, Colombia

26 killed

A landslide hit a passenger train between Armenia and Pereia. It was believed that the vibration of the train was sufficient to loosen part of the mountainside which had been weakened by heavy rain.

RG **95** 419 (1951).

12 November 1951
Evanston, Wyoming, United States of America (Union Pacific)

26 killed, 200 injured

Two of the Union Pacific's streamliners – the 'City of Los Angeles' and the 'City of San Francisco', both bound for Chicago, collided in a blizzard.

RG **95** 559 (1951).

17 December 1951
Fortale, Brazil

40 killed

Four coaches of a passenger train overturned after a derailment.

RG **95** 696 (1951).

4 March 1952
Anchieta, Brazil (Estrada de Ferro Central do Brasil)

119 killed, (200) injured

A train from Belo Horizonte to Minas Geraes was derailed in the suburbs of Rio de Janeiro on a bridge across the Pavuna River, and overturned. It was then hit by an electric suburban train from Nova Iguaço to Rio de Janeiro on the other track. Nearly all the coaches of both trains were wrecked. This nationalised railway was frequently criticised for negligence because of its poor safety record. The preliminary investigation indicated that the derailment resulted from a broken rail on the bridge, where another train had been derailed a few days earlier. Even though the former accident did not have any serious consequences, the failure to check the track thoroughly hardly inspired confidence in the administration. After the subsequent inquiry, the President approved a five-year project to up-grade the country's railways. Heavier-section rail was to be installed, with more sleepers, and authority was given for tenders to be sought for up to 200 new electric multiple-unit cars.

In 1952 100 people were killed on the railway, and 429 injured, but in the first six months of the following year, the figures were down to 18 and 120 respectively, so the changes seem to have had their effect on the safety record.

RG **96** 277, 345 (1952), **99** 541 (1953).

18 May 1952

Turkey

26 killed

Details are somewhat scanty about this accident, which occurred when a mixed train was derailed on or about this date between Ulukiska and Adana.

18 May 1952

Bikaner, India (Northern)

45 killed, 67 injured

A head-on collision took place between a passenger and a goods train seven miles on the Jodhupur side of Bikaner. Both trains had been allowed to enter the block section without permission being obtained.

RG **100** 542 (1954).

8 October 1952

Harrow & Wealdstone, England (British Railways, London Midland Region)

112 killed, 157 injured

During the morning rush-hour, an up outer-suburban train from Tring to Euston was struck violently in the rear by an overnight sleeping-car train from Perth, after it had been standing in the up fast platform at Harrow & Wealdstone for just over a minute. The wreckage was strewn across the down fast line, where, seconds later, it was hit by a double-headed Euston–Liverpool express, the locomotives of which mounted one of the platforms and finished foul of the up local electric line. Sixteen coaches were demolished or very badly damaged, thirteen of them being '. . . compressed into a compact heap of wreckage about 45 yards long, 18 yards wide, and 30 feet high, completely burying the engine of the Perth train . . .', to quote the inspecting officer's report.

In terms of fatalities, this was the second-worst accident to occur on the railways of the United Kingdom, the death roll only being exceeded by the double collision at Quintinshill in May 1915. However, while the Scottish one was caused by a number of irregularities which led to a signalman's error, the Harrow disaster was due to the failure of the Perth train's driver to obey the signal indications. The locomotive was one of the 'Princess Coronation' class 4-6-2s, No. 46242 *City of Glasgow*, and its eleven-coach train was running over half-an-hour late. The eight-coach commuter train from Tring was hauled by a 2-6-4 tank, and the signalman at Harrow had routed it into the fast-line platform from the up slow line just north of the station, as laid down in the working timetable. The cross-over behind it was still in the reversed position, which automatically locked the fast-line signals to danger or caution. It was easy to show too that there was insufficient time for him to have changed his mind about the order of the up trains, so the priority of trains could not have been changed after the express driver had seen the colour-light distant at clear. Once the first collision had happened, no one could have prevented the Liverpool train hitting the wreckage.

Some of the late running of the overnight expresses from Scotland was due to widespread fog, but visibility was not too bad in the Harrow area at the time of the collision, although the

Above *The aftermath of an accident which occurred near Campania, 27 miles north of Hobart, Tasmania on 29 February 1916. The Garratt on a passenger train left the track and rolled down the low embankment. Most of the damage occurred to the first three coaches of the train, resulting in seven fatalities. As was standard practice before the days of widespread use of road vehicles, rescue trains were sent to the scene of the accident from both directions.* (Author's Collection)

Below *The head on collision, between Moat Lane and Abermule on 26 January 1921, resulted from the combined carelessness of the station staff and the driver of the train which set off with the wrong tablet for the single-line section ahead. The two enginemen on the locomotive coming the other way were killed, together with 15 passengers, one of whom was a director of the Cambrian Railways. It used to be said that all the railwaymen in Wales could always recall where they were when the news of the disaster reached them.* (National Railway Museum)

Above 'La charcutière ' *(the butcheress). The front of the Est 'Mountain' 4-8-2 after it had ploughed its way through the wooden coaches of the local train at Lagny-Pomponne, France on 23 December 1933, killing 230 passengers.* (Author's Collection)

Below *A typical washout caused by monsoon floods on the East India Railway in 1934. As often occurred, the rails were left suspended over the gap, and some of the more adventurous locals used them to cross the still swollen river. On this occasion traffic was stopped before any accident occurred, but the fact that the telegraph wires remained intact shows how easily a train could have approached the washout at night without anyone being aware of the danger.* (National Railway Museum, L. D. J. Turnbull Collection)

Two almost identical accidents occurred 14 years apart at Billingham, Teesside, when drivers of trains on the northbound slow line misread the signals. Thinking they were on the main line, they failed to stop, and hit the buffer-stops in the short bay behind the platform. In the 1953 incident, word got around the author's factory during the morning of 2 December, and he was alongside John Phillips when the photograph of the 'Austerity' was taken. When looking through photographs in the Library of the National Railway Museum, he was surprised to find the illustration of the other incident that occurred on 14 December 1939. This was in the early days of World War II, and the blackout may have disorientated the driver, but there was no similar excuse in 1953.

(*Above,* the late J. S Phillips, *below,* National Railway Museum)

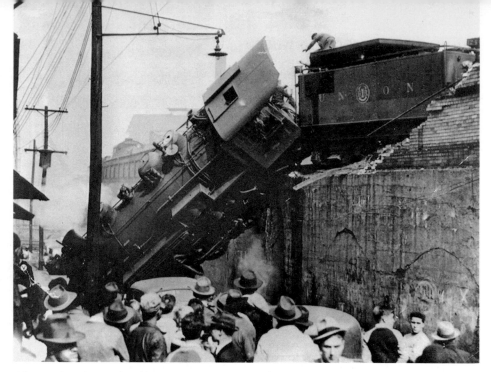

Above *A Union Railroad locomotive photographed only minutes after it had plunged off a bridge abutment in Homestead, Pennsylvania in October 1943. The fireman was the only casualty, being injured when he was thrown from the cab. The contemporary press caption referred to the fact that the street below was due to be thronged a few minutes later when war workers left a nearby plant, but one wonders about the dangers to the onlookers. With the inner-firebox likely to be uncovered because of the angle of the boiler, an explosion was a distinct possibility.*   (The Railway Magazine)

Below *The Naperville collision on the Burlington Railroad, which took place on 25 April 1946. The 'Exposition Flyer' failed to obey the signal indications, and hit the train ahead, which had stopped for an examination. A high proportion of the casualties occurred in the crumpled dining-car, bent into a U-shape ahead of the diesel locomotives.*   (Popperfoto)

Two views of the Goswick derailment in Northumberland, which occurred on Sunday 26 October 1947. The upper view, taken from the air, shows how straight the line is through the station, which misled the driver as he approached the booked change on to the slow line, after he had failed to note the diversion in the 'Tortnightly Notice'. It will be noted that the fourth of the overturned coaches slid for a considerable distance along the tracks, passing the locomotive, which was on its side in the gully. Aerial views can disguise the severity of the accident, and the lower illustration shows the extent of the destruction. The locomotive lies beyond the coach with the three windows still intact.
(Above, National Railway Museum, below, The Railway Magazine)

Above *An aerial view of the disaster at Woodbridge, New Jersey on 6 February 1951, when an evening commuter train failed to slow for some engineering work, and plunged off the track, travelling at over 60mph, instead of at the temporary maximum of 25 allowed.* (Popperfoto)

Above left *The aftermath of the collision between the Nancy–Dijon express and a light engine at Pont d'Atelier in France on 18 February 1949. The locomotive on its side is one of the Class 141R 2-8-2s manufactured in North America to make up for the wartime losses on the French railways.* (Popperfoto)

Left *Rescue work in progress at Rockville Center, Long Island, New York, on 17 February 1950, after the collision between two electric multiple-units on a temporarily-singled stretch of track. The telescoping that took place is very obvious.* (Popperfoto)

Overleaf *Looking down on Harrow & Wealdstone station after the double collision on 8 October 1952. The hole torn in the footbridge marks the point where* City of Glasgow *on the overnight sleeper, travelling from left to right, hit the rear coach of the stationary suburban train. This was also approximately where the double-headed express for Liverpool ran into the wreckage, and its locomotives were deflected to their left across the down fast platform. The pilot,* Windward Islands, *is scarcely recognisable behind the jib of the breakdown crane, but the newly rebuilt and named* Princess Anne *can be made out.* (The Railway Magazine)

Two of the wrecked locomotives after being recovered from the scene of the Harrow disaster. In spite of the extensive damage, 'Princess Coronation', No. 46242 City of Glasgow (above) was repaired and re-entered service, but the 'Jubilee', No. 45637 Windward Islands (below) was scrapped, as was No. 46202 Princess Anne. (*Both* National Railway Museum)

Above *The Pennsylvania Railroad Class GG1 electric locomotive after crashing through the buffer stops at Union Station in Washington on 15 January 1953. It can be seen how it and two of its coaches fell through the concourse, into the basement. The train could not stop in time because the cock on the brake pipe between the third and fourth coaches had been closed by coming into contact with the underframe.* (Popperfoto)

Below *Some of the wreckage after the double collision at Conneaut, Ohio, which took place on 27 March 1953. A badly-loaded pipe in a freight train became dislodged, and it then distorted the adjacent track. An overtaking passenger train was derailed and the wreckage was then hit by a third train travelling in the opposite direction.* (Popperfoto)

Above *A train wreck caused by a natural disaster. The locomotive and some of coaches which crashed into the river at Walouru in New Zealand, after the volcanic eruption caused a lahar to sweep down the valley on 24 December 1953. The locomotive has lost part of the rear driving wheel. One of the bridge spans lies next to the locomotive, but the rails are on the near side, showing how turbulent had been the flow of water.* (Popperfoto)

Below *Some of the wreckage of the express from the Algarve to Lisbon which was derailed on 13 September 1954, with the loss of 27 lives. The phototograph shows how some designs of stainless-steel coaches did not withstand impacts in an accident.* (Popperfoto)

Above *Two expresses collided head-on in a blizzard at Kuurila in Finland on 15 March 1957. This photograph shows the bleak conditions under which rescue work took place, some of the people in the picture being on skis.*   (Popperfoto)

Below *On 20 October 1957 a steam-hauled train in Turkey collided with a diesel railcar travelling in the opposite direction at Ispartakule. The extensive damage explains the high death-toll.*
                                      (Popperfoto)

Above *In France, like the accident in Turkey, there were many casualties when a collision took place between a steam train and a diesel railcar. This occurred at Chantonnay on 16 November 1957 and one side of the railcar has been peeled away from the underframe and roof by the force of the impact.* (Popperfoto)

Below *Rescue work in progress in Newark Bay, New Jersey, where a train had plunged off the lifting section after it had been opened for the passage of a ship. Two of the coaches and the locomotive are submerged, and the third coach, perilously suspended from the bridge abutment, later fell into the water. There were separate lifting spans for the two tracks, which was a fairly common North American feature.* (Popperfoto)

Above *The wreckage of a leave train for the British Forces in Germany which crashed at Woerden in the Netherlands on 21 November 1960. Resignalling work had involved a temporary diversion, and the driver failed to reduce his speed to the 40km/h (25mph) required. Two passengers were killed and ten injured. These trains, running to and from the Hook of Holland, operated for a long time after World War II, and old British coaches were used for many years until the Continental railways had recovered from their wartime devastation.* (Popperfoto)

Below *Some of the wrecked coaches after the derailment of a Strasbourg–Paris express at Vitry-le-François in France on 18 June 1961. Some of the locally-based United States Air Force personnel, who helped the rescue work, can be seen standing on the side of one of the overturned coaches.* (Popperfoto)

Above *The head-on collision on 8 January 1962 at Harmelen, just east of Woerden, caused the highest number of fatalities (93) of any railway accident in the Netherlands. The driver of a locomotive-hauled train missed the distant signal and could not stop before the junction, where an electric multiple-unit had been given the road.* (Popperfoto)

Below *In the early hours of 9 March 1962 a train from Lecce to Milan in Italy failed to slow over a section of track under repair at Castel Bolognese, and the resulting derailment caused 13 deaths, with over 100 passengers being injured.* (Popperfoto)

Above *After part of a Paris–Marseilles train had been derailed on a curve, the rear coach plunged off this lofty viaduct at Velars-sur-Ouche in France on 23 July 1962. Thirty-nine people were killed.*
(Popperfoto)

Below *Tidal waves from a freak storm on 23 December 1964 swept away a narrow-gauge train as it crossed from Raneswaran Island to Dhanashodi on the mainland of southern India. As will be seen the waves turned the train upside-down and destroyed the coach bodies. All the passengers and crew were drowned, but the 128 train fatalities only formed a small proportion of those killed by the storm in the area.*
(Popperfoto)

signalman there had adopted the fog working arrangements for a while earlier in his shift. However, he first spotted the Perth express as it was '. . . coming out of the mist and passing my Outer Home signal on the Up Fast'. That was nearly 600 yards from the signal box, and he had time to put down detonators ahead of it by pulling the lever in box. However thick the mist or fog might have been, the fact that the distant was a colour-light meant it was exempt from fog-signalling restrictions, as such installations are today. The brakes of the express were applied just before the collision, but that was far too late. As in many earlier accidents, the failure of the driver to see, or act upon, the warning and danger aspects was never satisfactorily explained. However, the Harrow & Wealdstone disaster did result in greater impetus being given to the introduction of the BR Automatic Warning System, with its siren sounding in the cab whenever the train approaches a signal at caution.

Although *City of Glasgow* was badly mangled in the crash, it was rebuilt, and remained in service until 1962. On the other hand, the two locomotives on the Liverpool train were both scrapped. They were the 'Jubilee' 4-6-0 No. 45637 *Windward Islands*, and the unique 4-6-2 No. 46202 *Princess Anne*, which had only recently been converted from its 'Turbomotive' form to an ordinary reciprocating design.

Hamilton, p92/93, 156. Nock, p160/161, 199. Rolt, p132/133, 287.

15 October 1952
21 miles south of Ibadan, Nigeria (NRC)

34+ killed

A goods train had been derailed, and the breakdown crane had been sent for to carry out the rerailing. On its way to the scene of the accident it broke free from the locomotive hauling it, and ran back three miles down a falling gradient before hitting the following passenger train. In the collision the first coach of

the latter was wrecked and the next two telescoped. After a young Nigerian had run three miles to the nearest road to report the accident, the first two cars he stopped happened to have the district officer and his senior medical officer in them. The rescue work was hampered, however, by the fact that the nearest *usable* breakdown crane was at Enugu, 1,000 miles away.

RG **96** 474 (1952).

20 October 1952
Heavitree, South Africa (SAR)

21 killed, about 50 injured

The Durban–Johannesburg night mail had just passed through Heavitree station, ten miles from Eastcourt, when the first ten coaches left the track on a curve. One of them slewed round and finished up on top of the next. Considerable damage was caused to the overhead electrification masts and wires. Until the ambulances arrived from Eastcourt and Ladysmith, help was provided from nearby farms. The reports in England referred to the fact that 'None of the European passengers was seriously injured, but 30 were treated for minor wounds'.

RG **97** 473 (1952).

15 January 1953
Washington DC, United States of America (Pennsylvania)

87 injured

This accident, fortunately without any fatalities, was an extremely spectacular one. A runaway Class GG1 2-Co-Co-2 electric locomotive, at the head of the 'Federal Limited', crashed through the buffer-stops at 35mph, and careered into the concourse of the Union Station in Washington. It and the first two coaches then plunged through the floor into the basement. The 16-coach express had been unable to stop after a fault had developed in the braking system. It was found that the cock on the brake-pipe between the third and fourth coaches had come into contact with part of the underframe, and had been turned off. Fortunately the fact that the train was running away was realised, and the leading coaches were cleared of passengers. Part of the station and offices were evacuated before the train arrived with its whistle blowing and bell sounding. President Eisenhower's Inauguration was due to take place only two days later, so the hole in the floor was quickly covered over, and the locomotive was not lifted out until some appreciable time later.

Reed, p144, *151*. RG **98** 111, 389 (1953).

15 February 1953
Benevento, Italy (FS)
23 killed

In the early hours a semi-fast train from Lecce to Naples and Rome was derailed when it entered the station at an excessive speed. The driver later claimed that, because of its smooth running, he had not checked the speedometer, but the brakes failed when he tried to apply them. As a result the locomotive left the track at some points. Considerable damage was caused to the front vehicles in the train, and all except one were overturned. The first passenger coach, an old third-class one, hit the wall of the parcels office, and the majority of the fatalities occurred in it.

Schneider, p129.

15 February 1953
Comodoro Rivadavia, Argentina
23 killed, 42 injured

A railbus was derailed and fell down an embankment in Patagonia. The local

Mardi Gras carnival festivities were suspended as a token of mourning.

RG **98** 222 (1953).

27 March 1953
Conneaut, Ohio, United States of America (New York Central)
21 killed

This accident occurred on a four-track main line, and was caused by a number of large pipes, 31 feet long and 13 inches in diameter, being dislodged from a gondola wagon (an open bogie type with sides) of an eastbound 'extra' freight train. One of them became wedged between the vehicle carrying it and the next track, which was pushed sideways by about 18 inches. This distortion was sufficient to derail the westbound, diesel-hauled 'Mohawk', which was passing at a speed of 75mph, and it hit the freight, scattering wreckage across the whole width of the railway. Before anyone could protect the other tracks, the eastbound 'Southwestern Limited' collided with it at 70mph, and all except its last three coaches were derailed. Seven passenger coaches were destroyed in the two trains. It was discovered that the pipes had not been properly loaded at a steel works in Aliquippa, Pennsylvania. The top of the pile was over five feet above the wagon's sides, and the pipes had not been securely fixed to the side stakes. This should have been detected by the railway inspectors at several interchange points *en route*.

Reed, *p67*. Shaw, p212.

24 December 1953
Walouru, New Zealand (NZR)
151 killed

This accident was the indirect result of a volcanic eruption. The 9,000ft Mount

Ruapehu had a lake in its crater, and the waters from this were suddenly released through a cave underneath the Whangaehu Glacier. The huge mass of water, plus volcanic ash from the eruption and lumps of ice, roared down the river. Quantities of silt and boulders were picked up as it went, forming what is known as a lahar. There was a railway bridge across the river at Walouru, and this was swept away just before the arrival of an express. The postmaster at the small railway town of Taihape had seen the damaged bridge, and ran along the line waving a torch to try and stop the train. The driver failed to see him, and he had to jump out of the way. The locomotive and six coaches fell into the raging waters. So fierce was the flow that one coach was swept down the river for five miles, while some of the drowned bodies were picked up 30 miles away. After the train had plunged into the gap, the postmaster climbed on to the sixth coach as it hung over the river, shouting to its occupants to get out, but the vehicle fell into the water before any could do so. In view of the on-going volcanic activity, it was decided to install warning equipment on all the railway bridges in the area, as any future lehar could sweep down several different river valleys.

RG **100** 2, 23, 55, 64, *102*, 176, 232 (1954), **101** 58, 77 (1954), **102** 40 (1955).

25 December 1953

Sakvice, Czechoslovakia (ČSD)

(186) killed

A Prague–Bratislava express collided with the rear of a local train in Sakvice station, near Brno. It was caused by the 'gross negligence' of a railwayman, who was arrested.

21 January 1954

Between Jhampir and Braudabad, Pakistan (North Western)

(60) killed

The Lahore–Karachi mail train, with the Pakistan Foreign Minister aboard, collided with a derailed petrol tank-wagon on the Kotri section of the railway. Fire broke out, and spread to the coaches of the mail, as well as to the other wagons of the freight train alongside.

30 January 1954

Kafr-el-Zayyat, Egypt

28 killed

President Negulb was visiting a village in the Nile Delta which had been destroyed by a fire. The crowd surged across the tracks to greet him just as the Cairo–Alexandria diesel express ran through the station, mowing them down.

RG **100** 222 (1954).

31 January 1954

Between Suwon and Osan, South Korea (KNR)

57 killed, 100+ injured

A collision occurred between a passenger train and an empty wagon, 20 miles south of Seoul. Varying numbers of fatalities were quoted by different sources.

RG **100** 194 (1954).

31 March 1954

Jagatbels, Uttar Pradesh, India

37 killed, 40 injured

An explosion destroyed a coach of a passenger train in somewhat bizarre circumstances. Fifteen hundred sticks of gelignite in compartments occupied by five policemen were said to have been ignited by an exposed electric wire, however improbable this may sound.

3 July 1954

Tournon, France (SNCF)

33 killed

A local diesel railcar from Lyon to Nimes was involved in a head-on collision with a goods train six miles north of Tournon. The railcar and the first of its trailers were badly damaged, but the rear vehicle, containing a party of children on their way to a holiday camp, was relatively undamaged. A statement by the Director-General of the SNCF said that the accident occurred because of an error by a local pointsman. Earlier in the day trains in both directions were using one of the tracks while repairs were taking place on the other. Normal working had been resumed, but the pointsman routed one of the trains over the wrong line. He was arrested.

RG **101** 54 (1954).

2 September 1954

Fabrica, Negros Island, Phillipines (Insula Lumbar Company)

139 killed

A train owned by the largest logging company in the Phillipines was taking timber from a mountain forest to a sawmill. It was derailed, and fell into a ravine. Many of the fatalities were unauthorised passengers getting a free ride. (The number of casualties differs in some reports.)

RG **101** 305 (1954).

9 September 1954

Odendaalsrust, South Africa (Loraine Mine)

10 killed, 3 injured

A diesel locomotive hauling a load of steel plunged down the shaft of the Loraine gold mine, where it hit a double-deck cage containing 72 African miners at a depth of 4,700 feet. It was not stated whether the locomotive had been operating at the surface or on one of the underground levels, but few railway accidents will have occurred nearer the centre of the earth.

RG **101** 333 (1954).

13 September 1954

Odemira, Portugal (CP)

27 killed

Three coaches of an express from the Algarve to Lisbon left the rails near Odemira, some 170 miles north of its destination. (Through trains from the southern half of the country have to make a long detour to cross the River Tagus, although there is a station on the south bank opposite Lisbon, connected by railway-operated passenger ferries.)

27 September 1954

Jangaon, India (Central)

139 killed

A steel bridge between Secunderabad and Kazipet, which had been weakened by recent floods, collapsed under the weight of a train. Nearly all the coaches were involved, two ending up in the bed of the river, while a third was swept away by the current. Bodies were still being recovered from the river several days later. This accident occurred on what was formerly part of the Nizam's State Railway.

RG **101** 390 (1954).

2 December 1954

Wilsele, Belgium
(SNCB/NMBS)

21 killed

A special train, carrying supporters home from an England v West Germany international football match in London, was derailed on some points at Wilsele, near Louvain. The locomotive and the first three coaches left the track, the second one being completely wrecked. The driver and fireman were among those killed. The accident occurred 200 yards from a bridge over the River Dyle, where single-line working was in force to permit engineering work. The train may have taken the cross-over at too high a speed.

1955–1959

3 April 1955

Guadalajara, Mexico
(FNdeM)

(300) killed

A passenger train was derailed near Guadalajara, and fell into a gorge.

17 July 1955

San Bernando, Chile
(EFE)

(30–70) killed

In fog a fast train ran into the back of another standing in San Bernando station, twelve miles from Santiago.

23 August 1955

Ciudadela, Argentina
(FA)

21 killed, 50 injured

On the western outskirts of Buenos Aires, an express hit the rear of a slow train in a station, telescoping a first-class coach.

13 January 1956

Near Ludvika, Sweden

20+ killed, 9 injured

An iron-ore train collided with a railcar, most of whose passengers were school-children. The freight had failed to stop at Ställdelen to cross the railcar in the loop. Wreckage from the passenger train was found spread along several hundred yards of the line.

RG **104** 90 (1956).

22 January 1956

Los Angeles, California, United States of America
(Santa Fé)

30 killed

Four miles from Los Angeles station, a two-car Budd diesel railcar entered a 15mph curve at a speed of 69mph, as registered by its recorder. Although this was below the theoretical overturning speed for the amount of super-elevation, the train pitched over on to its side, and slid 550 feet along the track. The driver said he had reduced speed at an earlier 35mph warning board, but then blacked out. A subsequent medical examination showed that he had a concealed epileptic condition, and the second man in the cab had been too slow to realise what was happening. As the accident occurred in the suburbs of

'Tinsel City', newsreel cameramen were quickly on the scene, and the number of fatalities was initially put as high as 88.

Although the stainless-steel vehicles were not badly damaged structurally in the accident, many of the passengers fell through the shattered windows, and were crushed. On a much smaller scale, the same occurred when the BR diesel multiple-units were derailed on Lockington level-crossing in 1986.

Shaw, p302.

(7 August 1956)

Barra do Pirai, Brazil
(Central Railway of Brazil)

20+ killed

A fast goods train hit a passenger train outside the station, 70 miles from Rio de Janeiro.

RG **105** 176 (1956).

25 February 1956

Bornitz, German
Democratic Republic
(DR)

43 killed

An express from Dresden to Leipzig was hit by a fast goods train which had run past signals in fog. The local traffic superintendent and the driver of the goods train were arrested immediately, and five months later it was announced that four railwaymen had been given prison sentences of one to five years for their part in causing the crash.

30 June 1956

Near Oaxaca, Mexico

30 killed

Two coaches in a train from Mexico City were derailed and fell into a ravine. It was thought that the accident was caused by a landslide following the recent heavy rain.

RG **105** 63 (1956).

2 September 1956

Mahububnagar, India
(Central)

At least 112 killed

Two coaches of a metre-gauge train from Secunderabad to Dronachalam were precipitated into the swollen river when a bridge collapsed. Everyone in the first coach was thought to have died, but the five postal sorters in the second survived and were able to rescue the mail, although some of the passengers in the ordinary section of this coach were killed. A villager cycled five miles to Mahububnagar, the nearest station, to raise the alarm, but heavy rain impeded the rescue work.

5 September 1956

Robinson, New Mexico,
United States of America
(Santa Fé)

20 killed

Two expresses, each hauled by four diesel locomotives, were given orders to pass at Robinson in the early hours of the morning. As the station was closed, this meant the fireman had to get out to work the points. The first train to arrive was the 16-car eastbound one, and, although it was 'superior' by direction, it was specifically instructed to take the siding. After the fireman had unlocked and changed the points, he went on ahead and unlocked those at the other end of the loop. He also remained by the lever, both these actions violating the rule which stated, 'At meeting or passing points, the employee attending the switch must not unlock the derail or main-track switch, nor station himself nearer to the main-track switch than the clearance point, . . . , until expected train has been met or passed'. As the westbound train approached at speed, the driver of the stationary train sounded his horn, and flashed his headlight, possibly as a warning to the fireman. However, these actions confused the latter, and he ran forward to reverse the points. As a result the trains collided at 60mph, all the fatalities being railway employees. The majority were off-duty restaurant-car staff in the dormitory car marshalled second behind the locomotive of the westbound train.

Shaw, p114.

15 October 1956

Rokken, Japan (JNR)

40 killed, 96 injured

A head-on collision occurred between two steam-hauled passenger trains near Nagoya. Police later arrested two drivers and a fireman, on a charge of manslaughter, for over-running signals.

23 November 1956

Ariyalur, India (Southern)

150 killed

An express for Tuticorin was derailed on the approach to a bridge near Ariyalur, 170 miles from Madras. The locomotive, seven coaches and a parcels van fell into the swollen Marudaiyar River. A commission of inquiry found that the approach to the bridge had collapsed under pressure from the flood water. They blamed the regional engineer, the patrol man on duty, the stationmaster, the permanent-way inspector and his assistant, for failing to discharge their duties properly.

9 February 1957

Chapel-en-le-Frith, England (British Railways, London Midland Region)

2 killed

After leaving Buxton, the pipe supplying steam to the brake system on a Class 8F 2-8-0 locomotive at the head of a freight train fractured. This filled the cab with steam and put the brake out of action. Although Driver John Axon told his fireman to jump off and apply as many hand brakes on the wagons as possible, on the subsequent long descent the train ran away. It finally collided violently with the rear of another freight train in Chapel-en-le-Frith station, the guard of which was killed in addition to Driver Axon. The latter was postumously awarded the George Cross for his outstanding example of courage and devotion to duty. There was a subsequent BBC radio programme, 'The Ballad of John Axon', which was later produced as a long-playing record. In 1981 a Class 86 electric locomotive (No. 86261) was named after him.

Rolt, p266. Vaughan, p146.

25 February 1957

Cordoba, Argentina

15–40 killed, 100+ injured

A train full of tourists was derailed on a sharp curve near Cordoba, seven coaches overturning. Excessive speed was apparently the cause.

4 March 1957

Burma

30+ killed

A Mandalay–Rangoon mail train was derailed, sabotage by Communist insurgents being blamed. Their offer to negotiate with the government had been refused, and this was their fourth subsequent attack on the railway.

15 March 1957
Kuurila, Finland (VR)

24 + killed, 50 injured

Two expresses, both running late and travelling at speed, collided on a stretch of single track about 80 miles north of Helsinki. The accident, which was the worst peacetime one so far experienced in Finland, occurred during a blizzard. To reach the site in a lonely forest area, some of the rescuers had to travel on skis, or by horse and sleigh.

8 April 1957
Woodstock, South Africa (SAR)

20 + killed, 45 injured

Two suburban electric trains collided at Woodstock, near Cape Town.

3 July 1957
Between Mauvres and St Péray, France (SNCF)

35 killed, 42 injured

A collision occurred just outside Valance.

19 July 1957
Bollène, France (SNCF)

31 killed, 69 injured

In the early hours of the morning, a Nice–Paris express was diverted into a siding. Although the driver was able to reduce speed from 75 to 60mph, the locomotive overturned on a cross-over limited to 20mph. An escape of steam from the locomotive scalded a number of passengers in a sleeping car. A high proportion of the deaths occurred subsequently in hospital, rising from 19 to 30 within a few days. One passenger who survived the accident telephoned his wife to say he was all right, only to collapse and die from a stroke.

4 August 1957
Villa Verde, Spain (RENFE)

22 + killed, 51 injured

A double-headed troop train, loaded with 800 soldiers returning from manoeuvres in the Pyrenees, collided with a light engine at Villa Verde, four miles from Madrid. All three locomotives were derailed, together with most of the coaches. Large numbers of men were trapped in a heap of wreckage composed of three coaches and two flat wagons.

2 September 1957
Kendal, Jamaica (Jamaica Government)

179 killed

Late at night, an excursion train, with some 1,500 people aboard, left the rails on a curve a short distance outside Kendal station, 75 miles from Kingston, wrecking eight of its twelve coaches. Five fell into a lineside ditch, two were wedged into a narrow cutting, and the other lost its roof and sides. In addition to the rescue services, large numbers of volunteers assisted the survivors out of the wreckage. There was no access to the site, so initially the locomotives shuttled backwards and forwards carrying the injured and unharmed passengers in two wagons. Later a bulldozer cut a half-mile track to the nearest road. Many victims went home after receiving treatment, so there was no official total of the injured, but the figure was estimated as several hundred.

Initially it was stated that the derailment was due to excessive speed on the curve, and the driver said he had been unable to apply the brakes. It was discovered that one of the cocks on the air pipes between coaches had been closed, the first story being that this was done by a passenger who objected to the noise caused by the brakes. It was also stated that the brakes should have been tested by the crew at Greenvale, the last station before the accident, and that the driver and guard subsequently made up a bogus brake certificate.

A high-level commission was set up by the government, and Brig. C. A. Langley, the Chief Inspecting Officer of Railways in Britain, was invited to assist with the investigation. He discovered that the cocks on the brake-pipes were loose enough to be easily turned, and that they could come into contact with the coupler on a curve, which caused them to shut. The guard and one of the brakesmen had been riding on the locomotive, contrary to instructions, and the other brakesmen failed to take any action when the speed became excessive.

Brig. Langley was praised for his work, it being stated that:

'Had it not been for his persistence in conducting these enquiries it might well have been that the we may not have discovered the cause of failure of the brakes. We cannot express too strongly our appreciation of the services he has rendered, not only to the commission in making its enquiries but also to the Management of the Jamaica Government Railway for the very thorough examination he has made into its working, particularly in relation to the safety of trains and condition of the brake equipment.'

One could not wish for a better tribute than this to the old British Railway Inspectorate.

RG **107** 266, 288, 318, 495 (1957), **109** 120 (1958).

7 September 1957

Nozières-Brignon, France (SNCF)

26 killed, 70 injured

An express from Paris to Nimes left the rails as it was entering the station. The locomotive hit a bridge, and several coaches were telescoped.

29 September 1957

Gambar, Pakistan (PR)

(250) killed

A Karachi-bound express was due to cross an oil train in the loop at Gambar, near Montgomery. Because of an error by the pointsman, it was diverted into the loop at a speed of about 45mph, colliding head-on with the freight. Fire broke out, which consumed the front coaches, only three passengers managing to escape from the leading two vehicles.

29 September 1957

North of Ibadan, Nigeria (NRC)

66 killed, 122 injured

Some 20 miles north of Ibadan, an embankment was washed away by torrential rain, which derailed seven of the 16 coaches of a Lagos–Kano passenger train. First reports spoke of more than 300 people missing, feared carried away by the flood water, but many had just walked home. A report on the accident was published within a month, and went into the causes in considerable detail. The derailment occurred during the early hours of the morning, after several days of heavy rain. Reports of unsafe conditions along the line had delayed the train, which was being driven carefully within the laid-down speed limits. Two hour earlier a goods train had passed over the same stretch of line and its crew had seen nothing unusual. In the intervening period, however, a culvert through the embankment had become blocked, and the water rose to the level of the permanent way, washing out some of the formation. As the train reached this point the track collapsed, and the first seven coaches finished up on top of the locomotive. The floods continued to erode the embankment, which added to the destruction.

RG **107** 529 (1957).

20 October 1957
Ispartakule, Turkey (TCDD)

83 killed, 100+ injured

Apparently as a result of a signalling error, two trains collided in the province of Thrace. The Istanbul–Edirne (Adrianople) train included a through coach for Greece, and hit one travelling in the opposite direction between the same cities.

16 November 1957
Chantonnay, France (SNCF)

23 killed, 30 injured

A two-coach local diesel train collided head-on with a steam-hauled freight on a stretch of single track near Chantonnay in the Vendée. In the raised cab of the diesel locomotive the crew both survived, but all the passengers in the first coach were killed. The press did not give the cause of the accident, but the examining magistrate at La Roche-sur-Yon ordered the detention of the driver of the passenger train and one of the station staff at Chantonnay.

4 December 1957
St Johns, Lewisham, England (British Railways, Southern Region)

90 killed, 109 seriously injured

In very thick fog, an express from Cannon Street to Ramsgate, hauled by the 'Battle of Britain' Pacific No. 34066 *Spitfire*, ran past a double-yellow and then a yellow signal on the four-track Eastern Section main line of the Southern Region without checking its speed. Only when the following red aspect was seen by the fireman at short range did the driver start to brake. There was then insufficient room to stop, and the train collided with the rear of a ten-coach electric multiple-unit at an estimated speed of 30mph. Because of the rising gradient, this Charing Cross–Hayes electric train had its brakes full on, as it was being held at a red signal because of confusion about the routeing of another train ahead. This made the impact of the collision more severe, the whole of the body of its eighth coach being destroyed when the ninth was forced into it.

The rapid deceleration of the steam-hauled train caused the front coach to crush the rear of the locomotive's tender, and both were forced sideways, dislodging the centre pillar of the bridge above, which carried the Nunhead–Lewisham line. Two of its girders subsided on the train below, completing the destruction of the first coach, and badly crushing the second and the front half of the third. The number of fatalities made this the third worst railway accident to occur on the railways of Britain. It could have been even worse, because two minutes later another electric multiple-unit, on a Holborn Viaduct–Dartford service, approached the bridge from above. Fortunately it had already been checked by signals, and the driver, seeing the displaced girders, managed to stop clear.

Throughout the area, visibility had been bad during the afternoon and evening of the day concerned, and was causing considerable delays to trains leaving the London termini during the rush-hour. The Hayes train involved in the accident had left 30 minutes late, but the Ramsgate one had been delayed much more, and was running 76 minutes late at the time of the collision. The visibility was particularly bad in the area where the accident occurred, and the signal positioning was very difficult along this curved four-track stretch. It had been installed in the late 1920s when most locomotives were driven from the right, but the groups of four lenses were sited as near eye-level as possible.

While the signals were clearly visible from the cabs of electric and diesel trains, the boiler of a steam locomotive with left-hand drive hid them at close range. From the left-hand side of a Bulleid Pacific the two vital 'distant' signals could have been seen from 324 and 150 yards away in clear weather, but were obscured by the boiler at a range of just over 100 yards in each case. With the visibility as it was on the night of the accident, they could thus not have been seen by the driver unless he moved across the cab. However, he did not do this, nor did he ask the fireman to look out for him until they were approaching the signal which was showing red behind the stationary electric train ahead. When the fireman shouted a warning, there was no time for the speed to be significantly checked before the collision occurred. In his subsequent evidence, the driver said he had never been stopped at this signal before, and one wonders how much that might subconsciously have influenced his actions.

In November 1956 the British Railways standard Automatic Warning System had been approved, and was to be installed on the country's main lines. This was bound to be a progressive process, and on the Southern Region priority was being given to the Western Section line out of Waterloo, because of its semaphore signals. It was likely that, had it been installed on the Eastern Section main line, it would have prevented this disaster.

Clearing the tracks after such a destructive collision was difficult and prolonged, one of the coaches of the Ramsgate train being cut up on the spot, as were the distorted girders of the overbridge. All told the line was closed for $7\frac{1}{2}$ days, which considerably disorganised the Southern's busy suburban services.

The driver of the Ramsgate train was tried twice for manslaughter. On the first occasion the jury disagreed, and at the second trial the prosecution, in the light of his mental and physical health, offered no evidence, and he was acquitted.

Hamilton, p164, *opposite p92*. Nock, p*160/ 161*, 203. Rolt, p*132/133*, 288. Vaughan, p116, inc. *p.* RM **139** *xii* (April 1993).

1 January 1958

Mohri, India

32 killed, 85 injured

In thick fog an Ambala–Delhi stopping train collided with a Delhi–Pathankot express standing in Mohri station, six miles from Ambala.

7 March 1958

Pacienca, Brazil

58 killed, (120) injured

There were two brief reports in the English press of a collision between three trains in a suburb of Rio de Janeiro.

8 May 1958

Rio de Janeiro, Brazil (Centro do Brasil)

112 killed, 315 injured, 50 seriously

A evening suburban train collided with an empty one near Rio de Janeiro. The cause was stated to be a faulty signalling system, which failed to register the presence of the passenger train, and so permitted the empty-stock working to enter the single-line section. Shortly afterwards three of the railway's directors resigned, and the President of Brazil called a meeting with the Ministry of Transport and the head of the federal railways, to discuss safety.

21 May 1958
Chamraj, India

30 killed

A Rajkot–Viramsam express was derailed in Chamraj station, close to its starting point.

28 July 1958
Between Shepherds Bush and Holland Park, London, England (London Transport)

1 killed, 51 injured

While a tube train was in tunnel betweeen Shepherds Bush and Holland Park, an electric arc started between two cables in a power-receptacle box on one of its cars which dated from 1928. These boxes are provided to enable power to be supplied to the train when it is separated from the conductor rails in maintenance depots. A crack in the insulation of the box is thought to have caused the initial arc, which, being on a dc supply, then burnt its way through a bulkhead, and into the interior of the vehicle. It also made a hole in the nearby air pipe, which automatically applied the brake. There was some unnecessary delay in evacuating the train, and most of the passengers and crew suffered from the effects of the dense smoke and acrid fumes. One passenger subsequently died in hospital.

14 September 1958
Königswinter, West Germany (Drachenfels)

17 killed, 94 injured

There is a short rack railway from the town of Königswinter to the ruined Drachenfels Castle on a hilltop overlooking the Rhine opposite Bonn. After 70 years operation, it was electrified in 1953, but steam was still used in the summer. The locomotive on one of these trains left the track and the three coaches behind it broke away and overturned. State proceedings were later started against four of the railway staff. The line is still in operation with its electric motive power, and one of the steam locomotives is preserved on a plinth near the lower terminus.

RG **111** 9 (1959).

15 September 1958
Newark Bay, New Jersey, United States of America (Central of New Jersey)

48 killed

When the line into the New York area from the south was opened in 1864, it spanned Newark Bay on a two-mile, double-track trestle, the longest bridge in the world at that time. In 1926 it was replaced by a pair of parallel twin-track high-level bridges of all steel construction, each of which included a pair of vertical-lift spans over navigation channels. These were protected with two automatic signals, a 'distant' situated 1,562 yards from the near-end of the opening span, and a stop one 187 yards from the lift. As recommended after the accident on the Pennsylvania Railroad near Atlantic City on 28 October 1906, there was also a derailer 70 feet beyond the second signal.

On the morning concerned, a small freighter had whistled for the bridge to be opened shortly before Train No. 3314 from Bay Head Junction was due to leave Elizabethport, its last stop before the bridge. Shipping had priority, and the opening spans were lifted, their protecting signals remaining against the train, as these were not normally cleared until it was approaching. Train No. 3314 consisted of five steel coaches, hauled by a pair of diesel locomotives. For reasons never determined, it failed to slow or stop at the two signals, and hit the derailer at over 40mph. The train then bumped along the sleepers before the locomotives and the first two coaches plunged into the gap and disappeared beneath the water. The third vehicle was caught by the pier of the bridge, and hung there for several hours before being dislodged by the tide and sinking. Many of its passengers got out and were rescued by a flotilla of small boats. Fortunately there were no passengers in the leading coach, but nearly all those in the second were drowned. The driver, fireman, conductor and head brakesman were all killed, and no satisfactory explanation was discovered for their failure to obey the signals.

Several of the businessmen on the train had been survivors of the Woodbridge accident in February 1951. As in that case, there was a discontinuity in the operating practices part-way along the line. On the New York & Long Branch section, automatic train control was provided, which ensured that speed was held at 20mph after a signal had been passed at caution. This system, however, stopped twelve miles south of the bridge, so there was not the same degree of protection for the vital opening spans. When these were *fully* raised, the concrete counter-weights descended to track level and blocked the line. It was only customary for the bridge to be raised far enough to clear the approaching ship. Conscious of the extra delay a full lift would have caused to the 140+ daily trains using the bridge, the railway resisted recommendations for this to be done each of the 28 times a day, on average, when the span had to be opened. On 8 May 1974 a double-headed freight of 94 wagons failed to stop at the signal protecting a similar bridge at Cleveland, Ohio. The bodies of both diesels were sheared off their underframes, the first of which narrowly missed the passing vessel as it fell into the water. The rest of the train however, remained on the bridge.

In later years, the Newark Bridge suffered badly from the increased shipping movements in the Bay, being rammed by passing vessels rather more frequently than once a year. One of the lifting spans was rendered permanently inoperative after a French freighter hit it in May 1966. In this country the swing bridge across the River Ouse at Goole has also been badly damaged by ships on several occasions, to the detriment of Hull's train connections with the south.

Reed, p90, *101*. Shaw, p194.

8 November 1958

Buenos Aires, Argentina (General Mitre Railway)

22 killed, 100 injured

During the evening peak, a steam train from Retiro to Pergamino collided with an electric suburban service. The latter had left Retiro for Tigre a few minutes earlier, and had stopped for signals at Empalme Maldonado. It was thought that a signalling failure had occurred. Some of the casualties were caused by the electric power supply not being switched off promptly. On 28 October 23 passengers had been injured in another collision, and two signalmen had been taken to a police station for questioning. All the others immediately went on strike until their colleagues were released.

RG **109** 599, 680 (1958).

8 May 1959

Tasikmalaja, Indonesia (NJKA)

92 killed, 14 injured

A Bandjar to Bandung express left the track and fell into a ravine near Tasikmalaja. The Minister of Communications announced that the investigation had shown that some unknown person had been responsible for the accident, presumably implying that it had been sabotage.

RG **110** 657 (1959).

5 June 1959

Engenheiro Goulart, Brazil

43 + killed

Two trains were involved in a head-on collision in the São Paulo district, due, it was stated, to a signal defect.

7 February 1959

Sewell, Chile (EFE)

33 killed, 55 injured

According to *The Times*, a passenger train left the track in the mountains south-east of Santiago.

1960–1964

7 January 1960

Monza, Italy (FS)

30 killed, 70 injured

The train left the rails on a curve which was subject to a speed restriction of 60mph.

15 May 1960

Leipzig, German Democratic Republic (DR)

54 killed, 206 injured

A collision occurred in the evening outside Leipzig station. As usual with the communist countries, few details emerged, but the Minister of Transport immediately left for the scene, having been given special powers by the Prime Minister to investigate its cause. The violence of the collision made rescue work difficult. The 1-Do-1 electric locomotive, No. E17 123, which was hauling one of the trains, was badly damaged, with both cabs crushed and one of its pony-trucks ripped off. Four railwaymen were subsequently given prison sentences of between eight and 15 years.

Ritzau, p173, *175*. RG **113** 301 (1960).

8 July 1960

Yamuna, India (North Eastern)

25 killed

A train was so over-crowded that passengers were travelling on the coach roofs as it crossed the Yamuna Bridge, where the top bracings swept 25 of them to their death.

RG **120** 513 (1964).

Passengers riding on the roofs of trains are not the only ones who have been killed through their own foolhardiness. In the 18 months up to the end of 1956, more than 800 people riding on the footboards of trains in India had fallen to their deaths. Two other unusual fatal accidents in that country are also worth reporting, this time only involving people on the ground. In 1955 a fight was taking place on the line between two lots of villagers to determine which of their communities should be sacrificed to save the other from flood water. A passing train killed seven of the combatants, and injured another four. The second incident took place shortly afterwards in more peaceful conditions, six people being killed and eight injured when a train hit a crowd of refugees who were squatting on the track.

It is also worth commenting that in the mid-1990s, road fatalities in India were running at over 60,000 per year.

RG **103** 202, 292, (1955), **109** 505 (1958).

14 November 1960

Near Steblova, Czechoslovakia (CSD)

110 killed, 106 injured

This was a major disaster when two passenger trains collided at speed near Steblova station on the Paradubice–Hradec Kralove branch line, in eastern Bohemia. Few details were given, but the inquiry was headed by the Minister of Transport, assisted by members of the Communist Party. It was concluded that the cause was 'a crude violation of traffic regulations'. A further commission was set up to aid the relatives of those killed.

RG **113** 611 (1960).

9 January 1961

Barcelona, Spain (RENFE)

21+ killed, 50+ injured

The overnight express from Valencia to Barcelona collided with a goods train on a stretch of multiple track outside its destination. A pile of matchwood, 30ft high, was formed from the wooden bodies of the freight wagons, plus the second- and third-class coaches. Both drivers were killed, in addition to a number of students returning after the Christmas holidays, but the first-division Barcelona Español football team all escaped injury. A signalling fault was believed to have caused the accident.

26 March 1961

Burma

23 killed, 100 injured, 60 taken hostage

A Mandalay–Rangoon express was mined by Karen rebels about 150 miles from its destination. The passengers, who were mainly government officials and soldiers, were then attacked with automatic weapons.

RG **114** 676 (1961).

19 April 1961

Siliguri, West Bengal, India

23 killed, 77 injured, 28 seriously

A passenger train was derailed, the reason, according to the Indian Railways' Minister, was that there had been some tampering with the track.

13 June 1961

Esslingen, West Germany (DB)

35 killed

A head-on collision between two local trains occurred during the evening rush-hour, after temporary single-line working had been introduced in the outer suburbs of Stuttgart on the route to Munich via Ulm. The leading coaches of both trains fell down the embankment on to the bank of the River Nekar. One of the trains ran past two signals.

Ritzau, p113.

18 June 1961

Vitry-le-François, France (SNCF)

27 killed, 218 injured, 89 seriously

In the afternoon the rear 14 coaches of a Strasbourg–Paris express became derailed on a curve, although the locomotive and the four leading coaches remained on the track. Ten of the derailed vehicles plunged down the embankment, where three came to rest in marshy ground, which made rescue difficult. Firemen had to cut through the roofs of some of the coaches to release those trapped inside. A nearby United States air base provided help, and three of the most seriously injured were flown to hospital in Chalons-sur-Marne by helicopter.

5 October 1961

Hamburg, West Germany (DB)

28 killed, 55 injured

Late in the evening, an electric passenger train collided with an engineer's train on the Hamburg S-Bahn system, between Haupbahnhof and Berliner Tor. The engineering train consisted of a locomotive and a number of wagons loaded with 50ft girders, some of which penetrated the first coach of the passenger train for half its length. The accident was caused by the passenger train running past signals.

Ritzau, p113.

20 October 1961

Between Ghatsila and Dalbhumgarh, India (South Eastern)

27 killed, 105 injured

A Howrah–Ranchi express was derailed, the locomotive and seven carriages leaving the track. The provisional findings of the investigation into the crash was that someone had tampered with the track. In the year 1961/62, 87 were killed and 324 injured in three acts of sabotage against the railways.

RG **115** 523 (1961), **116** 101 (1962), **120** 513 (1964).

29 October 1961

Between Mainpuri and Bhongaon, India (Northern)

22 killed, 62 injured

A train was derailed because of excessive speed on open line.

RG **120** 514 (1964).

26 October 1961

Between Oita and Beppu, Japan (Oita Kotsu Corporation)

32 killed, 35 injured

Two days of torrential rain caused a landslide, 90ft wide, 60ft long and 45ft high. The slip contained many pine trees, and buried a single-car electric coach. All 66 passengers were either killed or injured. This was more of a tramway operation than a railway, and has since been closed and replaced by a bus service.

RG **115** 523 (1961).

23 December 1961

Cantanzaro, Italy (FS)

70 killed

One of the vehicles in a two-coach train fell 100 feet into the ravine from a curved viaduct across the River Fiumarella, on the outskirts of Catanzaro, in southern Italy. The disaster resulted in violent demonstrations against the railway, one lot of protestors damaging rolling stock in the station at Sovaria Manelli, until dispersed by *carabineri*. Communist deputies in the Italian parliament called for a 'democratic inquiry' into the cause of the accident, claiming that it was the inevitable result of the policy of neglecting secondary lines in the south of the country. The driver and conductor of the train were arrested and charged with manslaughter, as the train was found to have been doing 35mph over a stretch limited to 22mph.

RG **116** 32 (1962).

8 January 1962

Harmelen, Netherlands (NS)

93 killed

In morning fog a Utrecht–Rotterdam express travelling at 66mph was in head-on collision with a Rotterdam–Amsterdam stopping train doing 45mph as it approached the junction at Harmelen, just east of Woerden. The layout here required trains from Woerden to Amsterdam to travel along the westbound track for 20 metres before diverging, and the collision occurred on this stretch. The impact of the Class 1100 electric locomotive, No. 1131, destroyed three coaches of the emu, which consisted of a four-car unit, plus a two-car set. Six of the eleven coaches in the express, which had about 900 passengers aboard on the Monday morning, were wrecked. Rescue work took all day. The driver of the express missed the distant signal, and was only able to brake from 125 to 107km/h (78 to 66mph) after sighting the stop signal at danger. From the fatality point of view, this was the worst railway accident to take place in the Netherlands, and prompted the introduction of their Automatic Train Protection system.

RG **116** 64 (1962).

22 February 1962
Cari, Colombia

40 killed, 67 injured

A fast goods collided with a crowded passenger train near Cari, all the fatalities occurring in the first four coaches of the latter.

3 May 1962
Mikawashima, Japan (JNR)

160 killed, 296 injured

This was an unusual disaster, which resulted from a minor mishap to a steam-hauled goods train in the outskirts of Tokyo. This failed to stop at the end of the siding, and the impact with the buffers derailed the locomotive and the first wagon. On the next track, the front coach of an electric train, full of passengers returning home after the Constitution Day holiday, was derailed, and fouled the opposite running line. Five

minutes later a second electric train hit the wreckage, after running down a number of the passengers who had got out of the first train involved and were still standing on the track. Other passengers had got clear by climbing down the side of the embankment, only to be struck by the derailed coaches of the second train as they were pushed sideways off the line when it collided with the debris. Four railwaymen were later given prison sentences of 14 months to three years for causing the disaster through negligence and operating errors. Following this accident the Japan National Railways took the decision to install their Automatic Train Stop system (ATS).

Shaw, p412.

31 May 1962
Voghera, Italy (FS)

64 killed, 15 seriously injured

In the early hours of the morning an overnight passenger train stopped to change locomotives in Voghera station, this being a junction between the newer 3,000 Volt dc electric system, and the old three-phase ac one. While this was happening, a special train, conveying 39 empty cement wagons, ran past two colour-light signals without braking, and the driver also failed to notice the frantic waving by the signalman in the box on the Milan side of the station. An emergency brake application was only made at the last minute, and the locomotive demolished the rear half of the passenger train, which was heavily loaded because of the Ascension Day holiday.

8 June 1962
Bhilai, India (South Eastern)

9 killed, 123 injured

Eleven coaches of a passenger train were blown over by the wind during a particularly severe cyclonic storm.

RG **122** 473 (1966).

21 July 1962

Dumraon, Bihar, India
(Eastern)

48+ killed, 55 seriously injured

The Amritsar–Howrah mail train collided head-on with a goods train near Buxar, which had moved on to the main line during a shunting operation. The operators in the east and west cabins were both reported to have absconded afterwards. During the following August it was reported that, including this disaster, 72 people had been killed and 164 injured in 15 different accidents between 23 June and three August.

This was one of the periods when the Indian railways suffered a series of bad accidents, and a special commission was set up to improve safety. One of their recommendations to reduce sabotage to the track was to use half-mile lengths of continuously-welded rail, and CST-9 sleepers.

RG **117** 245, 504 (1962), **118** 180 (1962), **120** 514 (1964).

22 July 1962

Between Bucharest and Mogosoaia, Roumania
(CFR)

32 killed

A passenger train was derailed because of excessive speed over a curve. As usual with a communist country, few details were available, but the Ministry of Transport announced that it would take all legal steps to punish those responsible for it.

23 July 1962

Velars-sur-Ouche, France
(SNCF)

39 killed, 46 injured

An overnight Paris–Marseilles train was partly derailed on a curve leading to a viaduct near Dijon. Most of it continued for several hundred yards, but the seventh coach plunged over the parapet, falling 60 feet on to the wooded slope below. It then slid down to the bottom of the valley, its front half being badly damaged. The recorder in the locomotive's cab registered over 80mph, showing that the derailment was caused by excessive speed.

9 October 1962

Piotrkow, Poland (PKP)

34 killed

Three coaches of an international express from Sofia to Warsaw were derailed, fouling the other track, where they were struck by a Rome–Moscow express travelling at about 65mph. A total of 16 coaches finished up off the rails. Although this was at the height of the Cold War, there were three British passengers in the two trains, one of them, a businesswoman from London, being slightly injured.

5 November 1962

Near Kumanov, Yugoslavia (JŽ)

23+ killed, 17 injured

Shortly after a train had been derailed, the Yugoslav news agency announced the preliminary casualty list, and added that the cause of the accident was under investigation.

11 November 1962

Gogra, India (North Eastern)

28 killed

In spite of the repeated efforts by railway staff and police to de-roof passengers travelling on top of a train, 28 of them were swept off as it crossed the Gogra Bridge.

RG **120** 514 (1964).

4 January 1963
Umeshnagar, India (North Eastern)

37 killed, 86 injured

Two trains collided in the Monghyr district of Bihar province.

RG **120** 514 (1964).

11 April 1963
Near Bandung, Indonesia (PJKA)

37 killed

According to the press report, the 'engine and leading wagons' of a Jakarta–Bandung express left the track and one of the vehicles, heavily loaded with passengers, rolled over several times as it plunged into a ravine.

26 July 1963
Skopje, Yugoslavia (JŽ)

20 killed

During the severe earthquake which devastated the capital of Macedonia, a train entering the city's main railway station was derailed. Although 20 of its passengers were killed, their numbers were small compared with those who died elsewhere in the area. The station was also destroyed by the shock wave.

4 August 1963
Montevideo, Uruguay

(40) killed

A passenger train was derailed at 40mph, seven miles outside the city of Montevideo, and two of its carriages were wrecked. The cause of the accident was officially given as sabotage.

9 November 1963
Yokohama, Japan (JNR)

161 killed, 119 injured

A goods train was derailed when it collided with a lorry on a level-crossing. The wreckage was then hit by two passenger trains running in opposite directions. The first was bound for Tokyo and was well filled with Saturday-night crowds. By coincidence, on the same day there was a major explosion in a coal mine at Omuta, which killed over 400 people.

24 December 1963
Szolnok, Hungary (MÁV)

45 killed

A collision occurred near Szolnok in the eastern part of the country. One of the drivers was subsequently held responsible for the accident, and given an eleven-year prison sentence.

(9 March 1964)
Baudpur, India (South East)

22 killed

A Madras–Calcutta express collided head-on with a stationary goods train.

RG **121** 677 (1965).

26 July 1964
Custoias, Portugal (CP)

94 killed, 79 seriously injured

A heavily-loaded twin-car diesel railcar was derailed on a curve three miles outside Oporto. The second coach hit the stone piers of a viaduct carrying a road over the line, and was wrecked, but the other stopped undamaged. The train was full of passengers returning from a Sunday on the beach at Póvoa de Varzim, and rescue work in the dark was difficult in the narrow cutting. The injured had to be carried up the steep slope on the backs of rescuers or on improvised stretchers. The bodies of the dead were hauled up with ropes. More than 500 people answered an appeal for blood donors. The size of the casualty list was partially due to the overcrowding, but most of the crowds had got on the first of the two metre-gauge trains laid on to take them back to Trindade terminus in Oporto. As a result it was carrying three times its proper load, and the second train was nearly empty. The train was estimated to be doing over 60mph at the time of the accident, which is appreciably faster than normal on this line, so excessive speed was the most likely cause of the accident.

Media reports attributed the cause to the 'couplings parting', which is traditionally one of the incorrect reasons they ascribe for a derailment. If a passenger train comes uncoupled, both halves will normally come to a halt automatically, still on the track. Occasionally the rear portion can catch the front one up, sometimes with sufficient force to cause an accident. Should a coach at the rear of a train become derailed for some reason, the 'snatch' or lack of alignment may cause the couplings to break or come undone. There is then a strong possibility that the derailed vehicle(s) may turn sideways, which renders them more likely to suffer damage. This can occur from the others thrashing about, or from hitting lineside obstructions, such as bridge piers. If this happens on a viaduct, the derailed coach can also fall over the edge. Vehicles simply becoming uncoupled are most unlikely to be exposed to these dangers unless they are already derailed. (A press photograph in the National Railway Museum collection of the derail-

ment of a steam-hauled express at Slough some years ago is similarly wrongly captioned, the accident having been caused by a broken rail.)

29 July 1964
Randfontein, South Africa (SAR)

21 + killed

A passenger train was derailed three miles outside the mining town of Randfontein.

20 December 1964
Tacotalpa, Mexico (FNdeM)

46 + killed, 26 injured

A passenger train filled with Christmas shoppers, returning home from Mexico City, Pueblea, and Vera Cruz, was hit from the rear by a goods train travelling at approximately 45mph. Its last two coaches were wrecked, the majority of the casualties being in the inner one. Five members of the crew of the goods train were detained by the police after the accident, but the driver could not immediately be traced. The apparent need for as many men as this to operate a goods train would indicate that productivity on the Mexican railways was even less than that in the United States.

23 December 1964
Near Dhanushkodi, India (Southern)

128 killed

A freak storm in the Palk Strait raised a tidal wave which overwhelmed a train.

RG **112** 473 (1966).

1965–1969

10 February 1965

Grisen, Spain (RENFE)

30 killed

Fire broke out in the woooden coaches of a Madrid–Barcelona train, shortly after it had left Grisen at 6.15am. The flames spread very quickly among the sleeping passengers, and some leapt from the train before it stopped. Several of the rear coaches were completely gutted, only the steel underframes and bogies remaining. The undamaged front portion of the train was used to transfer some of the injured to hospital in Zaragossa.

28 March 1965

Commendador, Brazil

21 killed, 40 injured

A passenger train collided with the derailed wagons of a goods train near Rio de Janeiro, its first two coaches being derailed.

4 October 1965

Effingham, South Africa (SAR)

89 killed

Three coaches of a crowded train carrying some 1,500 workers back to the black township of Kwa Mashu were derailed, for reasons which were not recorded in the British press. Shortly afterwards a crowd of blacks attacked and killed a white signalman, while another white man was able to escape.

9 December 1965

Toungoo, Burma

76 killed

A collision occurred between two trains.

20 December 1965

Lisbon, Portugal (CP)

20+ killed

A suburban train taking workers and Christmas shoppers home was in head-on collision with a goods train on the suburban line from Rossio station in Lisbon.

February 1966

India

37 killed

This was the first of three terrorist attacks by Naga tribesmen from Assam on passenger trains. A bomb exploded on the 'Assam Mail', but the location and the exact date were not reported.

20 April 1966

Lumding, India

57 killed

In spite of talks having been held the previous week between the Indian Prime Minister and the Naga leaders, a bomb was placed on a train while it was standing in the station at Lumding.

26 April 1966

Diphu, India

39 killed, (60) injured

This was a similar incident to the one six days earlier, and took place near the borders of Nagaland.

26 May 1966

Belgaum, India (Southern)

22 killed, 21 injured

An early-morning train from Banglapore to Poona was derailed. After visiting the site, the railway's Chief Engineer said the accident resulted from someone removing a fishplate.

31 May 1966

Near Bucharest, Roumania (CFR)

38 killed, 65 injured

A Bucharest–Galati express collided with a local train about five miles after starting. As a result, the country's Railways Minister was dismissed for allowing 'repeated cases of indiscipline on the railways'.

13 June 1966

Matunga, Bombay, India (Central)

60 killed

Two suburban electric trains collided head-on. No cause of the accident was given at the time, although two railwaymen were suspended from duty pending the results of the inquiry. The previous month the Central Railway had been judged to have the best safety record of the country's eight regional railways. Less than a week later, there was another railway collision, near Ajnmer, and the Minister of Railways called a meeting of the chief operating superintendents, mechanical engineers, and signalling and telecommunication engineers of all the country's railways to discuss the series of accidents which had claimed 247 lives so far that year. It is not known whether this total included those killed in the three terrorist attacks by the Nagas in Feruary and April.

16 November 1966

Nilopolis, Brazil

38 killed

Two suburban trains collided 18 miles north-west of Rio de Janeiro, the front two coaches of each being almost completely demolished. It was thought that the heavily-loaded up train had run past two signals at danger.

18 December 1966

Between Santa Eulalis and Villafranco del Campo, Spain (RENFE)

29 killed

A head-on collision took place between a train of empty fruit vans and a diesel railcar on a cold, foggy morning. The goods train was running eight hours late, and the driver failed to obey the signal indications at Villafranco, as well as missing the emergency hand-signals given by the station staff. He may have been misled by the fact that trains did not normally cross at this particular point. Having incorrectly entered the stretch of single track, the steam-hauled train collided with a diesel railcar travelling from Terueo to Saragossa. Fire broke out after the accident, most of the fatalities occurring in the leading coach, where most of the passengers were travelling because it had better heating.

6 July 1967

Langenweddingen, German Democratic Republic (DR)

94 killed

The barrier at a level-crossing on the line between Magdeburg and Halberstadt was catching on some telephone wires which stopped it descending to close the road when trains were approaching. As a result a petrol tanker was rammed by a train, which was then enveloped by the ensuing fire. The stationmaster and the gatekeeper were both given five-year prison sentences.

5 November 1967

Hither Green, England (British Railways, Southern Region)

49 killed, 78 injured, 27 seriously

On a Sunday evening a heavily-loaded diesel-electric train from Hastings to Charing Cross was derailed by a broken rail as it was approching Hither Green at about 70mph. Initially only the leading axle of the third coach was forced off the track by the 5-inch wedge of rail which had broken away at a joint. The other wheels jumped the gap, but a quarter of a mile later nearly the whole train was dragged off the track when the derailed wheelset hit a diamond cross-over.

Only the leading power car remained on the track, with four of the other eleven vehicles finishing up on their sides.

The stretch of line concerned is a very busy one, and took a lot of pounding from the nose-suspended traction motors of the electric and diesel-electric multiple-units. Work was going on to up-grade the track, and four months earlier the line speed had been put up from 75 to 90 for electric trains with modern bogies, although the Hastings diesels had their own general maximum of 75mph. This was partly because their bogie suspensions had been stiffened to avoid the coaches swaying too much in the tight-to-gauge tunnels. At the time of the derailment, the train had just started slowing from full speed to conform with the 60mph limit which began at Hither Green station.

The broken rail occurred where two short 'closure rails' had been laid between lengths of continuously-welded track (CWR) which was being installed as part of the line's up-grading. Because of inadequate support from the ballast, the rail joint was over-stressed by passing trains, and fatigue cracks in the rail and one of the fishplates caused both to fail by brittle fracture as the Hastings train passed over them. Col. D. McMullen, the Inspecting Officer, found that the general maintenance of the stretch of line concerned was inadequate for the speeds being attained, and a general limit of 60mph, imposed immediately after the accident, remained in force for some time. The installation of CWR was speeded up, and the use of 'closure rails' stopped. Comparative tests of the Hastings units, noted for their particularly rough riding, were carried out on the Southern and Eastern Regions. Although well within safety limits on the route where they were used, the ride was found to be significantly better on the East Coast Main Line. Col. McMullen also recommended the use of fully-suspended traction motors on all new stock.

Nock, p220. Rolt, p132/133, 254. RM **139** xiii (April 1993).

27 January 1968

General Gamara, Brazil

41 killed, 57 injured

No details were published in this country about this accident, which occurred in the province of Rio Grande do Sol.

15 March 1968

Between Robledo de Chavela and Santa Maria de la Alameda, Spain (RENFE)

25 killed, 80+ injured

One of the air-conditioned diesel-railcar express trains, known as *Tren Español Rapido*, or TER, hit a runaway engineering train as it was climbing the hills of the Sierra de Guadarrams, en route from Madrid to Avila. It consisted of two two-car sets, and its passengers were enjoying a meal. Engineering work was in progress on the northbound line beyond Robledo, with single-line working over the other track. After an engineer's train had finished unloading rails on this line, it was decided to run it back down the gradient as far as Santa Maria to get it out of the way of the approaching diesel, using a small 'tractor' as motive power. Unfortunately the crew lost control on the falling gradient, and it shot through the station, colliding with the passenger train two miles further on, just as coffee was being served. The leading coach of the diesel was badly damaged, and fire broke out in the wreckage. Helicopters flew the seriously injured to a football ground at El Scorial, but the others continued their journey in the undamaged rear two cars of the express.

19 March 1968

Yalvigi, India

40+ killed, 38 injured

The 'Deccan Express' from Poona to Bangalore collided head-on with a local train in the state of Mysore, 340 miles south of Bombay. Three doctors on the train worked by torchlight to treat the injured until a relief train arrived from Hubli.

1 October 1968

Corinth, Greece

34 killed, 150 injured

Two passenger trains collided on their way to Athens. They were carrying voters who had returned to their home towns to take part in the country's constitutional referendum. All that remained of one of the wrecked coaches was its frames.

22 December 1968

East of Budapest, Hungary (MÁV)

43 killed

It was reported by the Yugoslav news agency that a collision had occurred 20 miles east of Budapest. A goods and a passenger train were involved, the first three coaches of the latter being badly damaged.

15 July 1969

Near Cuttack, India

100+ killed

A goods train collided with the rear of a passenger train 25 miles north of Cuttack in the state of Orissa.

30 July 1969

Near Gostivar, Yugoslavia (JŽ)

29 killed, 17 injured

During shunting operations at Gostivar, on the line from Skopje, three 40-ton tank wagons got out of control and ran away down the steep incline towards Tetovo, 19 miles away. A two-car diesel railcar had already left this point, and there was no way of preventing a collision. The impact was so severe that the length of the leading coach was reduced from 32 feet to about six. The officials at Gostivar station were placed under arrest pending possible charges of negligence.

31 December 1969

Near Theis, Senegal

20 + killed

A Dakar—St Louis passenger train collided with a goods train near Theis, about 30 miles from Dakar.

1970–1974

1 February 1970

Benavidez, Argentina (General Mitre)

236 killed, (400) injured

A local train, loaded with about 1,000 people who had been visiting the resorts along the estuary of the River Platte, had to stop on its way into Buenos Aires because of trouble with a fuel injector. It should have been protected by signals, but, because of an error by the signalman, a double-headed Tucunan–Buenos Aires express behind it was not stopped, and hit the rear of the local at about 60mph. There were no fatalities among the passengers on the express, but the last two coaches of the local train completely disintegrated. The collision took place on a double-track stretch, provided with semaphore signals, but the staff at Benavidez had been held up at pistol-point earlier in the day, and this was believed to have been a contributory factor.

The accident occurred in an isolated and marshy area, and rescue work was difficult. The magnitude of the disaster was not realised at first, and work went on through the night and into the following morning. An emergency hospital was set up nearby, and air force helicopters were used to bring in medical supplies and evacuate some of the injured.

RG **126** 127 (1970).

16 February 1970

Langalanga, Nigeria

(150) killed

The diesel locomotive was derailed and plunged down an 80ft embankment at Langalanga, a remote site south of the town of Kaduna, taking four coaches with it. The accident occurred on the first day of the Muslim festival of Eid-al-Kabir, and the train was crowded with pilgrims. Cars and lorries parked nearby provided light for the rescue work, but 52 of the injured were said to have been killed when the lorry taking them to hospital crashed.

9 August 1970

Plencia, Spain

33 killed, (200) injured

A train returning to the industrial city of Bilbao on a Sunday with day-trippers from the coast collided with a goods train. Two stationmasters were arrested pending the outcome of an investigation into its cause. The wooden rolling-stock was badly splintered in the collision.

31 December 1970

Ardekan, Iran

70+ killed, 130 injured

Two trains collided on a stretch of new line on the edge of the desert, one of them carrying 300 railwaymen and miners on their way to Isfahan for the New Year holiday. Although a government spokesman would only confirm 15 deaths, journalists at the scene gave the higher figures quoted above. The collision was blamed on a signalman's error and poor communications.

9 February 1971

Aitrang, West Germany (DB)

28 killed

The Trans-Europ Express 'Bavaria', running from Münich to Zürich, was derailed in the dark when it took a curve near Aitrang station at far too high a speed. Some of the wreckage fouled the opposite line, where it was hit by a four-coach diesel multiple-unit running from Kempten to Kaufbeuren. There was a speed limit of 50mph over the curve, but the recorder on the locomotive of the express, whose driver was killed, registered more than 80mph. He had driven over the line for 20 years, but no reason was established for his failure to slow to the correct speed.

Ritzau, p151, *156.*

14 February 1971

Vranduk Tunnel, Yugoslavia (JŽ)

34+ killed

The diesel-electric locomotive on a train carrying some 200 passengers caught fire inside the mile-long Vranduk (or Vrandul) Tunnel between Zenica and Doboi in Bosnia. It stopped about 300 yards from the mouth of the tunnel, and the driver tried to fight the fire with an extinguisher, but it spread to the coaches. A number of passengers jumped out of the train and tried to escape, but some were overcome by the smoke as they groped their way through the darkness. Many of those killed were workers on their way to a Zenica steel mill, and volunteers from there helped with the rescue work.

27 May 1971

Radevormwald, West Germany (DB)

46 killed, 25 injured

A diesel railcar carrying a party of children home from a school outing to Bremen was in collision with a goods train. The latter was booked to cross the passenger train at Dahlerau, but the driver left the loop before the train in the other direction had arrived. He said he had stopped but then saw a sign from the stationmaster indicating he should depart, and accordingly entered the single line ahead. The stationmaster ran after the train waving a red light, but was unable to attract the driver's notice, so returned to the station and was able to warn the emergency services before the accident took place.

Ritzau, p119.

21 July 1971

Freiburg-im-Breisgau, West Germany (DB)

22 killed

The 'Schweis Express' from Basel to Copenhagen was completely derailed when it took a curve too fast on the main line from Switzerland along the valley of the Rhine. The locomotive and twelve coaches fell down a 15ft embankment and through a house, while the remaining two vehicles finished up broadside-on across the running lines.

Examination of the speed recorder showed that the train had been travelling at over 85mph at the time of the accident, almost twice the permitted speed. Survivors spoke of the coaches swaying from side to side beforehand, with luggage being dislodged from the racks. This accident, together with the one at Aitrang the previous February, made the railway authorities realise that, at the high speeds starting to be reached by trains, drivers could become disorientated at night, and fail to brake in time as they approached a permanent speed restriction. It was accordingly decided to replace the small kilometre-posts with large lineside boards with the distance figures on them every 200 meters. These have since become standard on the DB, and are affixed to the nearest mast for the overhead wires on electrified lines.

Ritzau, p153.

4 August 1971
Near Belgrade, Yugoslavia (JŽ)

35 killed

A goods train should have stopped at Lipe station south of Belgrade, to pass a passenger train taking some 300 people home after visiting a fair, and the two collided on the single-track stretch beyond. The driver of the freight and his assistant, as well as four railwaymen from Lipe station, were arrested after the accident.

26 October 1971
Between Nagoya and Osaka, Japan (Kinki Nippon Tetsudo)

23 killed

There was a head-on collision on a single-track line of the private Kinki Nippon Railway between the two

Japanese cities of Nagoya and Osaka, in the Kii Peninsula.

31 March 1972
Near Potgietersrus, Transvaal, South Africa (SAR)

38 killed, 174 injured

A passenger train was derailed on the approach to a bridge across a river, the diesel locomotive bumping along the sleepers until it fell into the almost-dry bed of the river, pulling some of the coaches with it. All the fatalities were 'non-whites'. Railway officials stated that, although there had been no explosion, signs of sabotage had been discovered at the scene.

26 April 1972
North of Bangalore, India

21 killed, 37 injured

The locomotive and four coaches of a passenger train were derailed.

4 June 1972
Jessore, Bangladesh (BRB)

76 killed, 500+ injured

A collision took place between a passenger train and a stationary goods one, at least ten coaches being wrecked.

17 June 1972
Vierzy Tunnel, France (SNCF)

108 killed, 240 injured

After 110 years, and without any warning, part of the roof of a 875-yard tunnel on the line between Paris and Soissons collapsed, blocking both tracks with a pile of rubble. Almost simultaneously trains in both directions between Gare du Nord in Paris and Laon, travelling at about 70mph, hit the obstruction, filling the bore of the tunnel with a plug of twisted metal. No sign of this double collision was visible outside the tunnel, the only unusual happening being the continual ringing of a warning bell at a level-crossing. Rescue work in the confined space was very difficult, with oxy-acetylene cutting equipment being ruled out because of the ventilation problems. There was also the danger of further roof-falls, and massive hydraulic jacks were used to provide support. The last two living passengers were released 40 hours after the accident, while the final body, that of one of the drivers, was only removed after five days. Several months elapsed before the tunnel was reopened.

Shaw, p412.

21 July 1972
Near Jerez, Spain (RENFE)

76 killed, 103 injured

A Madrid–Cadiz express, with some 500 passengers aboard, collided with a local train 19 miles from Jerez just after 7am. There were approximately 200 passengers on the local train, including 60 sailors on leave. The local train failed to obey a danger signal, and the position of the points made it collide with the express.

6 August 1972
Liaquatpur, Pakistan (PR)

38 killed

An express for Karachi was mistakenly diverted into a loop on the main line from Lahore, and collided head-on with a stationary goods train.

29 September 1972
Malmesbury, South Africa (SAR)

(100) killed

A nine-coach passenger train was derailed in the early morning near Malmesbury, about 40 miles north-east of Cape Town. Most, if not all, the victims were blacks.

5 October 1972
Saltillo, Mexico (FNdeM)

208 killed

A derailment occurred of part of one of the extra trains put on to take pilgrims and holidaymakers back from festivities in the mining centre of San Luis de Potosi. Nine of the 22 coaches were derailed through excessive speed, and four of them then caught fire. Six of the train crew were arrested, the disaster being ascribed to the locomotive crew being intoxicated. Another railwayman was said to be 'missing'.

Shaw, p409.

30 October 1972
Chicago, Illinois, United States of America (Illinois Central)

45 killed, 330 injured

The driver of one of the new double-deck 'Highliner' electric multiple-units failed to stop at a halt in Chicago, in spite of being told by the conductor before setting out. While 27th Street was shown in the timetable as a 'flag stop', made only on request, in practice this train always called there for the benefit of the staff at a nearby hospital. When the mistake was realised the train was braked, coming to a stand over 200 yards clear of the platform, and, significantly, more than 130 yards beyond an automatic block signal. The crew decided to reverse the train back into the platform, and, while this was happening, the next train, booked non-stop through 27th Street, collided with the rear of it at about 50mph. It consisted of conventional stock, and considerable damage was caused to the ends of those vehicles which took the brunt of the collision.

The second train received a yellow aspect at the previous signal, which only gave it permission to enter the block beyond at a maximum speed of 30mph. Although this was exceeded by a considerable margin, the driver still ought to have been able to see the train ahead and stop clear of the obstruction. He did not do so, but the prime cause of the accident was the failure of the crew of the 'Highliner' to take proper precautions before setting-back. In Britain there are very strict rules about setting back on normal lines, although on a single-line section the situation is different. When a train has the tablet or staff, or its electronic equivalent, for such a section, there is no objection to it setting back if required, without any formalities. In steam days it was not unknown for a train to make several attempts to climb a particularly steep bank, going back further each time to charge the gradient at a progressively higher speed.

Shaw, p361.

30 October 1972

Near Karl Marx Stadt, German Democratic Republic (DR)

25 killed, 70 injured

Two expresses collided in thick fog.

Ritzau, p180.

31 October 1972

Eskisehir, Turkey (TCDD)

30+ killed, (50) injured

A passenger train collided with an oil train. Several coaches rolled down a cliff, and fire broke out in the wreckage.

6 November 1972

Hokuriku Tunnel, Japan (JNR)

30 killed, 700+ injured

This twin-track tunnel is 13.87km long (just over $8\frac{1}{2}$ miles). In the early hours of the morning fire broke out in the dining car of the *'Kitaguni'* ('North Country') express while it was in the tunnel. The driver stopped to try to uncouple the blazing vehicle, but the power system failed and plunged the tunnel into darkness. The sleepy passengers climbed down and tried to make their way out of the tunnel. Some were picked up by a train travelling in the opposite direction, but others formed a human chain to make their way out. Later rescuers wearing breathing equipment backed open wagons into the tunnel from each end to rescue the survivors. There was some press criticism about the lack of ventilation equipment in the tunnel.

Since this disaster the Japanese railway rules have been changed, and, in case of fire, drivers do not voluntarily stop in a tunnel. The same basic philosophy applies in the Channel Tunnel, where, if fire should break out in any train, it will normally continue through the tunnel to the other end. Arrangements are provided for the affected section to be evacuated and then isolated by the internal fire doors. If, for any reason, a train is forced to stop, the central Service Tunnel will provide a refuge for those aboard, as it is fed from both ends by air at a higher pressure than that in the Rail Tunnels. This philosophy results in an unusual anomaly with the automatic doors of the 'Eurostar' inter-

Above *The broken rail at Hither Green, south of London, which derailed a diesel-electric mult-iple-unit from Hastings on 5 November 1967, killing 49 people. It will be seen that a crack spread through one of the bolt-holes, allowing a small triangular section to become detached. One wheel on the third coach was derailed at the gap, but several hundred yards further on this dragged the rest of the train off the track at a diamond crossing.* (Colin J. Marsden's Collection)

Below *Zagreb station was littered with derailed coaches on 30 August 1974 after a train from Belgrade to Dortmund had approached it at too high a speed. The crash killed 153 migrant workers returning to Germany at the end of their summer holiday. The driver was later sentenced to 15 years in prison after admitting he had fallen asleep.* (Popperfoto)

Left *Two trains collided head-on between Warngau and Schaftlach, south of Munich, on the evening of 8 June 1975. As shown by the extent of the damage, the closing speed was high, with wreckage from the coaches being piled on top of the two diesel-hydraulic locomotives. Errors by the station staff at both ends of the section caused the accident, and three of them were later given suspended prison sentences and fined.* (Popperfoto)

Below left *An aerial view of the rescue work going on in Sydney on 18 January 1977 after an inbound commuter train had been derailed near Granville. Two of the coaches caused a road over-bridge to collapse on to them, adding to the death toll. The far end of the failed span had clearly not been tied very firmly into the abutment.* (Popperfoto)

Right *A view of the wreckage after the head-on collision between two suburban trains outside Barcelona on 28 February 1977. It will be seen how the electric locomotive of the inbound train fell on to the adjoining main road.* (Popperfoto)

Below *The 'Romulus Express' from Rome failed near Vienna on 6 July 1982. While it was standing a local train crashed into its rear, killing four people.* (Popperfoto)

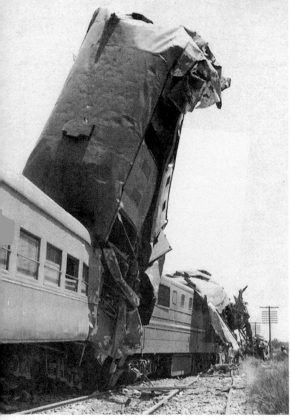

Above *The very unusual collapse of the bridge at Ishurdi in Bangladesh on 22 March 1983 is apparent from this photograph taken the following day. In the centre of the picture the diesel locomotive can be seen still on one span which has fallen at the run-on end, with further spans beyond having failed in the same way. On the right are two of the derailed coaches.* (Popperfoto)

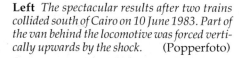

Left *The spectacular results after two trains collided south of Cairo on 10 June 1983. Part of the van behind the locomotive was forced vertically upwards by the shock.* (Popperfoto)

Above *On 14 September 1985 there was a collision at Rennens in Switzerland between a regional train and two light locomotives. The latter can be seen on their sides, while rescue work takes place on the leading vehicle of the passenger train. In spite of the devastation, only five people were killed, and 42 injured.* (Popperfoto)

Below *The collision at Argenton-sur-Creuse in France which occurred on 31 August 1985 after a train had been derailed because it failed to obey a temporary speed restriction.* (Author's Collection)

Above *A day after the disaster took place, smoke still rises from the wreckage caused by the head-on collision at Hinton in Alberta, Canada, on 8 February 1986. The passenger train was travelling from left to right, and hit a freight train which failed to wait for it in a siding. The locomotives, which burst into flames on impact, lie somewhere below the pile of debris.* (Popperfoto)

Below *The devastated area in Arzamas, USSR after 120 tons of industrial explosive blew up as a train approached a level-crossing on 4 June 1988. In the foreground is the crater, 85 feet deep, which marks where the three wagons were at the time.* (Popperfoto)

Right *In the confines of the low-level platforms at Gare de Lyon in Paris, rescue workers struggle to release victims after the collision between two suburban trains on 27 June 1988.* (Popperfoto)

Below *Another view of the point of collision between the two electric suburban trains at Gare de Lyon in June 1988. Debris has been forced back into the leading coach of the incoming train.* (Author's Collection)

Above *The only major accident involving one of the French TGVs occurred on 23 September 1988, when one hit a stalled lorry on a level-crossing at Voiron, between Lyon and Grenoble. One of the train drivers was killed and the other was among the 36 people injured. The accident occurred on an ordinary stretch of line, and there are no level-crossings on the actual* Lignes à Grandes Vitesse. *Two partial derailments have, however, taken place at full speed, but the articulation system adopted on these trains has kept the derailed bogies in line, and there were no serious casualties.*

(Popperfoto)

Below *The aftermath of the head-on collision at Pubail in Bangladesh on 15 January 1989. Some of the soldiers who assisted with the rescue work can be seen on the line-side.*   (Popperfoto)

Above *The wreckage of the trains on the Trans-Siberian railway which were engulfed by the natural-gas fireball on 4 June 1989. The force of the explosion is all too evident.*
(Popperfoto)

Right *Breakdown cranes clear the debris of the Guadalajara–Mexicali train which fell into the San Rafael de Bamoa River on 10 August 1989. There is no sign of the viaduct which collapsed, and the coaches which crashed into the river have been recovered.* (Popperfoto)

Above *The result of the rear-end collision at Miaoli in Taiwan on 15 November 1991, in which members of a tour party from Okinawa were involved. Several Japanese were among the killed and injured.* (Popperfoto)

Above left *Two diesel trains collided head-on in Shigaraki, central Japan, on 14 May 1991, killing 40 people and injuring more than 400. It was the country's worst railway accident for 28 years.* (Popperfoto)

Left *A breakdown crane helps to clear the wreckage in Ghotki station, Pakistan, after a passenger train collided with a stationary goods train on 8 June 1991.* (Popperfoto)

Above *A bogie and the diesel motor from the locomotive form the foreground to this picture of the debris caused by the collision between a Riga–Moscow express and a freight train at Tver on 3 March 1992.* (Popperfoto)

Left *When two trains collided head-on in Depok, a suburb of Jakarta, on 2 November 1993, the shock of the impact pushed their ends upwards. Troops helping with the rescue work await assistance to drag the trains apart to retrieve trapped bodies.* (Popperfoto)

Above *The disaster to Amtrak's 'Sunshine Limited' on 22 September 1993 was not of the railway's making. A tug and barges had hit the viaduct a few miles north of Mobile in Alabama, but the crewman in charge did not report it. An hour later, the viaduct collapsed under the train, and 47 passengers and crew died when several of the sleeping cars plunged into the bayou.* (Popperfoto)

Right *American circus trains have featured in some of the disasters listed in the Chronology, but there were fortunately no fatalities when 19 of the 59 vehicles in the Ringling Brothers and Barnum & Bailey Circus train were derailed on 13 January 1994, at Lakeland, Florida, en route from St Petersburg to Orlando. There were indications that the 'switch' (points) at a junction had been wrongly set for a very sharp turn-out.* (Popperfoto)

Trains have been derailed as a result of incorrect actions by road users as well as river craft. The illustration to the left shows the aftermath of a collision between Amtrak's 'Silver Meteor' near Kissimmee in Florida on 26 November 1993, when it hit an 80-ton electric turbine on a level-crossing. There were no fatalities, unlike the accident at Hixon in Staffordshire on 6 January 1968, when a road transporter with a 160-ton transformer tried to cross the railway at an automatic crossing, regardless of the fact that its maximum speed would not permit it to get clear if a train approached. The lower photograph shows an accident of a different sort that occurred in 1957, after a lorry had damaged the railway bridge in the background, derailing the Japanese National Railway 4-8-4 and several of its coaches. Three people were killed in this accident. (Both Popperfoto)

Above *One of the German ICE trains was involved in a most unusual accident in March 1993. As it traversed a junction near Hanau, the points changed under the last coach, and the rear power car took the other route. Speed was low, and the train stopped in the unusual position shown, without causing any injuries.*   (Popperfoto)

Below *Scottish North Eastern Railway 'Crewe-type' 2-4-0 No.48 after its boiler exploded near Bridge of Dunn on 23 March 1872. It had just assisted a goods train to Glasterlaw, and was returning down the bank when the explosion occurred. This was clearly not caused by too low a water level, and it was found that the boiler shell had been weakened by grooving.*

(J. A. Anderson/The Railway Magazine)

In the chapter on boiler explosions details are given of the unusual incident which occurred on a PLM 2-8-2 locomotive between Culoz and La Burbanche, France in August 1935. Its boiler was blown off the frames, and landed in a field 272 feet away, as shown in the upper photograph. The rest of the locomotive remained on the rails, and continued along the track with its train until being brought to a stand by the action of the automatic brake. The lower photograph shows the remains of the locomotive. (*Both* Popperfoto)

national trains. If anyone pulls the emergency release on one of these, it will sound an alarm, but will not stop the train. In contrast, on the British Inter-City 225s, pulling the door release sets off an automatic brake application. With each type of stock the door is only freed for opening when the train has been brought to a stop. This provides a good example of the way in which the risks of every potentially dangerous situation have to be assessed individually.

1 February 1973
Algeria (SNTF)

35 killed, 51 injured

A passenger train left the rails in the eastern part of the country.

27 March 1974
São Miguel, Mozambique

60 killed

A passenger train from Rhodesia collided head-on with a train carrying petroleum products near Lourenço Marques. Burning oil was sprayed over the passenger coaches, and the heat of the blaze prevented the fire tenders approaching the vehicles for some time. The injured were taken to hospital by helicopter.

30 August 1974
Zagreb, Yugoslavia (JŽ)

153 killed

An express from Belgrade to Dortmund, carrying some 400 migrant workers back to West Germany at the end of their holidays, was totally derailed after taking the curve on the approach to the station at over 55mph, instead of the 30mph permitted. It had also ran past a stop signal. A day of national mourning was proclaimed, President Tito intervening to ensure that it was observed. Subsequent tests with some similar coaches detached from a Munich–Belgrade express showed that the accident would not have occurred at the regulation speed. The crew of the locomotive maintained that the brakes had failed, but they were shown to be in order after the accident, so the staff were charged with causing the disaster. Seven months later, when the trial took place, the driver and his assistant admitted that they had both dozed off before reaching Zagreb, having worked for more than 300 hours during the previous month. They were found guilty, the driver being sentenced to 15 years in prison, and his assistant, eight.

31 October 1974
Mohanganj, India

43 killed, (60) injured

There was an explosion on the Delhi–Calcutta–Upper India express, apparently caused by fireworks being carried by a passenger. This set fire to the train, and many of the fatalities occurred when passengers tried to escape by jumping from it while it was still moving.

1975–1979

22 February 1975

Near Tretten, Norway (NSB)

29 killed

The Trondheim–Oslo express was booked to cross the corresponding train in the other direction at Tretten, north of Lillehammer. On this particular day the latter was running late, and the train from Trondheim was irregularly allowed on to the single-line section before the other had arrived.

28 February 1975

Moorgate, London, England (London Transport)

43 killed, 74 injured

In 1975 Moorgate station, as well as serving the well-known Inner Circle tracks, was also the terminus of a self-contained London Transport line stretching $2\frac{3}{4}$ miles north to Drayton Park. Unlike the normal deep-level lines, it had been constructed to take rolling-stock of main-line loading gauge, so trains from the Great Northern Railway's suburban routes could reach the City of London, but the connection had never been completed. Although another start had been made to adapt the route for this purpose in the early 1960s, nothing came of it, and the conversion was not to take place until a

couple of years after this disaster occurred. So, in its final years of working as part of London Transport, tube stock of the '1938' type was being used.

For reasons which were never determined, on the morning of 28 February the driver of a six-coach incoming train failed to slow down or stop as he brought his train into No. 9 platform at Moorgate. This was one of the terminal ones used by the Drayton Park shuttle, and, as customary at many stations of this sort, there was an over-run beyond the inner end of the platform. It was just under 67ft long, and a 36ft length was fitted with a sand-drag to help stop any train whose driver slightly misjudged his stop. On this occasion the train was going far too fast for this to have any material effect, and it hit the end-wall of the tunnel so fast that the first and second coaches were impacted to half their normal length. The front half of the third vehicle was affected in the same way, and all this wreckage filled the tunnel, making access for the rescue and medical teams extremely difficult. Although many of the passengers were killed outright, work went on for over 13 hours to free the last of those still alive, although that person unfortunately later died of his injuries. The last-but-one to be got out was a young woman police constable who was trapped in the wreckage by one leg, and was only freed after her foot had been amputated by a medical team sent in from one of the London hospitals. Her fortitude made a great impression on everyone, and she subsequently received more than 2,000 gifts and cards from all over the world, as well as being visited in hospital by the Prince of Wales.

The usual inspecting officer's inquiry took place, but Lt Col. I. K. A. McNaughton was unable to find any reason for the driver's action. When his body had been finally recovered, $4\frac{1}{2}$ days after the accident, no medical reasons could be determined for his failure to stop, and X-rays of the bones in his hands and arms showed his hands were on the controls at the time of impact. Nor was there anything wrong with the train. It was concluded that the responsibility for the accident lay entirely with the driver, even though the reason for his failure to stop could not be determined.

To prevent any similar future accidents, here or in other stations of the same type on the Underground, it was recommended that a control system should be provided to stop the train automatically if the driver failed to take the necessary action. London Transport already provided train-stops at each signal, which consist of an arm which rises beside the track when the signal is at danger. If one of these is passed in that position, it hits a lever on the leading bogie, which immediately applies the air brake along the train. Approaching a dead-end, one or more similar train-stops are provided, and the controls to lower them only operate if the speed of the train is below the safety-limit. These are now used widely on London Underground, and are known as 'Moorgate controls'. After the line became part of the Great Northern suburban system, the new rolling stock had a far higher top speed than the normal LT tube trains. As an added precaution, these Class 313 units are electrically prevented from running faster than 30mph in these tunnels, where they pick up their current from the third-rail system, rather than the overhead wires used north of Drayton Park.

This is one of the relatively few British railway accidents which has had a book written about it, the author being Sally Holloway.

Holloway. Rolt, p297.

22 May 1975

Near Kenitra, Morocco (ONCFM)

34+ killed

A passenger train left the track.

8 June 1975

Between Warngau and Schaftlach, West Germany (DB)

41 killed, 122 injured

Two passenger trains collided just before dusk one Sunday night, on a single-track section of line south of Munich. Some of the severely injured were flown to hospital in that city by helicopter, as the roads were badly congested as people returned after a weekend in the mountains. Errors by the station staff at the two ends of the section caused the accident, although the press made play of the fact that the Public Timetable showed trains were booked to arrive simultaneously at both ends of the single-line section. As most readers will know, for various reasons there are often differences between the times advertised to the public and those in the Working Timetables, this point being made by the DB President at a press conference. In the following year the two stationmasters and a clerk were given suspended prison sentences. Each of the former was also fined DM5,000, and the clerk, DM2,000, the money going to the Red Cross. (At the then rate of exchange, the Mark was worth about a third of what it is today relative to Sterling.)

Ritzau, p126.

20 October 1975

Mexico City

34+ killed

There was a rear-end collision between two trains in an underground station in Mexico City, the one in front having stopped because someone had pulled the communication cord. The collision took place at considerable speed, one of the coaches in the second train rising up and ripping open the roof of the station. As at Winsford in April 1948, the act of pulling the communication cord should not, of itself, be enough to cause a collision.

4 May 1976

Near Schiedam, Netherlands (NS)

24 killed

The 'Rhine Express' had been late leaving the Hook of Holland, and was switched to the left-hand track as it approached the Rotterdam–Den Haag line at Schiedam. (Now Rotterdam West-Schiedam.) Most of the Dutch main lines are fully signalled for use in either direction, and this particular switch was to enable the international train to overtake an eastbound, regular-interval stopping train on the right-hand track. A westbound train, consisting of two two-car 'Sprinter' electric multiple-units, failed to obey the signal stopping it entering the branch line to the Hook, and hit the Class 1300 electric locomotive head-on, just as it was overtaking the stationary local service. As a result all three trains were simultaneously in collision, the first coach of the westbound 'Sprinter' being crushed between the two opposing trains. By that time 25 per cent of the Dutch network had already been equipped with the continuous Automatic Train Control, and the installation programme was accelerated. As a result, 60 per cent had been equipped by 1987, and the figure rose to 85 per cent by 1992.

23 May 1976

Seoul, South Korea (KNR)

20 killed

A passenger train collided with a road tanker carrying inflammable material on a level-crossing in the capital, and fire broke out.

6 September 1976

Benoni, South Africa (SAR)

31 killed

While an express was stopped by signals, it was hit from the rear by a commuter train heading for the black township of Daveyton. All the fatalities were on the local train, and the only whites killed were the driver and ticket-collector. A railway spokesman ruled out sabotage as the cause, so the accident must have been either the result of a train failing to obey signals or a signalling error.

10 October 1976

Mexico (FNdeM)

20+ killed

A holiday excursion was in collision with a goods train, one of its coaches falling into a ravine. The accident occurred near the border with the United States.

18 January 1977

Sydney, Australia

83 killed, 213 injured

An inbound commuter train was derailed near Granville station on the outskirts of Sydney in New South Wales. Although the train was only travelling at about 20mph, the condition of the track was very poor, and two of the derailed coaches came into contact with the piers of a wide road bridge. This collapsed on to the train, causing many of the fatalities, and making the rescue work much more difficult, so that it lasted into the following night. The operation was complicated by the need to control an estimated 5,000 sightseers, which required the services of some 250 police at the site. Another unfortunate aspect was the fact that a number of death threats were received by the driver of the train, who was completely exonerated from blame at the subsequent inquiry.

19 January 1977
Varanasi (Benares), India

28 killed, 78 injured

A passenger train collided with a stationary one ahead near the Hindu sacred city of Benares or Varanasi, in the province of Uttar Pradesh.

28 February 1977
Near Barcelona, Spain
(Ferrocariles Catalanes)

22 killed

There was a head-on collision between two crowded suburban trains about twelve miles from the city centre. The inbound working was full of workers who had just finished their shift at the large SEAT car factory. This train was derailed and fell across a main road, blocking it for several hours.

30 May 1977
Assam, India

85 killed

Heavy rains had caused floods which weakened a bridge across a river about 70 miles from Gauhati in Assam. The locomotive and four coaches fell into the swollen river.

27 June 1977
Lebus, German Democratic Republic (DR)

29 killed

A steam-hauled express from Zittau to the Baltic port of Stralsund collided with a diesel-hauled freight train near the Polish frontier in the early hours of the morning. Fire broke out, gutting both locomotives, and the line was still blocked twelve hours later by smouldering wreckage. The express had been routed on to the wrong line as it passed through the junctions at Bossen. With the easing of secrecy about disasters in communist countries, western newspaper correspondents were allowed to visit the site during the afternoon.

Ritzau, p181.

8 September 1977
Assiut, Egypt (ER)

25 killed

Eight of the eleven coaches of a Cairo–Aswan express were derailed while the train was travelling at about 70mph in Upper Egypt. Buses, taxis and private cars were used to transfer the uninjured passengers into Assiut. The figure of 25 fatalities was given by the country's transport minister, although a Cairo newspaper was quoting a death-role of at least 70 three days after the accident.

10 October 1977
Naini, India

61+ killed, 151 injured, 81 seriously

During the early hours of the morning, a passenger train collided with the rear of a freight working in Naini station, near Allahabad in northern India.

(12 November 1977)
Mexico (FNdeM)

37 killed, (12) injured

A train hit a fuel tanker on a level-crossing about 60 miles from Cuidad Juarez.

4 January 1978
Esenkoy, Turkey (TCD)

30 + killed, 100 + injured

Two passenger trains collided head-on in a remote part of the country. There had been over 400 passengers aboard them, and on the following day people were still trapped in some of the seven coaches, three of which were piled on top of each other. Rescue work had to be carried out from the railway lines on either side, as access by road or air was impossible because of winter storms.

25 February 1978
Near Santa Fé, Argentina

53 killed, 56 injured

This was another level-crossing collision where a large number of fatalities occurred among those travelling on the train.

15 April 1978
Vado, Italy (FS)

47 killed, (200) injured

This disaster began with the derailment of a northbound local train in a pass about 20 miles south of Bologna. The locomotive finished up foul of the other line, where it was hit by the Venice–Rome 'Arrow of the Lagoon' express, its

coaches rolling down a steep embankment.

9 January 1979
Ankara, Turkey (TCDD)

30 killed, (100) injured

A commuter train ran into the rear of another near the capital, Ankara. The coaches of the stationary train caught fire. Only five days previously 16 people had been killed in another railway accident near the same city.

26 January 1979
Chuadunga, Bangladesh (BRB)

70 + killed, 200 + injured

A crowded train left the track and overturned near Chuadunga, 200 miles west of Dhaka.

21 August 1979
Taling Chan, Thailand (SRT)

52 killed, (200) injured

A passenger train collided head-on with a goods train. One of the coaches in the former overturned and rolled down an embankment. Afterwards it was reported that the police were looking for the driver of the goods train, as well as the signalman, both of whom had disappeared. The chairman of the railway made it clear that they were not being charged in connection with the accident, but their statements were required for the inquiry into its cause.

13 September 1979
Stalac, Yugoslavia (JŽ)

60 killed

The driver of a goods train ran past a signal, probably because he had fallen asleep. As a result his train was in collision with a passenger express for Skopje. Many of the passengers aboard were young army recruits travelling from Belgrade to training camps in southern Yugoslavia. As a result of the collision some of the coaches were reduced to a quarter of their original length. Commenting on the accident, *The Times* said that country's railways had a poor safety record, although there had been an improvement in the previous two years. Some 700 people had been killed and 2,000 injured between 1971 and 1976.

(31 October 1979)

Djibouti

50 killed, 30 injured

A train was derailed in the former French colony of Somaliland, south-west of the capital.

3 December 1979

Londa, India

23 killed, 12 + injured

A passenger train was derailed in the southern part of the sub-continent.

1980–1984

10 June 1980

Kampuchea

150 + killed, (250) injured

After many years of war and revolution, guerillas, who were supporting the Khmer Rouge regime after it had been ousted from government, carried out a campaign against the country's communications. On this date they attacked a train carrying civilians between Battanbang and Phnom Penh, 43 miles northwest of the capital. After bringing it to a halt by a mine or a missile attack, it was fired on by groups of guerillas.

19 August 1980

Torun, Poland (PKP)

69 killed, 50 injured

A passenger train from the port of Kolobrzeg on the Baltic collided head-on with a freight train near Torun, 120 miles north-west of Warsaw. The Polish communist leader and the Prime Minister visited the site of the accident, which was provisionally blamed on a signalling failure. It was not indicated whether this was a human or technical one.

21 November 1980

Lamezia Terme, Italy (FS)

28 + killed

A 41-wagon southbound freight train became divided, and, although fitted with continuous brakes, the front portion was not brought to a stand. The 28 wagons which had become uncoupled stopped, and were hit by an express bound for Syracruse in Sicily. As a result of this collision the locomotive and four coaches were strewn across the northbound line, where, half a minute later, there was a second collision with a train travelling in the opposite direction. Clearly several irregularities had taken place, the first being the failure to ensure that the continuous brake was working throughout the length of the train. Secondly, there had been a failure to check the tail light on the front portion before the southbound express was allowed to follow the freight train. To add to the saga of mismanagement, two other freight trains collided after the first of them had been stopped because of the accident ahead. There were no additional casualties, but the wreckage caught fire.

The main collision occurred in an isolated area of farmland. One of the passengers was trapped by his leg in the wreckage, and the rescuers sent for a surgeon to amputate it so he could be released. In the long time the medical team took to reach the site, the firemen managed to free the passenger, so the remoteness proved beneficial for him.

13 December 1980

Bosanka Krupa, Yugoslavia (JŽ)

23 killed

As a result of its crew not following the rules, a freight train left a crossing-loop before the arrival of a passenger one travelling in the opposite direction, and collided with it.

14 January 1981

Ghana (GRC)

21+ killed, (200) injured

An express left the rails between Accra and Kumasi.

14 May 1981

Taegu, South Korea (KNR)

54 killed

This disaster followed a minor collision between a Pusan–Seoul express and a motorcycle on a level-crossing near Taegu. The train came to a stand beyond the crossing, and was then hit from behind by a local train before it had restarted. This presumably happened either because of a signalling irregularity or the failure of the following driver to obey the signal indications.

6 June 1981

Samastipur, India

212+ killed

Seven coaches of an overcrowded passenger train fell into the River Bagmati in Bihar province, many passengers being drowned. Immediately after the accident officials said that the death-toll could be over 1,000, and might even exceed 3,000. As *The Times* commented, this could make it not only the worst railway accident in the world, but the worst to occur with any form of transport. Five days afterwards only 212 bodies had been recovered, but the head of the Indian Navy said his frogmen were planning to plant underwater explosive charges to enable them to retrieve a further 500 bodies still trapped in the train. Local divers and boatmen had refused offers of £5 for every body recovered because of caste taboos.

The reports in circulation after this major disaster in many ways epitomise the difficulty of obtaining accurate information about railway accidents which have occurred in India. In addition to the conflicting fatality estimates, two, quite different, reasons were given officially for its cause. The province's Rural Development Minister stated that the train was derailed after a sudden brake application, this story being amplified by an Indian news agency correspondent who said the driver had to brake hard to avoid hitting a buffalo. On the other hand, the chairman of the Indian Railways Board stated that the train had been blown into the river during a storm. Hard braking, in itself, is unlikely to derail a passenger train, although there is a slightly higher risk of that happening to a freight, with adjacent wagons possibly having widely differing axle-loads and/or braking abilities. Trains have been blown off bridges by very high winds, but, if this had occurred in this case, one would have expected the provincial authorities to have been aware of such extreme weather conditions.

(25 June 1981)

Near Gagra, Georgia, USSR (SZhD)

70 killed, 100+ injured

Although there was no official news about this accident, foreign travellers reaching Moscow told western correspondents of a collision between an express and a local train near the resort of Gagra.

16 July 1981

Bilaspur, Madhya Pradesh, India

38 killed, 42 injured

A collision occurred between a passenger and a goods train.

18 July 1981

Dangarva, India

35 killed

In the country's second major railway accident in two days, a passenger train was derailed half a mile from the station at Dangarva after some fishplates had been removed from the track. This was presumably sabotage, rather than carelessness on the part of the local track-gang.

31 July 1981

Bahawalpur, Pakistan (PR)

30 + killed

The 15-coach Awam express was carrying a large number of Muslim passengers from Karachi to Lahore and Peshawar for weekend celebrations to mark the end of the Ramadan fast. It was derailed near Bahawalpur, a report stating that two fishplates were missing from the track. The accident could thus have resulted from racial terrorism or sabotage, or alternatively this explanation could have been a cover-up for inadequate maintenance of the track.

31 August 1981

Asifabad Road, India

25 + killed, 40 + injured

A Madras–Delhi express was derailed near Asifabad Road station in southern India.

27 January 1982

Beni Helouane, Algeria (SNTF)

130 + killed, 140 injured

Shortly after midnight, an overnight express from Algiers to Oran ground to halt on a steep incline beyond Beni Helouane. A second locomotive was obtained from a freight train standing in that station, but this was not simply added at one or other end of the stalled train. Instead, the original train locomotive was uncoupled from the front, and the coaches, which clearly had not been properly secured, ran back down the incline, colliding with the stationary freight train. Ninety-two years on, it would appear that the lessons of the Armagh disaster were still not appreciated by railwaymen everywhere in the world.

27 January 1982

Agra, India

63 killed, 41 injured

An express running three hours late collided with a goods train near Agra in thick fog. Initially the railway authorities said the accident might have been due to the bad visibility and the use of oil lamps in electric signals after a power failure. Later it was stated by the Federal Railways Minister that the driver of the express, who was killed in the accident, had disregarded signalling regulations. The use of oil lamps in place of electric lights in railway signals is hardly a commonplace happening, and the mind boggles at the basic mechanics needed to do it, let alone the staff's ability to make the change after a power failure.

12 July 1982

Tepic, Mexico (FNdeM)

52 + killed, 120 + injured

A passenger train from Nogales to Guadalajara was derailed, and plunged into a ravine near Tepic, in a remote mountainous area.

22 March 1983

Ishurdi, Bangladesh
(BRB)

(60) killed

A girder bridge collapsed under a passenger train, and two coaches fell 75 feet on to a dry section of the river bed. Unlike many we have met in this chronology, this particular single-line structure had not been weakened by floods, and, as shown in the illustration on page 188, the bridge failed in a very unusual way after the diesel locomotive had become derailed. Its resulting impact on the structure caused the spans ahead to move in the direction of travel, and their nearer ends were no longer supported by the piers, so became dislodged. The locomotive remained on its half-collapsed span, but the next one behind it remained in position, although the sudden deceleration threw the following coaches off the track.

10 June 1983

Cairo, Egypt (ER)

22 + killed, 46 injured

A rear-end collision took place south of Cairo, when a stationary train was hit by another, causing some spectacular damage to the rolling-stock.

6 April 1984

Burma (BRC)

31 + killed

A train crashed while crossing a bridge 80 miles north of Rangoon.

14 July 1984

Divaca, Yugoslavia (JŽ)

31 killed

An express from Belgrade to the Adriatic coastal resorts of Koper and Pula was standing in Divaca station, with some 1,400 passengers in its 14 coaches. A freight train ran past two stop signals and collided with the rear of the express at a speed of about 40mph, badly damaging the last three coaches. The financial cost of the accident, in which 16 of the goods wagons were also destroyed, was given as 64 million Dinars (£340,000). The driver of the freight train survived and was arrested.

16 August 1984

Between Jabalpur and Gondia, Madhya Pradesh, India

104 killed

A bridge, weakened by the floods caused by the monsoon, collapsed under a train.

23 November 1984

Byculla, Bombay, India

25 killed, 47 injured

A packed commuter train was derailed as it was passing through Byculla station. Seven of its coaches left the track, four of them overturning.

1985–1989

13 January 1985

Bangladesh (BRB)

27 killed, 58+ injured

Two passenger coaches and a mail van in the 'Samanta' express caught fire. The train was on its way from the port of Khulna to Parbatipur in Dinajpur district, near the Indian frontier. Attempts were made to stop the train by pulling the communication cord, but nothing happened. An official later explained that drivers would not stop their trains in that particular area because there had been a number of robberies, but the driver and four other railwaymen were arrested pending the results of the government inquiry into the disaster. There was considerable dispute about the numbers killed, the figure of 27 being the official one. Several Dhaka newspapers were quoting a total of over 150, while one passenger claimed that at least 200 people were crammed into the small compartment he occupied, and most of them had been killed. This again demonstrates the difficulty in obtaining accurate information about railway accidents in Third World countries.

13 January 1985

Awash, Ethiopia (CDE)

428 killed

A four-coach train, with some 1,000 passengers aboard, left the track at a level-crossing near Awash, on the main line between Addis Ababa and Djibouti. The vehicles then fell from an ajoining bridge into a ravine. The cause was not immediately known, but it was thought that the train's speed had been too high. The driver, who was unhurt, was reported to be 'under investigation'.

20 January 1985

Between Mankulam and Murukandy, Sri Lanka (SLR)

(36) killed

As part of their campaign for independence, Tamil-separatist guerillas attacked a train in the dense jungle between Mankulam and Murukandy. The train should have begun its journey at the north-coast port of Jaffna, but an earlier sabotage incident necessitated it starting at Kilinochchi, some 30 miles further south. Mines were exploded, wrecking it, and the guerillas then fired on the passengers from both sides. Although there were 200 soldiers on the train, some civilians were also killed, so the details are given here, rather than in the chapter on Wars & Revolutions.

23 February 1985

India

34 killed

A fire broke out on a train in eastern India, and, as in the Bangladesh disaster in the previous month, pulling the communication cord failed to bring it to a stand. In this case the reason given was that the equipment had been deliberately disconnected to prevent possible misuse. The location of the accident was not mentioned, but the train was en route to Nagpur. Again there was some dispute about the number of fatalities. The official figure was 34, but news-agency reports put the total between 60 and 100.

2 August 1985

Mozambique

58 killed, 160 injured

Very little information about this disaster appeared in the British press, and then most of it was speculation whether it was an accident (the government version), or an act of sabotage, as claimed by the rebel guerillas.

3 August 1985

Flaujac, France (SNCF)

35 killed, 165 injured, 29 seriously

A relief stationmaster at Flaujac failed to realise that a Paris–Capdenac express had not yet passed through his station, and dispatched a Rodez–Brive local on to the same single-line stretch. He remembered almost immediately and his words, 'Je suis foutu! C'est une catastrophe!' ('I'm finished! It is a catastrophe!') were overheard by a couple who had just seen their young daughter off on the local train. Having realised a disaster was imminent, the parents had to wait for over an hour before she telephoned to say she had escaped almost unhurt.

Trains on most French single-track rural lines at that time were only controlled by telephone, but steps were immediately taken to improve the safety of the system, many lines being provided with a form of 'Tokenless Block'. Even in Corsica, the stationmistresses took to putting striped marker boards on poles in the middle of the track when a train had to await the arrival of one from the opposite direction.

The stationmaster at Flaujac was taken into custody for questioning. The disaster, coming less than a month after eight people had died in a level-crossing accident at St Pierre-du-Vauvray, caused considerable concern. It also provided an opportunity for the unions and the Communist Party to make a lot of political capital about expenditure on the French railways. The government and the SNCF were accused of starving the local lines of money, cutting back on staff, and concentrating expenditure on projects like the Trains à Grande Vitesse (TGVs).

31 August 1985

Argenton-sur-Creuse, France (SNCF)

43 killed, 38 injured

A train from Paris to Port Bou, on the Mediterranean coast close to the Spanish frontier, was derailed as it travelled too fast at night over a stretch of line which was being upgraded. The driver received the cab warning-signal for the ordinary 66mph restriction over the curve, and braked from 87. When he got the second warning for the temporary check to 20mph, he momentarily thought it was a reminder, and continued at the normal speed, only making an emergency brake application at the last moment. His train was comprehensively derailed, and, although he tried to warn the driver of the approaching Brive–Paris postal train by flashing his lights, it hit the wreckage at speed. Among those killed was an engaged English couple from Hampshire. Following this third major accident within a space of less than two months, the President of the SNCF resigned.

11 September 1985

Between Nelas and Alcafache, Portugal (CP)

45 killed

Although separated by Spain, there is a strong affinity between France and Portugal, with many migrant workers travelling north to take advantage of the better job opportunities. The most direct railway route between the two countries is the Beira Alta route, which links Pampilhosa on the Lisbon–Oporto line with the Spanish frontier at Vilar Formoso. Formidable gradients are required as the single-line snakes its way into the mountains, adding to the operating difficulties. At the time of this accident, trains were dispatched by telephone, and a misunderstanding occurred between the stationmasters at Nelas and Alcafache while they were rearranging the crossing points to cope with the late running of an express bound for France. As a result it collided with a Guarda–Coimbra local train at high speed, the latter being completely destroyed. The locomotive of the express, together with five of its eight coaches, fell down a 30ft high embankment, and then burst into flames. The fire spread to the first three wrecked coaches before setting the pine forests alight. Twenty-four hours after the accident the rescuers were still recovering the remains of passengers among the twisted steelwork, and there are still doubts about the exact number killed. Subsequently, as one of the investments to benefit the peripheral members of the European Community, the line was electrified and the signalling system up-graded.

1 February 1986

Kwa Mashu, South Africa

39 killed, (70) injured

Probably as a result of a faulty signal, two commuter trains collided near Durban. Rescue work took a considerable time, some of the injured being trapped for twelve hours.

8 February 1986

Hinton, Alberta, Canada (Canadian National)

29 killed

The crew of a 114-car freight train failed to wait in a 'siding' in the foothills of the Rockies as instructed, and entered the single-line section ahead. They then collided at high speed with a passenger train travelling in the opposite direction, the force of the impact making the locomotives explode into a fireball. The front coaches of the passenger train were also wrecked, and were 'welded by the flames into a tangled mass 40 feet high'. A load of sulphur in the freight train also caught fire, the resulting sulphur-dioxide fumes adding to the difficulties of the rescuers. The injured were flown by helicopter to Hinton, ten miles away, while buses ferried the other passengers to Edmonton.

17 February 1986

Limache, Chile (EFE)

58 killed

A train from the coastal towns of Valparaiso and Vina del Mar, bound for the capital of Santiago, collided with another passenger train taking holiday-makers in the opposite direction from Los Andes to the coastal resorts. Both locomotives were badly damaged, one finishing up on top of the other, while many of the coaches were reduced to a mass of twisted steel. The collision occurred on a stretch of line which had been singled after being damaged by a guerilla bomb a year earlier. A few hours before the disaster 300 yards of signalling cable had been stolen, so an emergency telephone dispatching system had been adopted. A misunderstanding then led to the collision. The stationmaster and three dispatchers were arrested while inquiries were made into the cause of the accident.

15 May 1986
Near Bheramara, Bangladesh (BRB)

25+ killed, 45 injured

A crowded express was derailed near the western frontier of the country. Several of the coaches fell into a flooded canal alongside the line. Sabotage was claimed to have been the cause, fish-plates having been removed from the track. The underground Marxist Sarbahara group, which had attacked a number of police stations in the area, was blamed

6 August 1986
Near Palamau, Bihar, India

(50) killed

An express from Tatangar to Amritsar collided with some wagons which had become detached from a goods train. Its coaches fell into a flooded gully, and 150 passengers were trapped in them for up to 18 hours after the accident.

6 November 1986
Koristovka, USSR (SZhD)

41 killed

Two passenger trains met head-on in the early hours of the morning when one of them had run past a red signal after the locomotive crew had fallen asleep. The trains involved were travelling from Kiev to Donetsk, and from Krivoi to Kiev, the incident occurring near the city of Kirovograd in the Ukraine.

16 January 1987
Kosti, Sudan (SRC)

21 killed, 45 injured

The details of this accident in central Sudan were not reported in the British press.

17 February 1987
São Paulo, Brazil (CBTU)

69+ killed, 150+ injured

Two crowded commuter trains were in sidelong collision in heavy rain, which impeded the subsequent rescue work. The local hospitals found it difficult to cope with the number of injured. The Brazilian urban train company stated that the accident had occurred because of a 'technical function caused by maintenance work'. Other reports blamed faulty points, a signal failure and human error, neither of the first two being incompatible with the official announcement.

2 July 1987
Kasumbalesa, Zaïre (SNCZ)

128 killed

As a train was going over a level-crossing, its first coach was hit by a Zambian lorry and trailer. The railway vehicle was knocked off the line and overturned, dragging the second vehicle off the track as well. The Zaïre government declared two days of mourning for the victims.

9 July 1987
River Ganderanagi, Andhra Pradesh, India

53+ killed

Before dawn many of the coaches in the 'Dakshin' express from Hyderabad to

Delhi were derailed on the approach to the river bridge, and two of them fell into the river, which was swollen by the monsoon. Continuing heavy rain hampered rescue work. As in so many previous similar disasters reported from India, while the potential for flood-damage to bridges was well recorded, the railway seemed unable to provide any means of checking the condition of the structure or the approach embankments. Nor was the simple precaution taken of stopping trains using the bridge during such abnormal conditions.

7 August 1987

Kamensk-Shakhtinsky, USSR (SZhD)

106 killed

A heavy freight train of more than 50 wagons, loaded with some 5,000 tons of grain, ran away down a twelve-mile incline. The driver — 'a veteran of the war in Afganistan and a party member' — radioed an emergency message to the preceding passenger train, which was carrying young people back to Moscow from the resort area and due to stop in Kamensk station. The driver of this train picked up the warning on his radio and tried to restart his train immediately to get it out of the way. Unfortunately the conductors had not received the information, and as some of the passengers were still alighting, one of them applied the emergency brake. The freight train, by this time doing 'about 80mph', hit the back of the standing train, and the two rear coaches were badly crushed. The driver of the freight locomotive was seriously injured when he was thrown from his cab into a poplar tree, and then fell to the ground.

According to the first report, investigations showed that the most likely cause of the brake failure which lead to the train running away was the closure of the brake-pipe by some unknown person, possibly one of the many 'free-riders who steal lifts on Soviet freight trains'. Reminiscent of the North American hobos, some 7,000 of these had been removed from Russian freight trains in the first part of 1987, and at least two other accidents had been caused by their interference with the brake-pipe.

A number of points in this story did not entirely make sense. It ought to have been possible to check where along the train the brake-pipe cock had been closed. If this could not be done by physically examining the position of all of them, valuable information would have been available from how hot the brake-blocks were. There should then be a positive cause of the runaway, rather than a 'most likely' one. It would have been unusual if the cock had been turned during the journey, in which case, why did it not show up in the brake test? So, in spite of *Glasnost*, this official information looked very much like a 'cover-up' for a party member, and this was later confirmed to be the case.

The report of the inquiry became available, and this stated that no brake-continuity test had been carried out, which would have revealed that the air-line had not been connected with the rear of the train. Although the driver noticed some irregularities during earlier brake applications, he ignored them until the train began to accelerate, out of control, down the long gradient. A warning was radioed ahead, giving the station staff at Kamenskaya sufficient time to have got the passenger train moving. However, 'they lost their heads and failed to do so', all the passengers in the two rear coaches of the standing train being killed. Five senior executives of the Southeastern Railway Directorate were sacked, together with various supervisors. A year later, in November 1988 a further report said that two railwaymen had been sentenced to twelve years in prison for negligence.

RGI **143** 718 (1987), T, (18 November 1988).

19 October 1987

Jakarta, Indonesia (PJKA)

155 + killed, (300) injured

Two crowded commuter trains collided head-on in a southern suburb of Jakata, as a result of a signalling error. Many of the casualties had, as usual, been riding on the roofs of the coaches, or hanging from their sides and ends. A nurse who worked at the site said the carnage was like a scene from Vietnam. Rescue work continued after night-fall, emergency lighting being used to help the large number of troops involved. Two boys were the last to be released from the wreckage, 18 hours after the accident ocurred. The Minister of Communications said a thorough investigation would be carried out into the disaster, and a check would be made on the signalling equipment on the country's railways.

28 November 1987

Kishangarh, Rajasthan, India

22 + killed, 16 injured

Fire broke out late at night near Kishangarh, in a second-class coach of a Ajmer–Delhi train, some 185 miles south-west of Delhi.

29 November 1987

Between Garabni and Beyuk-Kyasik, Georgia, USSR

30 killed, 66 injured

In the early morning a freight train collided with a stationary passenger one in the Caucasus mountains, after its driver had fallen asleep. *Pravda* reported that a meeting of the Georgian Communist Party Central Committee had been held after the accident, and decided that two officials on the Thibisi–Baku line

should be sacked *and thrown out of the Communist Party*. Five other employees were blamed for negligence connected with this particular accident. However, problems with the railways in that state were apparently widespread, as the committee also denounced slack discipline among workers on the Georgia–Azerbaijan main line.

31 December 1987

Pessene, Mozambique (CFM)

22 + killed, 71 injured

A train carrying some 1,500 migrant workers home from South Africa was attacked by guerillas. They derailed it with a land-mine and then opened fire. In addition to those killed and injured, some of those aboard were abducted.

7 January 1988

Hunan Province, China (CPPR)

34 killed, 30 injured

A fire was started accidentally in a crowded coach of a Canton–Xian train when a railwayman dropped a lighted cigarette into a bucket of inflammable banana oil. He was later sent to prison for life.

24 January 1988

Qiewu, China (CPPR)

90 + killed, 66 seriously injured

A special express from Kumning to Shanghai was derailed in the early morning near Qiewu station, about 22 miles from Kumning. At the time of the report in the British press, some passengers were still trapped in the overturned coaches, so the death-roll was likely to rise.

This was the third serious train accident in China within three weeks. In addition to the one in Hunan province, a head-on collision had taken place on 17 January, with the loss of 18 lives. Two days earlier the acting Prime Minister had ordered safety measures to be increased, and after this accident the Vice-Minister of Railways apologised to the State Council. He asked to be punished for causing accidents through lax work, and in early March the Minister himself had to resign, being held responsible for the accidents through his negligence.

24 March 1988
Shanghai, China (CPPR)

28 killed, 1,209 injured

There appeared to be something very wrong with the Chinese Railways at this time, as a fourth major accident occurred two months after that at Qiewu. All but one of those killed were Japanese high-school students travelling from Nanjing to Hangzhou after crossing by ship from Kochi in their native country. Their train appeared to have run past signals. Later the Director of the Jinan Railway Administration in the province of Shandong said that 70 per cent of the accidents in his area were due to slack discipline, although management problems and obsolete equipment were also significant factors.

20 May 1988
Takli, Thailand (SRT)

27 killed, 22 + injured

A heavily-loaded 10-ton lorry crashed through the gates of a level-crossing into the side of a passing train near Takli, in Nakon Sawan Province. The collision badly damaged the coaches on the train, and derailed some of them. Just ahead was a bridge over a deep irrigation canal, and some of the vehicles fell into the water, with others left hanging from the bridge or the bank of the canal.

4 June 1988
Arazamas, Russia (SZhD)

(100) killed, (200) injured

Three freight wagons containing 120 tons of industrial explosive blew up as a freight train was approaching a level-crossing at Arazamas, 250 miles east of Moscow. The explosion flattened 150 houses, and damaged another 250, leaving 600 families homeless. The windows of the Communist Party's headquarters, $1\frac{1}{4}$ miles away, were blown out, and damage was caused to the local gas pipeline and other transport facilities. Many of those killed were in their cars waiting to go over the level-crossing. One of the Soviet Deputy Prime Ministers was sent to the area in charge of a 14-member committee to investigate the cause of the explosion. As a result of *Glasnost*, far more information about the disaster was available than had been the case for decades previously, the Tass newsagency making reports from the spot.

T, 6 June 1988.

27 June 1988
Gare de Lyon, Paris (SNCF)

59 killed, 32 seriously injured

A runaway electric multiple-unit collided with another similar train in one of the sub-surface platforms at Gare de Lyon towards the end of the evening rush-hour. On its way in from Melun, a woman passenger on the train had pulled the communication cord at Vert-de-Maisons, five miles from the terminus. She needed to get home quickly, and thought the train was due to stop at her station, although it was not booked to do so. Following this, the driver had difficulty resetting the brake system, and finally left with most of it inoperative. He had lost 26 minutes in the process and was anxious to make up lost time, and realised as he approached the terminus at nearly 60mph that he had little brake-power available from the air system. Although the rheostatic brake was available, he did not use it because he erroneously thought it would not be effective as the rails were wet. He was, however, able to radio an emergency message to the controller from just over a mile out. Because a guard had been late booking on, a loaded departure for Melun had been delayed, and the runaway train ploughed through the first coach of it, standing on the track adjacent to the side-wall of the station. This cramped position complicated the rescue work, which went on through the night, the last survivor only being released as dawn broke.

The French legal system swung into action, and a major trial took place in the autumn of 1992. The prosecutor, Mme Marie-Odile Person, called for stiff sentences, on manslaughter charges, for the driver of the runaway train, the woman who pulled the communication cord, the guard who was late on duty, and the controller, who had failed to order the evacuation of the station. In the words of the defending lawyers, her comments humiliated the driver, adding that 'lack of presence of mind' was not an offence under the manslaughter law. Public reaction was extremely adverse, and the court decided to reconsider their verdicts. In December they acquitted the passenger and the controller, but gave the driver a four-year prison sentence (of which he had to serve six months), and the guard, who had been late on duty, received a suspended two-year sentence. These verdicts caused a country-wide strike by SNCF staff, and prompted some hard words from the railway's new President, Jacques Fourier. He said the verdict was 'deeply resented', because it included a jail sentence for a staff member who had no intention of committing an offence, and whose previous record was faultless. The guard appealed, and in late 1993 his suspended sentence was reduced from two years to two months, regardless of the fact that his late arrival on duty had no safety implications, whatsoever! Lt Col. Wilson's remarks after the Winsford collision in April 1948 are equally pertinent to the responsibility of the woman who had pulled the communication cord at Vert-de-Maisons.

The 1988 Gare de Lyon disaster was followed a few weeks later by two other, less serious, accidents at Toulouse and Gare de l'Est in Paris. As in 1985, the President of the SNCF resigned. A comprehensive safety package was, however, put into force, although some of the recommendations in the report went 'well beyond what might be considered reasonable', to quote the *Railway Gazette International*. By 1990 a geostationary satellite had started to provide continuous location reports for trains on the first of the Paris suburban routes, using lineside beacons and doppler radar on the trains.

RGI **144** 497, 726 (1988), **148** 815 (1992), **149** 5 (1993), **150** 5 (1994). T *1* (28 June 1988), 1, 24 (29 June 1988).

8 July 1988

Near Quilon, India

(140) killed

Yet another bridge collapse occurred in India during the monsoon. On this occasion a Bangalore–Trivandrum express was crossing the Perumon Bridge over Asthamundi Lake, ten miles north of the coastal town of Quilon, in the southern state of Kerala. Several of the coaches fell into the water, which was up to 30ft deep. The train had been carrying a thousand passengers, and, as in many previous disasters, there were differing reports about the casualty list. There were also two versions of the cause, one saying the train had been derailed, while the other, more generally accepted, was that the structure failed. The Indian Prime Minister expressed his 'deep shock and grief' at the disaster, and promised money would be available for the families of the victims.

16 August 1988

Near Bologoye, USSR (SZhD)

28 killed, 160 + injured

The 'Aurora', a Leningrad–Moscow express, was derailed while travelling at over 90mph on a stretch of track between Beresaika and Oplavenieto, where the speed limit had just been reduced to 60km/h (37mph). This restriction had been imposed after some ultrasonic tests made the previous day had shown the rails were defective, but the information had not been passed on to the driver. The derailed train caught fire, and there was no road access for fire-engines. A fire-fighting train was sent to the site, but used up the water available. The fire was finally put out after its supplies had been replenished.

It would appear that it was not Russian practice to indicate speed restrictions on the lineside. In Britain the regulations for an 'emergency' restriction of this sort used to call for a hand-signalman with a supply of detonators to be stationed on the side of the track a suitable distance away. This was additional to the usual warning boards, which remained after the information had been posted on the enginemen's notice boards. In recent years it has been permissible to use high-intensity 'strobe' lights in place of the man and the detonators.

With *Glasnost* making more information available about conditions in Russia, it became known that in the last quarter of 1987 there were 48 derailments on their railways, with a combined death toll of hundreds.

T, (18 August 1988).

9 October 1988

Lapovo, Yugoslavia (JŽ)

33 + killed, 15 injured

On a Sunday evening the rear two coaches of a Skopje–Belgrade express were derailed as it passed through Lapovo station, 49 miles south of the country's capital. They hit the locomotive of a stationary freight train and were badly damaged. Rescuers worked through the night, while the local inhabitants took some of the injured to hospital in their own cars. The initial investigation showed that the train was running at the correct speed, and under clear signals, so the cause may have been a technical one. The Serbian government announced that an award of 600,000 Dinars (approximately £120) would be made to those who had lost a relative in the disaster.

12 December 1988

Clapham Junction, England (British Railways, Southern Region)

35 killed, 69 seriously injured

Just after 8am on a Monday morning, the driver of a train from Basingstoke to Waterloo saw signal WF138 in the cutting just west of Clapham Junction suddenly change from green to red as he approached it. After making an emergency application of the brake, he let the train coast to the next signal, where he reported what had happened to the signal box by telephone. While he was doing this, the following train, usually referred to as the 'Poole' train, although it had actually started from Branksome, running under clear signals, collided with the rear of his at a speed of approximately 35mph. Some of the wreckage spread across the next track, where it was hit by a down empty-stock train, adding to the destruction and casualties.

The noise of the accident caused members of the public to make '999' calls, and when the Emergency Services arrived, they found that access to the site was difficult. The collision had occurred in a cutting, with a 10ft high retaining wall on the up side, against which the worst of the wreckage was piled. There were some 1,500 passengers on the two trains, many of them trapped by the distorted steelwork of the coaches and displaced seats. Amongst those who helped directly were the pupils and staff from a nearby school, and their building became a casualty centre. After the severity of the accident had been realised, a team from the British Association for Immediate Care (BASICS) was mobilised, some of their doctors being conveyed to the site by the Metropolitan Police's helicopter. The final five trapped passengers to be released were all looked after by BASICS' doctors, the last not being freed until five hours after the disaster. All survived.

It was quickly discovered that the false clear aspect being shown by signal WF138 had been caused by a wiring error made 15 days earlier. A formal investigation into the accident was carried out by Anthony Hidden QC, assisted by Major C. B. Holden of the Railway Inspectorate, Dr T. B. McCrirrick and Dr A. A. Wells, the report being published in the autumn of the following year.

At the end of the 1980s the London suburban services, then recently re-branded as Network SouthEast, were experiencing a travel boom. One of the busiest routes was that into Waterloo, and the colour-light signalling, installed in 1936, was overdue for replacement. After various renewal schemes had been studied for ten years, the final endorsement for the Waterloo Area Resignalling Scheme (WARS) was given by the BR Investment Committee in October 1984, and authorised by the Minister for Public Transport ten weeks later. Any project of this sort is extremely difficult to carry out without causing unacceptable disruption to services, particularly when the system is stretched to the limit, as in 1988. Installing the new signals along the line is the least of the problems: they also have to be wired into the control system, and arrangements made to switch from the old to the new at the appropriate time. To add to the difficulties in this case, the old wiring could not be disturbed, as its insulation had become fragile, and any major movement would have caused short-circuits.

On the Sunday two weeks before the accident, a replacement wire had been installed in the relay-room of Clapham Junction 'A' signal box. The senior technician doing this should have isolated the old one at its 'live' end, as well as cutting it short at the other, and binding that end with *new* insulating tape. He did none of these, but just pushed the disconnected end out of the way. On the day before the accident, the next relay on the rack had to be changed, and, while this was being carried out, the 'rogue' wire became free, and its end moved back so it again touched the terminal to which it had been attached for the previous 50 years. This provided a false feed, which kept signal WF138 at green, even when there was a train immediately beyond it.

It became clear, quite soon after the accident, that excessive demands were being made on the signalling staff carrying out WARS. As always, in times of high employment, keeping trained technicians on the railways was difficult, particularly in the London area. Excessive amounts of overtime were being worked, partly to get the job done, and partly to enable those concerned to increase their annual income. It appeared from the evidence that safety standards had slowly slipped over the years. Although the technician who failed to isolate the old wire considered he was totally responsible for the accident, Mr Hidden made it clear that others shared this because of their failure to check the work. British Railways was later fined under the Health & Safety at Work regulations.

As usual with these judicial inquiries, *all* the events connected with the accident were scrutinised. There were 93 recommendations in the Hidden report, 20 of them directed to improving the response of the Emergency Services. There had been some outside comment that the crash-worthiness of the Mk I vehicles in these trains was inadequate. This point was discussed in the appendix on the technical assessment of the rolling stock, but the penultimate paragraph concludes with the words, '. . . it could be forcibly argued that there are more rewarding candidates for large capital investment in the railway than would be incurred by early replacement of these vehicles'.

The fire at King's Cross Underground had happened eleven months earlier, and this, together with the much less severe collisions at Purley, on 6 March 1989 (see below), and Bellgrove, on the following day, (not included in this book), heightened concern about railway safety. As stated in my opening chapter, the clustering of these disasters caused the media and public to forget that death is the only certainty in life, and to overlook the constant attrition of fatal accidents on the roads and elsewhere. Not only did all this make people think that railways were far less safe than they are, but it became 'politically correct' to consider that money should be spent to prevent every type of railway accident. This ignored the danger of forcing more people on to the roads if fares were pushed up to cover the cost of safety-related investment that was not justified on a cost/benefit basis.

15 January 1989

Pubail, Bangladesh (BRB)

170 + killed, 400 + injured

An express for Chittagong collided with a northbound mail train near Pubail. Both trains were crowded, with many riding on the gangways or roofs of the coaches, the combined passenger loads being estimated at over 2,000. Many of the casualties were Muslims making an annual three-day pilgrimage to Tongi to attend the *Biswa Ejtema* (World Congregation), the largest Islamic gathering outside Mecca. Some of the derailed vehicles overturned and fell down the embankment into a paddy field. The bodywork of the leading diesel locomotive on one of the trains was very badly battered, although it remained on, or close to, the track. Scenes from the site were shown on television throughout the world, as soldiers from a nearby camp helped with the rescue work, or kept order among the crowds who flocked to the scene. It was the country's worst railway disaster, and the cause was given as the inability of the staff to operate the

newly-installed signalling system. A further accident occurred on the Bangladesh Railways on 2 February, when a derailment 20 miles from Chittagong killed at least 13 and injured about 100 passengers.

T, (16 January, 3 February 1989).

2 March 1989

Eastern Ethiopia (CDE)

57 killed, 54 injured

A goods train collided with three empty wagons, the casualties being mainly illegal passengers.

T, (3 March 1989).

4 March 1989

Purley, England (British Railways, Southern Region)

5 killed, 88 injured, 32 seriously

Although the number of fatalities was well below the total adopted for this Chronology, there were a number of important points that arose which make the accident worth including. On a Saturday afternoon, a four-car Class 423 (4VEP) electric train from Horsham to Victoria was struck in the rear by an eight-coach train of Class 421/2 (4CIG) stock running from Littlehampton to Victoria. The latter had over-run signals and collided with the train ahead, which had just crossed from the slow to the fast line after calling at the station. The front six vehicles of the Littlehampton train were deflected off the track, finishing up in various positions down the embankment behind some houses. One of the residents had just left his greenhouse to fill a watering can, when two of the coaches landed on top of it. The signalling had been installed five years before, and was of the route-relay type, but had given some problems. In addition to a number of 'right-side' failures, there had been an incident when one of the signals incorrectly displayed a green aspect instead of a red one. This was tracked down to a fault in the track-circuits, and rectified. After the accident the system was checked again, and all the tests showed it to be in order. The Inspecting Officer, Mr A. Cooksey, therefore concluded that the driver of the Littlehampton train had failed to heed the yellow aspect being shown by the signal two before the junction, as well as cancelling the audible warning he had received from the AWS (Automatic Warning System).

Although allowed limited immunity from prosecution so he could give evidence at the Inspecting Officer's Inquiry, the driver was subsequently charged with manslaughter and endangering life. This is hardly the way to encourage open cooperation to determine the cause of such accidents, and so avoid similar ones in the future. Eighteen months after the collision he was tried at the Central Criminal Court, where, on mistaken advice, he pleaded guilty. He was sentenced to 18 months' imprisonment, with twelve months suspended, but, as with the Gare de Lyon accident in Paris, this caused a considerable outcry, and his sentence was reduced on appeal.

The accident showed up one of the defects of the standard AWS, which could be cancelled semi-automatically, particularly as trains often have to be driven for considerable distances passing all the signals at caution. This reinforced the desirability of an Automatic Train Protection (ATP) system, which would stop the train in time, even if the driver failed to act on the audible warning. The development of such a scheme is currently in progress on the Great Western main line out of Paddington. 'Black-box' incident-recorders are also being fitted to many trains, which will facilitate technical inquiries after accidents, or incidents when signal indications are in dispute.

There was another unfortunate happening immediately after this particular accident, when the BR technical staff were denied access to the site by the police. When an accident occurs, suitably-qualified engineers can obtain a lot of important information on the spot, such as the positions of the controls, the temperature of brake-blocks, etc. As the Inspecting Officer put it in his report, 'Clearly the police officers have a responsibility to protect property and evidence at the scene but it is equally important that railway officers (and members of the Railway Inspectorate) have access to the site as well'. Welcoming the idea of police accompanying the railway officers as independent witnesses, he added that 'The respective roles were not fully understood at Purley'. Anthony Hidden, in the report on his public inquiry into the Clapham Junction accident, also commented on this matter. Fortunately action had already been taken to sort it out, but, as with the introduction of automatic half-barrier level-crossings (as shown by the Hixon accident in 1968), the police had been slow to appreciate the technology of railways.

RGI **146** 729 (1990), MR **47** 617 (1990).

19 April 1989

Jhansi, India

67+ killed, 137 injured

Twelve of the 20 coaches of an express from Bangalore to Delhi were derailed at speed near the town of Jhansi, in central India, 330 miles south of the capital. A photograph showed three of them lying on their sides in a zig-zag pattern, a considerable distance from the tracks. The Minister for Railways, after visiting the site, said the cause was not known, but sabotage had not been ruled out. An official inquiry was ordered into the accident.

T, (20 April 1989).

19 May 1989

Zambesia Province, Mozambique (CFM)

28+ killed, 48 injured

Two trains collided, the accident being ascribed to 'bad maintenance' of the rail line'.

24 May 1989
Thailand (SRT)

22 + killed

There was a report in *The Times* about this train accident in northern Thailand, but no other reference appeared in the British media.

4 June 1989
Near Ufa, USSR (SZhD)

Several hundred killed and injured

Two trains on the Trans-Siberian railway were engulfed in an explosion and fireball, west of the Urals mountains, after vast quantities of natural gas had leaked from a fractured pipeline. Some time earlier those operating it had detected a drop in the pressure, and had responded by speeding up the compressors, which merely increased the escape of the highly-inflammable gas. This was cold, and so flowed over the countryside and through the forests, forming two pockets in low-lying areas. As two trains were passing each other, a mile from the break, the explosive mixture ignited. A wall of flame, a mile and a quarter wide, hurled two locomotives and many coaches from the tracks. Over an area of several square miles, trees were felled, stripped of their leaves or set on fire. Most of the injured suffered severe burns, and some of the children involved were later brought to Britain for treatment. President Gorbachov visited the site, and a message of sympathy was sent by Mrs Thatcher to the families of the victims. A day of national mourning was immediately proclaimed in Russia, and the Congress of People's Deputies adjourned its meeting. There was praise for the efficiency of the rescue operation, helicopters ferrying the injured to hospital, while a special flight transferred some of them to Moscow later the same evening. Although most of the casualties were railway passengers, the disaster was clearly not of the railway's making.

T, (5, 6 June 1989).

26 June 1989
China (CPPR)

20 killed, 11 seriously injured

An explosion in a toilet of a Hangzhou–Shanghai train blew out part of the end of the coach. Dynamite had been put in the wash-basin, but it was not known whether this was a terrorist attack against the regime, or an accident. *The Times* reported that 'explosions on trains are not unusual in China'. Although it was illegal to take explosives on them, peasants wanting to do some quarrying or other similar work would hide explosives in the lavatories. There were also cases where explosions were set off with the intention of stopping the train for the purposes of robbery.

T, 13 (28 June 1988).

4 August 1989
Colon, Cuba (FdeC)

32 killed, 17 injured

Two passenger trains travelling at speed came into head-on collision just before dawn, 100 miles east of Havana. Two locomotives and four coaches were destroyed. The Provisional Defence Council were attempting to identify the dead and determine the cause of the accident.

10 August 1989
Puente del Rio Bamoa, Mexico (FNdeM)

100 + killed, (630) injured

An overnight train from Guadalajara to Mexicali, on the United States border, fell from a viaduct into the San Rafael de Bamoa River, about 50 miles south of Los Mochis. It appeared that the structure had been weakened by flood waters, several of the coaches finishing up in the swollen river. For most of the way from Mazatlan to the US frontier, the railway closely follows the eastern coast of the Gulf of California, crossing the various rivers running to the sea from the Sierra Madre. The train was known as 'El Burro' ('The Donkey'), because of its slow speed and the number of stops it made.

to 42. It was next put at 'possibly up to 100', and then finally fixed at 58, thus demonstrating how difficult it can be, even in recent years, to obtain accurate figures for deaths and casualties in foreign disasters. The cause of the derailment was not immediately apparent.

1 November 1989
Moghulsari, Uttar Pradesh, India

58 killed, 60 seriously injured

Ten out of the 18 coaches on the 'Toofan Express' left the rails and finished up in a ditch near the station. Reports of the number of fatalities varied widely to begin with, starting with 'at least 52', before being reduced

10 November 1989
South of Mosul, Iraq
(Iraqi Railways)

50 + killed

Government newspapers announced that a train had been derailed south of Mosul 'with many casualties'. Local residents' reports indicated that there were at least 50 killed, with many injured.

Wars & Revolutions

This book deals primarily with railway *accidents*, which are usually understood to be events which are not caused deliberately. In 1910, however, it was ruled that the widow of a clerk who was shot dead on a train in South Wales, carrying money for the colliery where he worked, was entitled to compensation on the basis that he had been 'killed in an accident arising out of, and in the course of, his employment'. It is thus not stretching the scope of this book unduly to include references to some railway disasters which were caused deliberately. Where they were carried out by individuals or groups acting in a purely criminal sense, they are included in the Chronology. Others, particularly those which have occurred as a direct result of hostile actions during wars or revolutions, are grouped together in this chapter to complete the story.

From their earliest days, railways became targets during a war, as they formed a vital means of moving large bodies of troops from place to place, and providing support for them in the field with rations and munitions. Although Buster Keaton's classic silent film, *The General*, was fiction, railway attacks did feature in the American Civil War, but these lie outside the dates covered in this book.

During World War I, however, numerous narrow gauge lines were built behind the trenches of the Western Front in France and Belgium, to transport supplies, and these were regularly subjected to bombardments by artillery and attacks from the air. As the capabilities of military aircraft increased, raids began to be made on railway systems and trains far behind the front lines. Between 1939 and 1945, many air strikes were thus launched against enemy trains in most theatres of war, causing much damage to rolling stock and railway installations. At times the daily *communiqué* from Bomber Command hardly seemed complete without mention of an attack on railway marshalling yards at Hamm, or elsewhere in the Ruhr.

In the fog of war there is no way in which more than a small proportion of such incidents would be recorded, and those details available are likely to be either suppressed or exaggerated, depending on which of the combatants supplied the information. Furthermore, such incidents rarely throw light on railway operating practices, nor do they demonstrate how safety standards have been improved from experience gained. However, in the course of research for this book, a number of 'accidents' caused by hostile action have come to light, and, to round off our examination of railway disasters, details of a few of these follow, giving readers an idea of what has taken place during the twentieth century.

Wartime conditions are not conducive to the maintenance of high safety standards, and the incidence of 'ordinary' railway accidents has often been greater during such periods. The over-crowding which so frequently occurred as larger-than-usual numbers of people travelled by train, on leave as well as on duty, could also increase the number of casualties. In the main Chronology there are reports of a number of such wartime accidents, and reference is made, where appropriate, to the effects of wartime conditions.

Over in the New World, Mexico was in a constant state of revolution for the best part of 30 years, from 1910 until 1940, and many bloody train wrecks were claimed to have taken place there during this period. Between 1912 and 1915, alone, six such incidents were reported in the press, the first two being in July 1912. In the earlier one, a mine exploded under a 22-coach troop train near the Bachimba Pass in Chihuahua. 'Virtually all the 1,100 soldiers aboard were killed or injured[1]'. A pilot engine had safely passed the point earlier, probably indicating that the mine was fired by hand.

Later press reports in July 1912 referred to a band of Zapista rebels mining a train and killing 30 Federal troops and nine second-class passengers, but it was not entirely clear whether this was another, less lurid, report of the incident referred to above. In September of the following year a passenger train was blown up by rebels 43 miles south of Saltillo, killing 50 of those aboard.

The first of three incidents in 1915 demonstrates the way information about such happenings often reached the outside world, the roundabout route throwing doubt on the accuracy of the report. On 11 January a troop train 'filled largely with the families of Carranza's soldiers who had taken Guardalajara, plunged into a chasm near that city', reputedly killing over 800 of those aboard. However, the news only reached the United States two months after the event in a letter from a missionary[2]. Like many of the other railway 'accidents' during the Mexican civil war, confirmation was lacking, and the details were almost certainly exaggerated. The most horrific incident reported during this period was in 1915, when Coqui Indians derailed a Southern Pacific train near Torres in the Mexican province of Sonora. They threw 80 of the passengers, mainly women and children, into a freight car loaded with hay, and set fire to it. Only 20 passengers were accounted for subsequently[3].

In an earlier arson incident, Maximo Castllo's 'bandits' sent a blazing goods train into Cumbre Tunnel as a passenger train was entering the other portal. Six United States' citizens and 40–50 Mexicans were suffocated[4]. Not long after this the train carrying a company of infantry to Jalapa, near Lima on the Inter-Oceanic Railway, was blown up. Among those killed were 55 officers and the English 'engineer' — presumably the driver[5]. Subsequently a 168ft long bridge across the Antigua River on the same railway was destroyed[6]. One cannot help wondering how much the long-term economic well-being of that country was set back by all this destruction, particularly in the light of the current troubles in Yugoslavia, Sudan and Somalia.

Aerial attacks on trains started to take place quite early in World War I, one such incident being reported in February 1915. On this occasion a French aircraft bombed a German troop train in occupied Belgium, killing 33 and wounding 52. Trains also featured as military targets in the Middle East during these hostilities, where the role of the railways influenced strategy to a considerable extent. Some of the more notable attacks of this sort were carried out by Lawrence of Arabia (T. E. Lawrence), his main target being the Hedjaz Railway. On 24 September 1917 British Forces carried out a raid on a bridge some 60 miles south of the Dead Sea and 90 miles south-east of Beersheba. Two German officers were among the 70 killed in the action, the remainder being Turkish troops, some 80 also being taken prisoner[7].

On 20 March the following year, Allied Arab forces mined and derailed a ten-wagon military train on the same railway, and then destroyed it with fire and explosives. Twenty Turkish troops were killed and ten made prisoner. The Hedjaz Railway was the only means of supplying the garrison at Medina, in what is now Saudi Arabia. In the main, Lawrence's tactics were not to destroy the link completely, but to make it difficult to work, and use it as a source of stores and munitions for his own troops. Had the outpost been completely cut off, its garrison would have had to surrender, and would then have had to be fed and guarded by the Allies.

After the war with Germany had finished in November 1918, the Russian revolution continued, and two attacks on trains in that country were reported in 1919. On 10 July one was derailed in the Ukraine, 'by bandits', who removed a length of rail between Bakhmatch and Pliski, east of Kieff, as it was then spelt. Among the thousand claimed victims, 600 were reported to have been burnt alive in the fire that followed. There was great confusion in the country at that time, with the civil war in progress between the 'Red' and 'White' Russians. As with the railway incidents in the Mexican conflict, considerable doubt must be cast on the accuracy of the reported figures.

On 27 October the same year, a 'Bolshevik' armoured train was attacked by Ukrainian 'insurgents', 30 people being killed and 200 wounded. Armoured trains featured in a number of conflicts as late as World War II, although their vulnerability was well demonstrated as early as 1899, when Winston Churchill was captured aboard one during the Boer War. He commented that 'Nothing looks more formidable and impressive than an armoured train; but nothing is in fact more vulnerable and helpless[8] '.

Claims of sabotage or actions by rebels have often been a convenient cover-up for railway accidents, or perhaps a useful peg for newspapers to use as the cause. Even in India, the derailment at Bihta on 17 July 1937 was initially blamed on sabotage, but was later tracked down to design shortcomings on the class of locomotive involved. In totalitarian regimes, the allocation of blame for railway accidents in this way can also be a useful means of deflecting charges of inefficiency, or a way of 'saving face'. For that reason the derailment of the 'Lenin Express' on its inaugural run in 1924 has been included in the Chronology.

Although none of the casualty lists were anywhere as long as those in Central America, the Irish railways were frequently attacked by Republicans during the 'Troubles' of the early 1920s, reports of numerous incidents appearing in The Railway Gazette. In June 1921 a troop train from Dublin to Belfast was derailed at Advoyle, Co. Armagh, when a mine exploded under it. The guard and several soldiers of the 10th Hussars were killed, together with some of their horses. By 1922 the railways in the country were heavily involved in the general lawlessness which so often occurs on the back of terrorism or a revolution. The Londonderry & Lough Swilly Railway was the target of no less than 300 robberies in three weeks, with parties of ten to twelve armed men stealing food, tobacco and general merchandise from trains. In May that year a Great Northern Railway of Ireland light engine taking £10,000 in cash to pay the wages of the locomotive staff at Windsor depot in Belfast was stopped and the money seized.

In 1923, at Liscahane on the Great Southern Railway, a few miles from Tralee in Co. Kerry, a goods train was derailed by armed men. The locomotive and most of the wagons fell down an embankment, both members of the fooplate crew being killed. Earlier, on 16 January, the 'Dublin Mail', with 200 passengers aboard, had a narrow escape when a culvert was mined between Lisduff in Co. Craven, and Templemoret. The train crossed the gap, and stopped without anything more toward than damage to the locomotive. On 12 February a large party of armed men opened fire on a Limerick–Nenagh train outside Castleconnell. The driver, two soldiers and a Boy Scout were wounded, and the locomotive badly damaged. After the train had been brought to a stop, passengers were forced to alight and it was then set on fire.

At Iniskeen on the Great Northern line from Dundalk to Enniskillen, the stationmaster was ambushed by armed men who placed a bomb in his office. As soon as they had left, he was able to throw it out of the room, but the detonator and fuse became detached. The resulting explosion was only a small one, but burnt him severely about the face and legs, although his wife and five children on the premises were saved from harm by his prompt action. In another explosion, the Riverstown Viaduct on the Dundalk, Newry & Greenore Railway was blown up on 6 March, closing the line. Three other trains were also wrecked at this time. At Tullamore in King's county, a train was driven into the gap where a bridge had been destroyed, and the wreckage subsequently burnt. Another train was also set on fire after the passengers had been ordered out, and it was then sent charging down the incline into Newcastle West station in Co. Limerick. Near Maryborough, in Queen's County, a goods train was derailed after a portion of the track had been lifted. Late in the evening of 28 April, an attack took place at Amiens Street station (now Connolly) in Dublin. An explosion occurred, and the troops protecting the station were fired on as they ran to the spot, while a number of people were wounded when a departing train was hit by gunfire.

In their recent terrorist campaign, the IRA has caused a number of disruptions on the Dublin–Belfast railway line. In a three-month period in 1988–89 no less than eight bombs were planted on it, of which five exploded[9]. This prompted a cross-border campaign to keep the line open, which included the running of the 'Peace Train' between the two capitals. Irish terrorism has also made itself felt in many countries during the last two decades, but relatively few direct attacks have been made on railways. Bombs have caused casualties in English stations, and a few have been planted on London suburban trains. In many cases prior warnings have enabled people to be evacuated before the explosion occurred. The ability of the security forces to operate in this way has, however, provided terrorists, and other misguided people, with the opportunity to use false alarms to cause disruptions. Considerable skill has been developed to identify many of the rogue calls. International terrorism has mainly turned to other modes of transport, but there was a very serious bomb explosion at Bologna station in Italy on 2 August 1980, which killed 85.

Contemporary with the Irish incidents of the 1920s referred to above, a number of acts of sabotage took place on the German railways in the Ruhr. Following World War I, that part of the country was occupied by Allied troops, and, in their sectors, the Belgians and French placed the railways under the control of a combined Franco-Belgian *Regié*, which sparked off the hostile reaction. In April 1923 a French *communiqué* reported two such incidents. Late one night, as three wagons were entering Merklinde station, an explosion took place in one of them, but the damage was slight and no one was injured. At Rolandseck station, on the main line just south of Bonn, the signal box was wrecked, the nature of the damage indicating it had been caused by people with expert knowledge. The levers were damaged and 'the electric control completely disorganised'. A more wholesale attempt at sabotage had taken place slightly earlier, when nine unmanned trains and two locomotives were dispatched from Friedriechfeld in the direction of Wesel, two stations on the line from

Emmerich to Oberhausen. The intention was to block the important junction ahead, but the pile-up took place at Lippe, where the seventh train crashed into the one ahead of it. Three suspects were arrested.

On 29 June an explosion took place in a Belgian troop train on the Hochfeld Bridge, which was attributed by the German press to the vehicle's own gas tanks. Both of these were, however, found to be still in one piece, although one had been holed. Traces of picric acid were detected in the wreck, and this was not an explosive used by the Allied armies. In July that year, the Inter-Allied Rhineland High Commission awarded the Franco-Belgian *Regié* considerable sums in compensation for earlier outrages at Bingenbrück and Wiesbaden. If the money was not forthcoming, it was to be seized from the German authorities. By November no payment had been made for the assassination of a Belgian officer on Hamborn station, and the Belgians seized railway rolling stock belonging to the German Government as it was being delivered from local factories. After the establishment of a new German Railway Board in 1924, the operation of the railways in the Ruhr was handed over to them, bringing to an end 'one of the most extrordinary chapters of railway operating history', to quote The *Railway Gazette*.

There do not seem to have been any similar incidents at the end of World War II, although the author did hear a story about some school children in northern Germany. They had found some cartridge detonators, and put them under the wheels of their school train after they had alighted. No damage was done, although the staff of the railway concerned locked up the boys while they sent for the police. Meanwhile the girls put down a second lot!

Serious explosions on trains have not been confined to Europe, nine people being killed and 14 injured when a coach blew up at Farron in Canada in 1924. It was initially thought that the gas-tank had been responsible, but it was later stated that this was intact, the blast being caused by high-explosive and taking place inside the vehicle. A number of serious incidents also took place on the railways in India at much the same time, during and after a strike. The Madras & Southern Mahratta Railway reported no less than eight in an eight-week period, the worst being a derailment which cost 14 lives, with 21 people being injured. As described in the Chronology, there have been few periods when the Indian railways did not suffer from sabotage to the track. The situation did not even change appreciably after Independence.

In December 1933, in advance of the Spanish Civil War, there was a short-lived 'Anarcho-Syndicalist' revolution in that country, and its supporters carried out two attempts at train wrecking in the first couple of days. A number of people were injured when one was derailed at Zuera, but, on the second occasion, a bomb was placed on a railway bridge between Puig and Puzel, near Valencia. It exploded when the daily Barcelona–Seville train was crossing the river, blowing the tender to pieces, while four coaches were hurled into the gorge. Some of the others were suspended across the gap, while the restaurant car finished up sideways across the line, with the remainder of the train piled on top of it. Thirty people were killed in the incident. There were several other attempts at sabotage before the revolution was suppressed.

During the Spanish Civil War, on 8 October 1938, a 'Fascist' seaplane bombed and wrecked a passenger train at San Vincente de Calvers, near the Mediterranean coast, 20 miles north-east of Tarragona. It was well loaded, mainly with women returning from a day in the country. No less than 182 were killed, and 400 injured[10]. On four January 1939, two months before the war finished, aircraft attacked two trains standing in the station at Tarragona, eleven days before that town fell to the 'Fascist' forces. Thirty passengers were killed. The Spanish railways have also suffered from terrorist attacks in recent years. Supporters of ETA, the Basque Separatist movement, have threatened long-distance lines with delayed-action bombs as well as actually laying some on the track[11].

During the late 1930s in Spain there was also a major disaster on a section of the Madrid Metro, where munitions were being stored. In 1936 services had been suspended over the branch from Goya station through Lista to Diego de Leon, and the line was guarded by armed sentries. An explosives factory was constructed at the Goya end, and the munitions it produced stored in a dump at the other. On 10 January 1938 there were three major explosions which killed 300–400 people, mainly local inhabitants. The blast shot down the tunnel and 'pushed over' a main-line train in Banco de España station, more than a mile away[12].

Over the years, railways have also been innocent victims of other major explosions. On 23 December 1917 the entire munitions dump for the Russian South-West Front blew up, completely destroying all buildings within a mile of it. This included the station, where two trains conveying Cossack troops were standing. It was estimated that 2,000 of them were killed[13]. Over in Nova Scotia, the explosion of the French ship *Mont Blanc* in Halifax harbour earlier in that month was more extensively reported. Loaded with 2,300 tons of picric acid, 200 tons of TNT, 10 tons of gun-cotton and 35 tons of benzol, the ship collided with another as it was leaving the harbour, and caught fire. After drifting – crewless – for 20 minutes, it exploded, the shock wave devastating the city. More than 1,700 people were killed, and 1,630 homes destroyed. Included in the fatalities were 55 employees of the Intercolonial Railway, of which six had been working on shunting locomotives in the various nearby yards. Sixty passengers waiting for their train in the railway station were also killed when the overall roof collapsed[14]. The Canadian Government Railways played a major part in the subsequent rescue work, operating 20 specials to the devastated city between 6 and 10 December alone. Many brought vital aid from the North-Eastern United States[15] [16].

Munitions were conveyed extensively by rail during both World

Wars, and a number of explosions occurred during transit. In this country a load of Admiralty explosives went up in Cumberland in March 1945[17], and a month later the fireman of a nearby light engine was killed when an LNER ammunition train exploded after a fire between Selby and Gascoine Wood[18]. Another similar train blew up in a siding at Savernake on the GWR in January 1946, killing seven soldiers[19]. Far better known is the explosion which occurred in 1945 at Soham in East Anglia, where the bravery of the Driver Gimbert and Fireman Nightall in taking the blazing train out of the town before it exploded was marked by awards of the George Cross[20]. Both have had Class 47 diesel-electric locomotives named in their honour. There was also an unexplained explosion at Catterick Bridge in February 1944, when ammunition went up in the station yard, killing twelve, including the stationmaster, and injuring 66[21].

Just before World War II a somewhat unusual explosion occurred on the Belgian Railways. The imposing Vierendeel Bridge across the Val Benôit at Liége had been mined by the military as part of their frontier defence plans. On 1 September 1939 there was a severe thunderstorm, and a flash of lightning hit the bridge, setting off the explosive as two trains were crossing the structure. Ten people were killed and twelve injured[22].

Not all explosions that have affected the railways have had military connections, and a few such disasters are listed in the Chronology. Some of them have not involved conventional explosives, either, two United States' incidents being somewhat unusual. In 1942 grain-dust exploded in an elevator at Superior, Wisconsin, owned by the Great Northern Railroad. Seven people were injured, but it was possible to keep the subsequent fire away from adjacent elevators and a nearby 16-million gallon petrol store[23]. In 1952 two tank wagons carrying butane exploded while they were crossing a bridge over the River Ogeechee, near Meldrum in Georgia. Some of the blazing liquid spread over the water below, killing at least 16 of those who were bathing in this swimming-hole[24]. The locomotive pulled the front portion of the train clear, but the rear 26 wagons caught fire.

Violent collisions involving vehicles carrying explosives can often set them off. In 1955 a train from Chihuahua to Torreon in Mexico hit two lorries loaded with dynamite on a level-crossing near Gomez Palacio. Twelve people were killed and over 50 seriously injured in the resulting explosion, which flung wreckage for distances of up to half-a-mile[25]. Four years later a Trans-Continental express on the Canadian National Railway was more fortunate when it had a narrow escape from being engulfed in an explosion. Its two diesel locomotives and the following three baggage cars were derailed on some points which were being repaired. The leading locomotive then hit a stationary wagon nearby, which was loaded with 100 cases of dynamite, forming a store for a nearby quarry. Although its body was torn off the wheels, the explosive did not detonate.

For their size, the railways of Palestine have probably been the target of more military and sabotage attacks than any others. As long ago as 1892 the locals from Bittir started attacking trains, and in World War I the railways were fought over by the Allies, while Lawrence's actions on the nearby Hedjaz Railway have been mentioned earlier. In the days of the British Mandate, Arab unrest from 1929 onwards resulted in numerous incidents, especially in the period 1936–39.

The sustained campaign of railway sabotage during the late 1930s was well documented by R. F. Scrivener, the railway's Chief Engineer from 1921 to 1948. A copy of his offical report for the period April 1936 to September 1939 was discovered in St Antony's College, Oxford, by Rabbi Walter Rothschild, the publisher and editor of *Harakevet*, the quarterly magazine on the railways of the Middle East. Over half-a-dozen different incidents were at times reported in a single day, but none caused even a minor disaster on the scale of those listed in the Chronology. They ranged from stones being placed on the line or telephone wires being cut, to the explosion of mines under trains or the blowing up of bridges. During these three-and-a-half years, more than 1,200 incidents were recorded. Keeping the railway running, even with military patrols, must have been a difficult task, and damage costing £P1,000 was frequently mentioned by Mr Scrivener in his report. To discourage the practice of blowing up the military patrol trolleys on the railway, the army made two local Arabs travel on a two-wheeled extension on the front[26].

After World War II, when the Haifa, Beirut & Tripoli Railway had been attacked *by a torpedo* fired by a German submarine, the Zionists turned on the Palestine railways and the British troops using them. Jewish immigration had been restricted, and various major incidents were recorded between 1946 and the formation of the state of Israel in May 1948. The two most serious ones involving railways took place in 1948. On 29 February 1948 the Cairo–Haifa passenger train was blown up by the Jewish Stern gang, just north of Rehoboth, killing 19 soldiers, and eight members of the RAF, travelling in the four special coaches which were normally attached to this daily train. Wires were found leading from a nearby orange grove to four mines under the track, positioned so that one would be under each of the military vehicles. Fortunately one of them did not explode. The second similar attack took place on the last day of March, but the 40 dead and 60 injured on this occasion were all civilians, most of them Arabs.

Sabotage of the railways in and around Israel has continued off and on since then, varying in intensity as Israeli–Arab relations have fluctuated. *Harakavet* has reported that a Katyusha rocket from Lebanon fell only a few metres away from the freight line north of Nahariyya during 1993[27]. Hopefully the current beginnings of an accord with the Palestinians may see stability return to the region.

During the 1930s the Japanese invaded the mainland of Asia, and various railway incidents were reported which were the result of hostile actions. One, listed in the Chronology, was undoubtedly a straight-forward attack by bandits, with robbery and kidnapping in mind, but three others are more appropriately mentioned here. On 23 September 1935 approximately 200 troops were killed when their train was deliberately derailed in Honan Province. Anti-bandit measures were adopted on a large scale, the police guards on the trains being provided with hand-grenades, machine-guns and wire-lesses. Their colleagues on the lineside had to make do with carrier pigeons and police dogs[28]. In spite of these precautions, a year later, another train carrying Japanese troops to their puppet state of Manchukuo was derailed and attacked by 'Chinese bandits' during the night. Immediately the train left the rails it was hit by a hail of bullets, killing 25 and wounding 55 of the troops. The survivors fought back, and repulsed the attackers, who left many of their number behind as casualties. Two years later the South Manchunian Railway announced that it was fitting bullet-proof windows to the coaches on its express trains. At £400 per coach, they were only being provided in the first-class.

On 3 November 1937 Japanese aircraft attacked a Chinese express, killing 25 and wounding 30 passengers. The train was stopped to enable those aboard to escape into the countryside, but a bomb demolished a third-class coach, killing some who had been too slow. The train was subsequently machine-gunned. By the time World War II had spread to Asia, the Chinese had the resources to make attacks on trains. On 30 August 1941 they were said to have killed and injured over 200 Japanese troops when their guerillas blew up a train in the north of Anhwei Province. Fourteen months later 500 casualties were claimed by the Chinese when a troop train from Nanchang to Kiukiang struck a mine near Shahsiatu.

In Europe, actions by partisans against military trains started quite early in World War II, a German troop train being blown up on a large bridge across the River Glomma in Norway on 24 April 1940. On the same day a Norwegian train with 165 troops aboard, travelling south from Röres, was attacked by a German aircraft, derailing all the coaches and setting them on fire.

Later in the war Greek partisans were particularly active at sabotaging their railways, aided by the geography of the country. In 1942 their exiled government in London announced that a German military train had been derailed on 29 March, killing a thousand enemy soldiers. Two further attacks took place in May and November that year. The deaths of 40 Axis soldiers were claimed on the first occasion, while, on the second, many of the coaches carrying 700 Italian soldiers were derailed and fell into a ravine. Some of the ammunition aboard exploded. In February 1944 details appeared in *The Times* of an operation by the Greek resistance, under the command of British liaison officers. Information had been obtained that an important German general would be travelling from Athens by train, and 300 yards of track were mined along the gorge of the River Pinies in the Olympus region. The explosions caused the locomotive, the leading armoured coach, and ten passenger vehicles to fall into the ravine. Only the rear armoured one remained on the line, and was quickly captured. The deaths of 400 German troops were reported, and the attack was said to have caused considerable confusion and dismay amongst the occupation forces, as well as closing the main Athens–Salonica line for four days.

At much the same time, Polish partisans wrecked a German train near Lipa, on the Lublin–Rozwadow line, the troops aboard suffering 350 casualties. Leaflets were left in the wreckage saying that the attack was in revenge for German cruelties. The train had been preceded by a 'pilot' locomotive, but the mine had been exploded by remote control under the train itself. This method could not always be used, and in World War II a special device was produced for use by the Special Air Services troops operating behind the German lines, and by the Resistance forces, which could be set to explode after a given number of trains had passed over it. This had the added advantage that days might elapse before the mine detonated, enabling those who planted it to get well away from the scene. It worked with a ratchet, but those responsible for its development discovered that a rail actually rises slightly as a train approaches, and the device had to take this into account. One of them – unarmed – was presented to the National Railway Museum in York a few years after it opened.

A number of train attacks by the French resistance was reported in the British press during the war. In the spring of 1942 a German munitions train was blown up near Vire, south of Cherbourg, but those killed included 21 French hostages made to travel on it. In addition a further 40 people were taken in the nearby towns of Caen and Romorantin, and shot. The following year the Raynal detachment, operating in the Chalons region, killed 250 when they derailed a fast-running German troop train at Chagny, in the valley of the Saône. Later that year another train was derailed in a tunnel elsewhere in France and, a few months before the Allied invasion started, the Paris–Irun train was mined near Poitiers. In addition to the 46 Germans killed, 13 civilians lost their lives, including the First Secretary at the Spanish embassy in Berlin.

There were also countless smaller acts of sabotage carried out by railwaymen and others in France during the war. The way this was done was conveyed very dramatically in John Frankheimer's 1964 film, *The Train*, which tells the fictional story of how a train full of French art treasures was prevented from getting to Germany. It includes a sequence of an attack by bombers on a French marshalling yard and, 50 years on, railway enthusiasts have described the conditions they discovered as the Allied armies rolled across France in 1944[29] [30]. The railway aspects of the making of this film have been described by John Huntley[31]. At one point the train just manages to take refuge in a tunnel when it is spotted by an RAF Spitfire. Attacks of this sort were made on numerous occasions during World War II by Allied aircraft on trains and railway installations in occupied Europe. This was particularly so during the final stages of hostilities, when fighter-bombers had the skies to themselves, and ranged widely, shooting-up anything that moved on rails.

The railways of this country have, over the years, suffered to a surprising extent from the attentions of 'friendly' aircraft. During World War II many military airfields were situated alongside railway lines, and the latter suffered from aircraft if they misjudged a landing or take-off. In the summer of 1944 a Halifax bomber overshot the landing area at White Waltham airfield, and crashed into the GWR's four-track cutting west of Maidenhead. The wrecked aircraft caught fire, and the bombs it had not been able to release over occupied Europe exploded in the heat, leaving a crater on the cutting side that was visible for many years. During the research for this book in the National Railway Museum Library, the author was introduced to an American visitor who had been based in Britain as a US Army Air Force navigator during World War II. He recounted the occasion in the same year when his B-17 Flying Fortress undershot while landing at Kimbolton. They realised their tailwheel had caught the lineside fencing on the single-track Huntingdon–Kettering branch, but when they went to look at the damage they found they had slewed the track as well, by three feet.

After a driver had been killed in another similar incident, the LNER installed special wires alongside vulnerable stretches of line. Supported on vertical poles some distance above the ground, they would be severed by any low-flying aircraft. The wires formed the equivalent of a track-circuit, and if they were cut, pairs of special colour-light signals immediately lit up on both sides of the affected stretch, giving trains enough warning to stop clear of any obstruction. Back in the United States, in 1943 two of their Air Force planes had collided in mid-air, and one of them crashed on the railway line between Worcester and Boston. The locomotive and five coaches of a train were derailed and although two of the vehicles caught fire, none of the 150 passengers was injured[32].

Even after the war, the railways in this country had to cope with aircraft crashing on them. In July 1954 an RAF Venom jet fighter actually hit the tender of a freight locomotive as it was landing at Broughton, near Chester. The driver and fireman saw it coming, and threw themselves to the floor. They were only slightly burnt from hot cinders, but the crew of the aircraft were taken to hospital with head injuries and shock. There were two more, unrelated, incidents in 1957 when military aircraft crashed on one of our railway lines. In the first, an RAF Hunter was involved in a mid-air collision on 7 June after taking off from North Weald airfield, and fell on the Epping–Ongar line, then still worked by steam. It buckled the track ahead of one of the push-pull trains, which was just unable to stop clear, and became derailed. No-one was injured, but three passengers suffered from shock and were taken to hospital[33]. The second incident was when a Fleet Air Arm Sea Hawk crashed on the Southern Region's line at Arundel Junction on 28 August, killing its pilot. The wreckage short-circuited the third-rail electrification system, completely cutting power off from the Littlehampton branch for a time[34]. There have also been occasions when airliners have overshot the runway at an airport close to a railway, and finished up teetering over the side of the tracks, fortunately without any serious consequences.

One of the longest-running wars in the last 30 years was that in South-East Asia, and the railways of the area suffered badly in consequence. Guerilla attacks on the South Vietnam railways began in 1960, and by September 1961 services over the inland branch from Saigon had been suspended. The insurgents then switched their attention to the main coastal line, which averaged almost one attack a day in succeeding years. The sabotage was carried out with considerable technical know-how, pictures in The Railway Gazette showing contemporary diesel-hauled trains derailed at awkward angles on bridges[35]. In 1989 the railway faced 'a mammoth rehabilitation task' according to Jane's World Railways, with many metal bridges restricted to a speed limit of 5km/h (3mph), nominally because of corrosion, but perhaps also as a result of bomb damage. There had been the promise of Russian financial aid, but it is doubtful if that has materialised. However, a special working was supposed to be taking passengers from London, through the Channel Tunnel and on to Saigon in 1994. A series of trains was to be used, one on each of the different gauges involved, to form the longest continuous train journey ever organised.

References have been made elsewhere in this book to hostages being taken after trains had been attacked in Third World countries, and it was former inhabitants of Molukker in Indonesia who introduced a new form of terrorism to the railways — hijacking. A number of people from that area had migrated to the northern areas of the Netherlands after the formation of Indonesia, and they considered their adopted country was not doing enough to promote an independent republic of Ambon. In December 1975 the Indonesian embassy in Amsterdam was beseiged, and on Tuesday, 2 December Intercity Train 734 from Groningen to Amsterdam was hijacked and brought to a halt near Beilen, between Assen and Hoogeveen. It consisted of a pair of two-car electric multiple units. On the first day the driver was killed, and this was followed by the the deaths of two passengers. The ticket inspector was intended to be the next victim, but freed himself from his bonds in the driver's cab, and escaped. The hijackers, after unsuccessfully demanding a 'Jumbo' jet to fly them to an unspecified destination, surrendered on Sunday 14 December. In the winter weather the train became very cold, and food and blankets had been brought for the 20 or so passengers remaining on the train, in addition to six hijackers. Throughout the policy had been to 'keep them talking', using specially installed telephone links.

Eighteen months later, on Monday, 23 May 1977 a second hijack took place, this time in parallel with the occupation of a junior school in Beilen. A four-car unit on a Den Haag–Groningen working was involved on this occasion. It had full-length access, whereas the previous hijack had involved a train that consisted of two, quite separate units. More hijackers were involved – 14 instead of six – as well as a larger number of passengers (55). After two weeks, three of the passengers were freed – two pregnant women and a man with a heart condition, and, on Saturday, 11 June, after a seige of 20 days, the train was stormed. The security forces had managed to monitor the whereabouts of the passengers and hijackers, and a simulated low-level attack by an air force fighter masked the ground forces storming the train. There were no casualties, and the school occupation, which had been coordinated from the train, then also ceased. Appropriate prison sentences were given to those responsible for both hijacks.

[1] Shaw, p408.
[2] Shaw, p408.
[3] RG **23** 338 (1915).
[4] RG **20** 226 (1914).
[5] RG **20** 317 (1914).
[6] RG **20** 717 (1914).
[7] RG **27** 362 (1917).
[8] Churchill, W. S., *My Early Life*.
[9] RG **145** 218 (1989).
[10] RG **69** 658 (1938).
[11] RG **145** 378 (1989).
[12] RG **68** 132 (1938).
[13] RG **28** 54 (1918).
[14] RG **28** 206 (1918).
[15] *The Halifax Explosion*: Maritime Museum of the Atlantic, Nova Scotia Museum, Halifax.
[16] *Canadian Rail* No. 431, 201-213 (November–December 1992): The Canadian Railroad History Association.
[17] RG **82** 529 (1945).
[18] RG **82** 434 (1945).
[19] RG **84** 50 (1946).
[20] RG **83** 149 (1945).
[21] RG **80** 151, 202 (1944).
[22] RG **71** 354 (1939).
[23] RG **76** 427 (1942).
[24] RG **111** 63 (1959).
[25] RG **103** 406 (1955).
[26] *Harakevet* No. 21, 2 (June 1993).
[27] *Harakevet* No. 22, 6 (September 1993).
[28] RG **62** 1247 (1935).
[29] Bayes, D. *The Railway Observer* **63** 333 (1993).
[30] Clingan, K. *The Railway Observer* **63** 470 (1993).
[31] Huntley, J. *Railways in the Cinema* 83 (Ian Allan ISBN 7110 0115 4).
[32] RG **79** 26 (1943).
[33] RG **106** 726 (1957).
[34] RG **107** 263 (1957).
[35] RG **120** 633 (1964).

Boiler Explosions

Few people realise that every steam boiler has the potential to be a highly destructive bomb. George Airy, the Astronomer Royal, calculated in 1863 that, even at a pressure of only 60 lb/in², every cubic foot of water has the same destructive energy as one 1 lb of gunpowder[1]. Such a volume of water weighs about 62 lb, which provides us with an approximate weight-for-weight relationship between the two substances' ability to cause destruction. When it is considered that the boiler of even a moderate-sized steam locomotive will contain upwards of 200 cu ft of water, its capacity to create a disaster quickly becomes apparent. The working pressure in latter-day steam locomotives reached five times that used in Airy's calculations, which raised the water's temperature correspondingly, both factors adding considerably to the locked-up energy in their boilers. The way in which we have learnt to deal with this over the last two centuries provides an object-lesson in the control of technological risk

Although an exploding boiler is very dangerous, they are routinely tested hydraulically at well over their working pressure, and even if a failure occurs under those conditions, the result is not catastrophic. One way of thinking about the differences between the boiler fracturing under these separate conditions is to remember that a considerable quantity of heat has to be put into a boiler to raise it from cold to working pressure. Virtually all this energy is released instantaneously if it bursts. When a boiler is pressurised with cold water, only a small amount of liquid will be discharged if any failure occurs. However, if the contents of the boiler are at working pressure and temperature, not only will any steam in the boiler expand rapidly to atmospheric pressure, but the water is well above its normal boiling point, which means a lot of it will also flash off as steam. Both these processes markedly increase the quantity of vapour streaming out of the fracture at high velocity. The resulting blast of superheated steam is highly dangerous to anything in its way, and, given the right conditions, it can provide rocket propulsion, turning parts of the boiler, or even the whole assembly, into projectiles capable of travelling considerable distances.

The early stationary engines built by Newcomen used steam at only a few pounds pressure, and the work was derived by letting atmospheric pressure move the piston against the vacuum obtained after the steam had been condensed. Watt's engines did the same, although he replaced the air on top of the piston with low-pressure steam. All these engines only had to cope with steam at very low pressures. The situation changed markedly when Trevithick started to employ 'strong steam', using higher pressures to move the piston directly. It was considered necessary to ensure that there was no loss of energy from condensation. This is why many of the early locomotives, such as his Penydarren one and, indeed, several of Stephenson's designs, including *Locomotion*, had their cylinder(s) inside the boiler, which would prevent any loss of heat and pressure.

Quite early on, Trevithick experienced boiler explosions with his stationary 'high-pressure' engines, and this was used by Watt and his partners as a good sales pitch to tell would-be users to stick with the old designs. But, while the large-diameter cylinders of the condensing engine could be tolerated in static installations, the need to lighten the whole ensemble was vital if steam locomotion was to become a practical proposition. Boiler pressures were thus set to rise inexorably during the era in which the steam locomotive held sway, even though the dangers increased and more precautions were needed to ensure that there were not too many catastrophes.

The two most likely causes of a boiler exploding are for the pressure-vessel to be stressed beyond the level at which it is known to be safe, or for the strength of a vital component to decrease without this being apparent. Safety valves are designed to take care of the first of these hazards, and, hopefully, inspections and hydraulic tests will be made sufficiently frequently to ensure there is no critical loss of strength, which can occur in several different ways. Both these points are worth considering in some detail.

A safety valve allows surplus steam to escape, and so ensures that the pressure in the boiler will not rise above the level at which it is set. In its simplest form, it consists of a valve which is held shut by a weight on a lever. Such an arrangement is easily open to abuse, by adding more weights, or even by just holding down the end of the lever. Drivers of the reproduction *Locomotion* know how annoying the intermittent discharge of steam from the safety valve is as the locomotive joggles over irregularities in the track, which, in itself, tempts the driver to try and hold it shut! (Which is why the locomotive also has one of the 'lock-up' variety!) Hackworth introduced a direct spring-loaded valve, and Salter actuated the lever with a spring, but Ramsbottom's design improved on these early arrangements. By using twin valves with a single spring operating on the lever that loaded them both, any attempt to hold either valve shut opened the other. In the latter days of steam, safety-valves of the 'Pop' variety were commonly used. Their advantage was that they closed positively when the pressure dropped, thus saving steam. On

SAFETY VALVES· RHYMNEY RLY ENGINE No 97

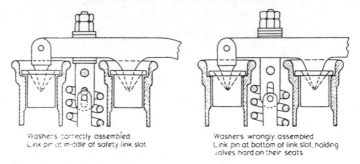

Washers correctly assembled.
Link pin at middle of safety link slot

Washers wrongly assembled
Link pin at bottom of link slot, holding
valves hard on their seats

Diagram of safety-valves of Rhymney Railway 0-6-2 tank locomotive, the boiler of which exploded at Cardiff in 1909. It can be seen how the washers had been incorrectly assembled, which prevented the valves from opening.

the other hand the sudden ear-splitting roar as they opened without warning was not 'user-friendly' for anyone standing nearby.

In spite of all the improvements which took place with safety valves, the last two major boiler explosions with railway locomotives in this country resulted from theirs failing to open. In 1909 the driver of a Rhymney Railway 0-6-2 tank could not get the injectors to work, and took the locomotive back to the depot in Cardiff. The pressure gauge had been seen registering 200 lb/in², which was well over the maximum working pressure of 160 lb/in², but this was put down to the instrument being faulty. (One standard precaution with these instruments is to ensure that the maximum permitted boiler pressure is less than that at which the pointer hits the 'stop'.) While the locomotive was standing in the depot, both sight-glasses shattered, but still no one realised the pressure was far higher than it should be, and the inevitable then happened. The entire firebox crown was blown out in one piece, and the discharge of steam wrenched the boiler – and the saddle-tank – from the frames and flung it 45 yards away. Three people were killed and the explosion was heard over much of Cardiff. The Board of Trade inspector quickly discovered that the Ramsbottom safety valves had been incorrectly assembled, as shown in the drawing, and were incapable of opening[2]. At the coroner's inquest, the jury came up with a different verdict, as mentioned in the Chronology, and this will be discussed later.

The other incident of this sort took place at Buxton in 1921, when the boiler of one of the LNWR 0-8-0 mineral locomotives blew up, just as it was setting off on its journey to Oldham at the head of a 34-wagon train. Again the pressure gauge had been assumed to be out of order, and had actually been changed *twice*. There was also difficulty with getting the injectors to work. (While this can be a symptom of too high a boiler pressure, these items are temperamental at the best of times for other reasons.) The over-pressure pushed the crown of the firebox down, and this tore the firebox and throat-plate out of the boiler, which then burst. Parts of it were found 200 yards away, and the force of the explosion threw the locomotive off the track, and the trailing wheels were torn away. Both of the crew were killed[3][4]. The safety valves had been overhauled by an outside contractor, and the machining had not left enough tolerance, so they jammed shut.

Although there were a number of other boiler incidents in the remaining 47 years that steam motive power was routinely used on our main-line railways, this was the last catastrophic one to occur in this country. The absence of any more over a period of nearly half a century is testimony to the way in which this particular hazard was managed. As an example of the well-established procedures, before any preserved steam locomotive is currently allowed on BR's tracks, one of the boxes on the form that has to be filled in by their inspector certifies that he has observed the safety valves lift. As we will see later, the same freedom from major boiler catastrophes was not the case in other countries.

This discussion about safety valves has taken the story of boiler failures well into the twentieth century, but we must return to the latter half of the 1800s to discuss the question of boiler strengths. As shown in the following table, a lot of British boilers or tubes burst during this period, although this type of accident formed a very small proportion of the total number of those taking place on the railways that were reported.

Boiler Accidents as a Proportion of Total Number of Railway Accidents, 1871–1900

	1871–75	1876–80	1881–85	1886–90	1891–95	1896–1900
Total Accidents	7,226	13,681	11,989	8,384	7,002	6,774
Boiler Accidents	41	38	16	10	13	17
(% of total)	0·6	0·3	0·1	0·1	0·2	0·3

Source: H. R. Wilson: *Railway Accidents:* Raynar Wilson, London (1925), Table 1.

There was still some confusion about the causes of these explosions, one theory being that the heat split the water into hydrogen and oxygen, which then recombined explosively. However, vastly higher temperatures than those *inside* the firebox would be needed to make water molecules dissociate directly. Certain heated metals can split the water molecule, by combining with the oxygen, but there is then no way for more oxygen to be introduced into the boiler to enable the hydrogen to explode.

Another theory put forward was that the introduction of cold feed water could cause a sudden evolution of steam, which raised the pressure too rapidly for the safety valves to respond. We all know the way in which water flashes off when drops fall on hot metal surfaces, but inside a boiler the same thing does not take place because of the existing pressure. Robert Stephenson doubted whether this was a feasible mechanism as early as 1856[5], and an experiment was carried out in the following year when a red-hot boiler was filled with water. There was no explosion[6]. In spite of this being done half a century before the Rhymney tank blew up, the jury inquiring into the deaths of those killed in the Cardiff incident concluded that the explosion was caused by someone managing to get the injectors to work, and so causing the rapid evolution of steam[7].

The best shape for a vessel to withstand internal pressure is a sphere, but this is not a practical proposition for a steam locomotive. With a sphere all the stresses caused by the pressure run along the metal shell in all three dimensions. By using a cylindrical barrel for the boiler, the same applies in two dimensions, leaving only the ends to require special attention. However, more problems arise with the inner and outer firebox, where the cylindrical surfaces give way to large areas which are nearly flat. To stop these from bulging as pressure rises, the two surfaces are joined together with stays. There are numerous different designs for these, but they have to be fixed securely at both ends, so they will not pull through the plate when fully stressed. This is relatively easy to ensure on the outside, but the end inside the firebox is exposed directly to the flames which slowly burn the fastening off, and this has to be monitored by the boiler inspector.

As the boiler is heated and cooled in service, differential expansion between the inner and outer fireboxes can cause racking stresses in the stays, which can cause them to fracture, and in extreme cases, special flexible stays had to be used. It is not easy to detect when an ordinary stay has broken, but the skilled boiler inspector gets a good idea by listening to the sounds made by his hammer. In other countries, notably the United States, it was customary to bore a narrow hole along the length of each stay. If such a stay fractures, a small jet of steam would appear, drawing attention to the trouble immediately. Locomotives so fitted tended not to have cladding on the outside of the firebox, to enable the location of any such trouble to be pin-pointed easily.

Corrosion of the metal in a boiler will obviously weaken it, and the majority of the areas where this is most likely to occur are inside the water space. Arrangements thus have to be provided to enable the critical areas to be examined at suitable intervals. In the last century problems used to arise through grooving taking place near joints in the metal. It was caused by flexing as the boilers heated and cooled, the problem being worsened by the difficulty of ensuring that the barrel was truly cylindrical. The visual results of an explosion from this cause were very different from the sort that was experienced more frequently in the fireboxes in this century. William Kirtley, the Midland's works superintendent, wrote a number of papers on the subject in the 1860s[8], but the problem was still rearing its head at the end of the century. The whole subject of locomotive boiler explosions in the second half of the nineteenth century has been extensively covered by Ian Winship in a paper to the Newcomen Society in 1989[9].

By the beginning of this century the design principles of boilers and the correct materials available for their construction were beginning

The remains of the Great Western Railway's 'Fire Fly' class 2-2-2, Actaeon after its boiler blew up at Gloucester on 7 February 1855. It will be seen that the shell of the boiler has disintegrated, indicating that the explosion was caused by notching rather than a low water-level. (GWR Magazine)

to be well known. However, the problem of sudden, and catastrophic, loss of strength in service was to remain a major problem, particularly in the United States of America. The critical area was the internal firebox, and this could overheat for two different reasons. Best-known was the crew's failure to keep the crown plates covered with water, but overheating could occur elsewhere because of the build-up of scale on the water side. In both cases there would be inadequate removal of heat from the outer side of the plating, in the first instance because of the absence of water, and in the other because scale was acting as a thermal insulator. Some interesting calculations were done by the LMS on the thermal gradients through the plates of the inner firebox, which showed how the temperature of the copper could rise to the point at which it started to lose its strength. With 1930s' technology and materials there was not a lot of scope left to increase the rate of heat generation in a conventional firebox.

In the part-work *Railway Wonders of the World* by F. A. Talbot, which appeared just before World War I, there is an article[10] about the Jacobs-Shupert boiler, which was specially designed to withstand the effects of an explosion caused by a low water level. In it the author states that '[in the United States], on average, a railway engine blows up once a week, and this class of calamity accounts for a long list of killed and maimed, as well as damage to the tune of several hundreds of thousands of pounds to property per annum.' One's first reaction is to assume this was the manufacturer's hype for their product, but the reality was perhaps even worse. In 1917 the Interstate Commerce Commission reported that there had been no less than 389 accidents caused by the failure of boilers or some part thereof, causing 52 deaths and 469 injuries. That was an average of more than one such incident *every day*.

An explosion on the Denver & Rio Grande Western in 1934 provides an example of a North American failure to ensure that boilers were always kept sufficiently clear of scale and sludge. The firebox of the 2-10-2 was torn free from the barrel and flung 212 feet ahead, while part of the smokebox and a section of the cab went even further in opposite directions. The ICC report's pithy conclusion[11] was that:

'. . . it is obvious that the overheating of the fire box sheets was caused by foul boiler water which was not in condition to absorb heat with sufficient rapidity to maintain the heating surfaces at a safe temperature. It is further evident that failure to wash the boiler as often as water conditions require was the primary cause of the accident.'

It also stated that 'The extracts from the carrier's [railway's] instructions covering blowing off and washing out of boilers show that extraordinary measures were taken to evade responsibility in the matter of washing out boilers as often as water conditions require.' Federal Rule 45 laid down that the *maximum* period between washouts was one month, but the D&RGW effectively prohibited this operation being carried out at any less interval, regardless of the quality of the water being used.

This was a somewhat unusual accident, and the most common cause of boiler explosions remained the crew's failure to maintain an adequate level of water above the top of the firebox. In this country there were a number of serious incidents of this sort, one of the 'Princess Coronation' Pacifics (No. 6224 *Duchess Alexandra*) being involved twice, in 1940[12] and 1948[13]. For a long time it has been mandatory for fusible plugs to be fitted to the top-sheet of locomotive fireboxes. If the water level got too low, the special alloy in the centre of these would melt, and so allow steam to blast into the firebox, thus giving the crew a warning. In the 1948 incident they had started blowing $8\frac{1}{2}$ miles after leaving Glasgow, but, even after stopping at Carstairs to have the boiler inspected, the crew carried on, but not for much longer.

Another requirement is for boilers to be provided with *two* independent means of checking the water level, which is why a pair of sight-glasses is normally prominent in a steam locomotive's cab. On the second occasion with the LMS Pacific, both were defective. In use, the glass in these could get so dirty that it was difficult to see the level of water inside it, and it was also possible to confuse a full glass of water with an empty one during a quick glance. In April 1945 the crown-sheet on the 'Lord Nelson' 4-6-0, No. 854 *Howard of Effingham*, overheated between Hinton Admiral and New Milton because the crew misread an empty sight-glass as a full one[14]. Another 'Princess Coronation', (No. 46238 *City of Carlisle*), also had its fusible plugs melt in 1962 because one of the gauge-glasses was dirty and could be misread. The LNER pioneered the use of a plate with diagonal black and white stripes behind the sight-glass. Seen through a column of water, the angle of the stripes was reversed, making a clear difference between the two conditions.

The GWR only fitted a single level-gauge, but supplemented this with a pair of try-cocks, which were not the most user-friendly bit of equipment to operate, although they were not liable to fail suddenly in the way a gauge-glass could. In 1952 the glass on No. 6859 *Yiewsley Grange*'s level-gauge had cracked inside its top housing, and the washer bulged out so it almost blocked the way through the glass tube. As a result it gave a misleading water-level, and the crown-sheet was allowed to get uncovered as the locomotive took a fitted freight up Gresford Bank[15]. The copper wrapper-plate split along its centre weld, and the fireman was badly injured, but there was no catastrophic damage to the locomotive.

During World War II a considerable number of United States 2-8-0s operated on our railway system, prior to the opening of the Second Front in Europe. In addition to having hollow stays, their level gauges were of American design, which differed from ours in a number of respects. Instead of glass tubes, a glass plate with prismatic ridges on the back was used, and, to British eyes, the appearance of an empty glass could look like a full one. In addition, valves, rather than cocks, were used on the top and bottom connections for the gauge, and had to be opened fully to work properly. As a result, three of the 756 locomotives landed in this country were involved in firebox collapses between November 1943 and the following August, at Honeybourne, Thurston and in South Harrow Tunnel[16].

There was also a lot of bad boiler explosions on locomotives in the United States during World War II. E. W. Lewcock described what happened in the *Journal of the Stephenson Locomotive Society*[17]. The worst fiscal year was 1943, when there were no less than 25 recorded explosions, all of which are listed. Illustrations of several of the incidents show the badly-mangled steelwork, often appreciably removed from the railway line. Some well-known classes of American locomotives have suffered in this way, not to mention famous trains. In September 1943 the locomotive on the 'Twentieth Century Limited' from Chicago to New York blew up while the train was travelling at 70mph, and came to rest 300 yards ahead of where it had

A Nathan Low-Water Alarm, as used on many North American steam locomotives in the 1940s.

parted company from the frames[18]. The locomotive, tender and eleven coaches were derailed. It became standard practice to fit low-level alarms on steam locomotives in that country, of the type shown in the illustration. However, even these did not prevent boilers exploding. One of the Chesapeake & Ohio's massive 2-6-6-6s blew up in 1953, but the warning had been heard sounding from the lineside some distance before, with the driver doing nothing about it[19].

One of the most spectacular boiler explosions in Europe occurred on the PLM in France during August 1935, when a standard 2-8-2 mixed-traffic locomotive (No. 141C623) was working a Geneva–Paris express. Between Culoz and La Burbanche there is a 15-mile bank with a maximum gradient of one in 83, and the line then descends at a similar inclination through Tenay. The train had averaged 31mph up the incline, and had passed the station of Tenay-Hauteville at 50, shortly before the boiler blew up. The crown sheet of the inner firebox burst downwards, and the discharge of steam, through a hole 17 sq ft in area, blew the whole 34½-ton boiler out of the frames, leaving them and the rest of the train to continue along the track. In its first leap forward, it reached a height of 59 feet, passing over a telegraph line and a row of trees in the process, before landing in a field 272 feet away. It then somersaulted three more times, making successive leaps of 72, 112, and 56 feet, before coming to rest on its side, facing the wrong direction. Part of the ruptured copper sheet was still hot enough to sag away from the side of the firebox, after several nuts from there had welded themselves to it[20].

Fortunately the line was on a curve at the point where the explosion occurred, and the train came to a stand without any injury to the passengers, the brake being applied automatically after the air pipes to the cab had been severed. The driver and fireman were both killed, their clothes being torn to shreds by the explosion, although there was no sign of burning.

A comprehensive report by Monsieur Chan, the railway's *Ingénieur Principal du Matériel*, was published in 1937[21][22][23], which reconstructed the events leading up to the explosion, as well as charting what happened after it occurred. It was concluded that the firebox crown had become uncovered some seven minutes before the summit was reached, and the change in gradient worsened the situation as the water tipped forward. The fusible plug must have melted on the climb, at least nine minutes before the explosion, but the driver made no attempt to stop and drop the fire as regulations demanded. It was calculated that there was 60 pounds weight of steam in the boiler when the explosion took place, together with 7 tonnes of water, all at 392°F (200°C) and 227 psi. The water contributed all but $2\frac{1}{2}$ per cent of the energy released in the explosion, and a mere one per cent of this was required to send the boiler somersaulting forward. One could not wish for a clearer quantification of the points made in the opening paragraphs of this chapter about the amounts of energy locked up in a locomotive's boiler.

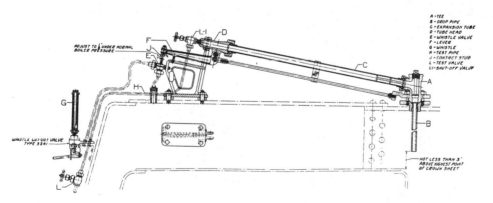

Diagram showing how a Nathan Low-Water Alarm worked. As long as the bottom end of the tube B was below the level of the water in the firebox, the tube C was full of water, which was cooled by the air outside the boiler. If the end of tube B came out of the water, the condensate in it and tube C flowed out, being replaced by hot steam. This made tube C expand, which rocked lever F, opening the valve E which admitted steam to the whistle G in the cab.

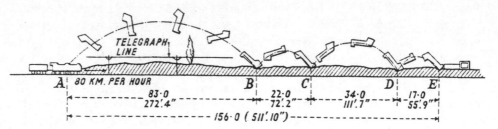

Diagram showing the trajectory of the boiler of the PLM 2-8-2 after it exploded on 2 August 1935. (Railway Gazette)

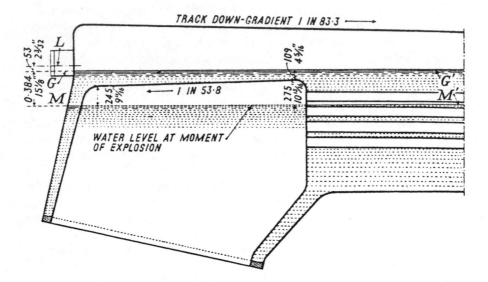

Diagram showing water-levels in the boiler of the PLM 2-8-2. G-G represents the lowest level the water should have been allowed to reach, while M-M is the calculated level at the time the boiler exploded. (Railway Gazette)

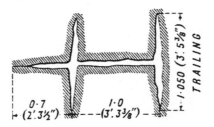

Diagram showing the splits which occurred in the crown of the inner firebox of the PLM 2-8-2 which caused the boiler to explode. (Railway Gazette)

[1] Airy, G. B: 'On the Numerical Expression of the Destructive Energy in the Explosion of Steam Boilers and on its Comparison with the Destructive Energy of Gunpowder': *Philosophical Magazine* **26** 329-336 (1863).

[2] Hewison, G.H.: *Locomotive Boiler Explosions*, p115.

[3] Hewison, *op cit*, p119.

[4] Garraway, A. G. W.: *Operating and Safety*, Proceedings of Railway Preservation Symposium, held by the Friends of the National Railway Museum, p15 (1978).

[5] Discussion following a paper by W. K. Hall: *On the Causes of Explosions of Steam Boilers*: MPICE **15** 281-308 (1855-56).

[6] Johnson, J.: letter 'Boiler Explosion': *Engineer* **3** 261 (3 April 1857).

[7] RG **10** 665 (1909).

[8] Kirtley, W.: 'On the Corrosion of Locomotive Boilers and the Means of Prevention': *PIME* 56-78 (1866).

[9] Winship, I. R.: 'the Decline in Locomotive Boiler Explosions in Britain 1850–1900': *Transactions of the Newcomen Society* **60** 73 (1988–89).

[10] F. A. Talbot: 'A Safety Locomotive Boiler': *Railway Wonders of the World*: Cassell & Co p82 (circa 1913).

[11] ICC *Report covering investigation of accident to Denver & Rio Grande Western Railroad Locomotive 1409 near Wellington, Utah, August 18, 1934.*

[12] Hewison, *op cit*, p121.

[13] Hewison, *op cit*, p132.

[14] Hewison, *op cit*, p128.

[15] Hewison, *op cit*, p138.

[16] Hewison, *op cit*, pp123–128.

[17] Lewcock, E. W.: 'Trading Water for Steam', *Journal of the Stephenson Locomotive Society* **62** 50, 82 (1986).

[18] RG **79** 295 (1943), **80** 109 (1944).

[19] Atkins, C. P.: *Railway World Annual 1983* p97.

[20] RG **63** 238 (1935).

[21] Chan: *Revue Générale des Chemins de Fer* p106 (1 February 1937).

[22] RM **80** 363 (1939).

[23] RG **69** 123 (1938).

Appendix

Major railway disasters since 1 January 1990

Date	Country	Location	Description	No. of Fatalities
1990				
4 January	Pakistan	Sangi, Sind	Collision after train diverted on to wrong line	306
16 January	India	Patna, Bihar	Fire	100
3 May	Mexico	Oaxaca	Derailment of runaway train	40
4 June	India	Near Vikarabad, Andhra Pradesh	Head-on collision	20
25 June	India	Bihar	Collision	45
7 August	Tunisia	Near Tunis	Collision	20
9 October	India	Near Hyderabad, Andhra Pradesh	Fire (arson)	47
17 October	Cambodia	Kompong, Sori	Train derailed and fired on by terrorists	50
1991				
4 March	Mozambique	Nacala, Nampula	Derailment of runaway train	96
6 April	Cuba	Villa Clara	Derailment	56
14 May	Japan	Near Shigarki	Head-on collision on single line	40
8 June	Pakistan	Ghorki	Probably rear-end collision	55
22 June	Ethiopia	Near Dire Dawa	Derailment	50
5 September	Congo	Near Dolisie	Head-on collision on single line	150
31 October	India	Near Bangalore	Train derailed by rock-fall	40
15 November	Taiwan	Miaoli	Rear-end collision	33
1992				
4 March	Russia	Tver	Collision followed by fire	?
4 September	India	Madhya Pradesh	Rear-end collision	37
1993				
18 January	Iran	Near Semnan	Collision	24
30 January	Kenya	Near Mtito Andrea	Bridge collapsed under train	65
28 March	South Korea	Near Pusan	Derailment due to track subsidence	79
27 May	Armenia	Near Gyumri	Collision with wagons	30
31 May	Angola	Quipungo	Derailment caused by Unita guerillas	355
1 June	India	(not stated)	Runaway wagons caused collision	24
4 August	India	Mairwa	Derailment	22
13 September	Mozambique	(Northern part)	Derailment	77
22 September	United States	Near Mobile, Alabama	Bridge collapsed after being hit by barge	44
2 November	Indonesia	Near Jakarta	Head-on collision	35
1994				
8 March	South Africa	Near Pinetown	Derailment probably due to excessive speed	63

Bibliography

Adams, C. F.:   *Notes on Railroad Accidents*: Putnams, 1879.
Bishop, Bill: *Off the Rails — A Detailed Account of Railway Accidents
                        & Derailments*: Bracken Books, 1984: (ISBN 1 85170
                        208 3).
Blythe, R.:   *Danger Ahead*: Newman Neame, 1951.
Bonnett, H.:   *The Grantham Rail Crash of 1906*: Bygone Grantham,
                        1978: (ISBN 0 906338 05 0).
Churchman, G. B.:   *Danger Ahead*: IPL Publishing Group, 1991: (ISBN
                        0-908876-74-2). [New Zealand railway accidents.]
Conly, G. and Stewart, G.: *Tragedy on the Track*: Graham House, 1986: (ISBN
                        1-86934-008-6). [New Zealand railway accidents.]
Coombes, L. F. E.:   *The Harrow Railway Disaster—Twenty-five Years On*:
                        David & Charles, 1977: (ISBN 0 7153 7409-5).
Currie, J. R. L.:   *The Runaway Train — Armagh 1889*: David & Charles,
                        1971: (ISBN 0 7153 5198 2).
Davey, Nancy: *The Tay Bridge Disaster 1879*: Dundee Art Gallery &
                        Museums, 1993: (ISBN 0 900344 55 5).
Gerard, M. and Hamilton, *Rails to Disaster — More British Steam Train Accidents
J. A. B.:   1906—1957*: George Allen & Unwin, 1984: (ISBN
                        0-04-385103-7).
Hall, Stanley: *Danger Signals — An Investigation into Modern Railway
                        Accidents*: Ian Allan, 1987: (ISBN 0 7110 1709 2).
                        Danger on the Line: Ian Allan, 1989: (ISBN 0 7110
                        1872 2).
                        *The Railway Detectives — 150 Years of the Railway
                        Inspectorate*: Ian Allan, 1990: (ISBN 0 7110 1929 0).
Hamilton, J. A. B.:   *Britain's Greatest Rail Disaster — The Quintinshill Blaze
                        of 1915*: George Allen & Unwin, 1969: (ISBN
                        04 625003 4).
                        *Trains to Nowhere — British Steam Train Accidents
                        1906—1960*: edited by Malcolm Gerard: George Allen
                        & Unwin, 1981: (ISBN 0-04-385084-7).
                        Disaster Down the Line!: George Allen & Unwin,
                        1967: (Paperback, Javelin Books, 1987: (ISBN 0 7137
                        1973 7)).
Hewison C. H.:   *Locomotive Boiler Explosions*: David & Charles, 1983:
                        (ISBN 0-7153 8305)
Holloway, S.:   *Moorgate — Anatomy of a Railway Disaster*: David &
                        Charles, 1988: (ISBN 0 7153 8913).
Johnson, C.:   *Learning the Hard Way*: The New Zealand Railway &
                        Locomotive Society, 1991 (ISBN 0-908573-57-X).
                        [New Zealand railway accidents.]

Jones, Elwyn V.:   *Mishaps on the Cambrian Railways (1864–1922)*:
                          Severn Press, 1972.
Jongerius, R.:   *Spoorweganvallen in Nederland 1839–1993*: Schuyt &
                          Co, 1993 (ISBN 90-6097-341-0).
Nock O. S.:   *Historic Railway Disasters*: Ian Allan, 1966:
                          (Paperback, Arrow Books, 1986: (ISBN 0 09 907720
                          5)). Fourth edition, revised by Cooper, B. K.: Ian
                          Allan, 1987 (ISBN 0-7110-1752-2).
Pearce, K.:   *Broken Journeys Volume I*: Railmac Publications, 1985:
                          (ISBN 0 949817 45 7).
                          Broken Journeys Volume II: Railmac Publications, 1989:
                          (ISBN 0 949817 79 1).
Prebble, John: *High Girders*: Martin Secker & Warburg, 1956: [The
                          Tay Bridge Disaster of 1879].
Püschel, Bernhard: *Historiche Eisenbahn-Katastrophen – Enie Unfallchronik
                          von 1840 bis 1926*: Eisenbahn-Kurier (ISBN 3-88255-
                          838-5).
Reed, Robert C.:   *Down Brakes*: First edition, P. R. MacMillan, 1960.
                          *Train Wrecks – A Pictorial History of Accidents on The
                          Main Line*: Bonanza Books, New York, 1968 (Library
                          of Congress card No. 68-13249).
Ritzau, H. J. and Hörstel, J.: *Die Katastrophenszene der Gegenwart – Eisenbahnunfälle
                          in Deutschland Band 2:* Verlag Zeit und Eisenbahn,
                          1953: (ISBN 3-921 304-50-4).
Ritzau, H. J.:   *Eisenbahn-Katastrophen in Deutschland*: Verlag Zeit &
                          Eisenbahn: 1979 (ISBN 3-921304-38-6).
Rolt, L. T. C.:   *Red for Danger*: Fourth edition, revised and with
                          additional material by Geoffrey Kichenside: Pan
                          Books, 1982: (ISBN 0 330 29189 0).
Schneider, A. and Mase, A.: *Railway Accidents of Great Britain & Europe*:
                          Translated from German by Dellow, E. L.: David &
                          Charles, 1970 (ISBN 7153 4791 8).
Shaw, Robert B.:   *A History of Railroad Accidents, Safety Precautions and
                          Operating Practices*: 1978.
Stretton, C. E.:   *Safe Railway Working*: Crosby Lockwood & Son,
                          1909.
Thomas, John: *Obstruction Danger – Stories of Memorable Railway
                          Disasters*: William Blackwood & Sons, 1937.
                          Great Britain's Worst Railway Disaster (1915): David &
                          Charles, 1962: (7153 4645-8).
                          *The Tay Bridge Disaster – New Light on the 1879
                          Tragedy*: David & Charles, 1972: (ISBN 0 7153
                          5198 2).
Vaughan, A.:   *Obstruction Danger – Significant British Railway
                          Accidents 1890–1986*: Patrick Stephens, 1989: (ISBN
                          1-85260-055-1).
Wells, J. A.:   *Signals to Danger – Railway Accidents at Newcastle
                          upon Tyne and in Northumberland*: Northumberland
                          County Library, 1992: (ISBN 1 874020 07 8).
Wilson, H. R.:   *The Safety of British Railways*: P. S. King & Son, 1909.

In Britain the annual and individual railway accident reports are published by Her Majesty's Stationery Office. The United States Department of Transportation offers several publications produced by the National Transportation Safety Board, there being, typically, ten reports each year on railway accidents. These publications are available in Britain from Microinfo Ltd, P.O. Box 3, Omega Park, Alton, Hampshire, GU34 2PG.

Acknowledgements

Australia
R. McAdams
J. Costigan
Canada
D. J. Nichol
Dr R. V. V. Nicholls
France
M. Doerr
J. Falaize
P. Jefford
Union Internationale des
  Chemins de fer
Germany
M. Grieves
Great Britain
W. Adams
C. P. Atkins
G. Bird
G. Duddridge
M. C. Holmes
M. Hughes
P. Kelly
J. Rintoul

L. Tyrrell
G. D. Towner
F. Voisey
Staff of the National Railway
  Museum Library, York
Japan
O. Nakayama
T. Suga
K. Usui
Netherlands
H. Hanenbergh
New Zealand
J. B. C. Taylor
Sweden
G. Dahlberg
L. Furuskar
United States of America
Mark J. Cedeck
John W. Barringer III, National
  Railroad Library, St Louis
Transport Museum Association,
  National Museum of Transport,
  St Louis

All photographs and diagrams are acknowledged individually.

Index

This index lists the location of the disasters referred to in the Chronology under the countries concerned. Where the accident took place between two places, these are given in the form **Onawa/Benson**. If the entry refers to it having occurred near a particular place, the index gives that name, marked with the **symbol** †. References to the accidents shown in the illustrations are given as **page numbers in italics.** Where the only information about the whereabouts of a particular disaster is the name of the railway concerned, that is given in brackets. Other accidents (where only the name of the country is known) are listed at the end of the entries for the appropriate section. Post-1989 disasters are listed in an appendix, rather than in the Chronology.

Sirhind	29 January 1950	Mikawashima	3 May 1962
Umeshnagar	4 January 1963	Nagoya/Osaka	26 October 1971
Vadamadura	21 August 1938	Oira†	7 April 1930
Varanasi (Benares)	19 January 1977	Oita/Beppu	26 October 1961
Vikarabad†	4 June 1990	Osaka	29 January 1940
Villupuram Junction	14 November 1943	Rokken	15 October 1956
Yalvigi	19 March 1968	Shigarki	14 May 1991, *194*
Yamuna	8 July 1960	Tadakuma	16 April 1936
—	23 July 1917	Yamagati Prefecture	4 March 1940
—	19 November 1921	Yokohama	24 April 1951
—	February 1966	—	9 November 1963
—	23 February 1985	—	25 February 1947
—	1 June 1993	—	*198*
—	*138*		

Jugoslavia (see Yugoslavia)

Indonesia

Bandung†	11 April 1963	**Kampuchea**	
Jakarta	19 October 1987	—	10 June 1980
Jakarta†	2 November 1993, *196*		
Tasikmalaja	8 May 1959	**Kenya**	
		Mitito Andrea†	30 January 1993

Iran

Ardekan	31 December 1970	**Manchuria**	
Semnan†	18 January 1993	Chengchitun/	17 March 1933
		Ssupingkai	
Iraq		Machungho	8 December 1926
Mosul†	10 November 1989	Tiehlong†	11 December 1926

Italy

		Mexico	
Arguata Scrivia	7 August 1917	Cazadero	1 February 1945
Armi Tunnel	2 March 1944	Encarnačion	19 September 1907
Benevento	15 February 1953	Gargantua Siding	25 April 1908
Cantanzaro.	23 December 1961	Guadalajara	3 April 1955
Castle Bolognese	*151*	Iguala†	December 1940
Como†	20 July 1941	(Manzanillo Line)	23 June 1910
Lambrate	30 October 1939	Mexico City	20 October 1975
Lamenzia Terme	21 November 1980	Oaxaca	3 May 1990
Monza	7 January 1960	Oaxaca†	30 June 1956
Naples	21 December 1941	Puente del Rio Bamoa	10 August 1989, *193*
Orvieto†	13 June 1945	Queretaro City†	February 1940
Populonia	18 February 1934	Saltillo	5 October 1972
Rome†	27 August 1921	Santa Lucrecia/Matias	21 October 1939
Spoleto	21 March 1948	Romero	
Torre Annunziata	30 December 1939	Tacotalpa	20 December 1964
Vado	15 April 1978	Tepic	12 July 1982
Venice	8 October 1920	—	5 October 1919
Voghera	31 May 1962	—	13 April 1939
		—	10 October 1976
Jamaica		—	12 November 1977
Balaclava	30 July 1938		
Kendal	2 September 1957	**Morocco**	
		Kenitra†	22 May 1975
Japan			
Aboshoi	16 September 1941	**Mozambique**	
Akinakano/Umitashi	23 September 1926	Pessene	
Hokuriku Tunnel	6 November 1972	December 1987	
Honshu (earthquake)	1 September 1923	Nacala	4 March 1991
Kyujo	May 1941	Säo Miguel	27 March 1974
Kyoto	8 January 1934	Zambesia Province	19 May 1989

Effingham	4 October 1965
Heavitree	20 October 1952
Heidelberg	27 July 1927
Johannesburg†	28 April 1949
Kwa Mashu	1 February 1986
Leeudoorn Stad	17 July 1932
Malmesbury	29 September 1972
Odendaalsrust	9 September 1954
Pinetown†	8 March 1994
Potgietersrus†	31 March 1972
Randfontein	29 July 1964
Salt River	9 June 1926
Watterval Boven†	15 November 1949
Woodstock	8 April 1957

South Korea

Pusan†	28 March 1993
Seoul	23 May 1976
Suwon/Osan	31 January 1954
Taegu	14 May 1981
Taejon†	14 September 1948

Southern Rhodesia

Plumtree/Tsessebe	4 April 1938

Spain

Anetlla/Ampolla	1 September 1926
Arevale†	11 January 1944
Barcelona	9 January 1961
Barcelona†	28 February 1977, 187
Barcelona, Las Planas	9 April 1925
Barcelona/Tortosa	16 July 1920
Fuensanta	15 November 1945
Grisen	10 February 1965
Hospitalet/Cambrile	25 November 1907
Jerez†	21 July 1972
Martorell	25 September 1938
Mons La Nueva†	13 February 1949
Neon Daroston	20 May 1920
Parades	11 July 1922
Plencia	9 August 1970
Robledo de Chavela/ Santa Maria de la Alameda	15 March 1968
San Asensio	27 June 1903
San Gervasio	11 February 1939
Santa Eulalis/ Villafranco del Campo	18 December 1966
Selerra	12 October 1918
Torre	3 January 1944
Valencia	4 December 1937
	29 March 1938
Velilla de Ebro	3 December 1940
Villa Verde	4 August 1957
Zumaya	15 February 1941

Sri Lanka (see Ceylon)

Styria

Trifail	27 January 1917

Sudan

Kosti	16 January 1987

Switzerland

Bellinzona	24 April 1924
Rennens	189
Wädenswill	22 February 1948

Sweden

Ludvika†	13 January 1956
Norrköpping	1 November 1918

Taiwan

Miaoli	15 November 1991, 195

Thailand

Takli	20 May 1988
Taling Chan	21 August 1979
—	24 May 1989

Tunisia

Tunis†	7 August 1990

Turkey

Ankara†	28 October 1948
Ankara	9 January 1979
Esenkoy	4 January 1978
Eskisehir	31 October 1972
Ispartakule	20 October 1957, 148
Istanbul	July 1943
—	18 May 1952

Uganda

Kampala†	23 April 1941

United States of America

Amherst, Ohio	29 March 1916
Atlantic City, New Jersey	28 October 1906
Bagley, Utah	31 December 1944
Berry, Alabama	1 September 1902
Bolivar, Texas	8 September 1900
The Bronx, New York City	16 February 1907
Brookdale, Pennsylvania	12 August 1916
Byron, California	20 December 1902
Canaan, New Hampshire	15 September 1907
Carlin, Nevada	12 August 1939
Castle Rock, Washington†	18/19 September 1944
Chicago, Illinois	30 October 1972
Colton, California	28 March 1907
Conneaut, Ohio	27 March 1953, 140